PEER RESPONSE GROUPS IN ACTION

Writing Together in Secondary Schools

KAREN SPEAR
and
Cheryl Ause
Heather E. B. Brunjes
Marjorie Coombs
Trudy Griffin
Nolyn Starbuck Hardy
Kristi Kraemer
Beth Johnson
Rebecca Laney
Becky L. Reimer
William Strong

BOYNTON/COOK PUBLISHERS
HEINEMANN
PORTSMOUTH, NH

Boynton/Cook Publishers, Inc.
A Subsidiary of Reed Publishing (USA) Inc.
361 Hanover Street   Portsmouth, NH 03801
Offices and agents throughout the world

Every effort has been made to contact the copyright holders and students for
permission to reprint borrowed material. We regret any oversights that may have
occurred and would be happy to rectify them in future printing of this work.

Chapter 8: "Salvation" from *The Big Sea* by Langston Hughes. Copyright 1940 by
Langston Hughes. Reprinted with permission of Hill and Wang (Now a division of
Farrar, Straus, & Giroux, Inc.).

Library of Congress Cataloging-in-Publication Data

Peer Response Groups in Action : writing together in secondary schools
  / Karen Spear . . . [et al.].
        p.   cm.
     Includes bibliographical references.
     ISBN 0-86709-318-8
     1. English language—Composition and exercises—Study and
teaching—United States.   2. Group Work in Education   3. Team
learning approach in education.   4. Language arts (Secondary)—
United States.   5. Language arts (Higher)—United States.
LB1631.P35   1993
808'.042'—dc20
                                                        93-13171
                                                           CIP

Cover design by Janet Patterson
Printed in the United States of America on acid-free paper
97 96 95 94 93   9 8 7 6 5 4 3 2 1

Contents

Acknowledgments

This is a book by and about friends, so much so that these acknowledgments need to trace the web of relationships through which I am connected with each of the contributors, as a way of foregrounding the personal, reflective tone of each chapter and, more importantly, as a way of illustrating the many layers of collaboration that underlie this project.

This book wouldn't even have been thought of without Peter Stillman. Pete brought up the idea of a follow-up to *Sharing Writing* during a walk along the Seattle waterfront at the 1989 Conference on College Composition and Communication. I always thought it a remarkable act of kindness for Boynton/Cook to publish *Sharing Writing* in the first place; the thought that anyone would want to hear more from me on the subject never occurred. At that time, I had left my faculty position at the University of Utah and was moving more fully into academic administration at another institution, so there wasn't much time in my life to think about another book, and my involvement in teaching was diminishing to the point of making me feel more like a bystander than a practitioner in composition. But it's pretty hard to ignore a respected editor's open invitation to "do something as a follow-up to *Sharing Writing*," particularly when that respected editor has become a friend and colleague who manages to combine just the right amounts of ego-building confidence and guilt-inducing encouragement.

Another career move brought me back to the West where I am, at least by western standards, in hailing distance of a group of old friends and colleagues who I wanted to work with me on this project. Though as a dean of arts and sciences I still administer more and teach less, my role in a liberal arts college allows me to keep the values of collaborative learning and classroom research at the forefront of my work as an administrator, teacher, and writer. I knew I wanted this project to embody the collaborative principles it espouses. I knew I wanted it to be more than an edited collection, but rather something that would be closer to a co-authored work. With some help from my long-time friend and team teacher, Heather Brunjes, we rounded up a team of writing project colleagues whose work with peer response and whose writing we respected and whose company we enjoyed. Next to Peter Stillman's nagging, Heather's efforts in bridging the four hundred miles between Durango and Salt Lake City have kept the project alive.

Heather and I co-directed the Salt Lake City site of the Utah Writing Project during the summer of 1986, while Heather was still teaching in a seventh-grade gifted and talented program. The following winter we team-taught a graduate seminar for Writing Project alums. Becky Laney was a member of that summer writing project and of the winter seminar, which focused on classroom research. Becky's seminar project became her M.A. thesis under Bill Strong's direction; she has reworked and extended it into her chapter here. Meanwhile, Heather and I were also working with Marjorie Coombs and Becky Reimer on a three-year writing across the curriculum project for the Salt Lake City schools. Marj was teaching in one of the district's intermediate schools and Becky in an elementary school. I'm still a member of Heather's dissertation committee, though more advisory now than official in function, and Heather has been one of the principal readers of drafts of my introductory chapter.

In addition to our collaboration in the school district, Marj and I worked together for many years on the Executive Board of the Utah Council of Teachers of English, and Becky and I worked together on her now temporarily-sidelined dissertation on collaboration among kindergarten children.

I first met Cheri Ause when she was a member of the faculty at Eisenhower Junior High where I offered a lengthy in-service program on writing across the curriculum. She subsequently enrolled in a summer writing workshop that I taught in 1985, and we worked together again in a graduate seminar on composition theory. Nolyn Hardy was also a member of that seminar. Their chapters began as seminar projects for that class.

Beth Johnson attended various writing workshops that I conducted; sometimes she was a student, sometimes a guest speaker, and later she organized a writing project in her school district. She invited me to be a member of her M.A. committee in 1986, a project on writing in computer labs that, contrary to her district administrators' visions of the economy of computer instruction, pushed Beth further into collaboration as a mode of teaching and learning.

Kristi Kraemer is our California colleague. I wanted this project to achieve a consistency of approach that would best be assured by contributors whose work I know well and who know each other's work. But I also wanted us to show that Salt Lake City is not a special case in which collaborative modes of teaching somehow flourish. (To the contrary, since teachers' salaries in Utah are consistently among the lowest in the country while the class size is among the largest, Salt Lake City is one of the last places one would expect to find this sort of teaching.) I knew of Kristi's work from a long review essay of *Sharing Writing* that she published in a University of California at Davis writing journal, *Visions and Revisions*, and invited her to join our group. Though at the time she held a university appointment that combined teacher training with writing instruction, she is currently teaching in the public schools, working full time and maintaining a mind-boggling schedule with seventh and twelfth graders.

So except for Heather, who is now working full time on her dissertation, all these contributors maintain full-time careers as teachers, second careers as graduate students or coordinators of in-service programs and teachers of teachers in various capacities, and third careers as parents, spouses, and active participants in community life. In one sense, their reflective observations of daily classroom life are part of how they have trained themselves to be effective teachers. Their practice models good teaching. Like the students these authors write about, they have the courage to open themselves to change when the outcome is far from certain and the process is fraught with risk.

In another sense, the time devoted to writing and rewriting, to weekend authors' sessions and evening telephone critiques is not built into their lives the way it is for the university faculty who generally produce the scholarship on writing. This is the time to acknowledge and celebrate their commitments to writing, to learning, and to the betterment of their profession that came at considerable personal sacrifice. Likewise, I would also like to thank Fort Lewis College and my faculty colleagues for supporting me in this work when I'm sure they would have preferred a dean who was not regularly driving off for extended weekends in Salt Lake City or hiding out to write and assemble this manuscript.

Finally, I would like to acknowledge and thank Bill Strong—not just for his contribution to this project—but in a much larger sense for being *the* force in Utah public education that has created, nurtured, and frequently battled for a professional climate conducive to the kind of inquiry reflected here. Either directly or indirectly, all of us have benefitted from Bill's leadership and dedication, always expressed in the form of friendship. Though he is surely as accurate as ever in characterizing writing project alums as a "guerilla force" in a jungle of R-bits (to use Frank Smith's term), Bill has nevertheless fostered the professional development of hundreds of public school teachers in Utah and across the country, always pushing for professional autonomy in a context of integrity, responsibility, and scholarship.

Speaking personally, I need to acknowledge Bill as my closest sustaining colleague for well over a decade. As was the case in his help with *Sharing Writing*, his thoughtful reading of the introductory chapter of this project got it headed in the right direction. More importantly, Bill pulled me into working with the public schools in the early 80s, creating associations that would not have occurred otherwise and that have certainly been among the most intellectually and personally rewarding associations in my career. I am grateful that he is a contributor and collaborator on a project that, in some very real ways, he made possible.

Part I

Response Groups
Starting with Teachers

1

Creating Contexts to Share Writing
Starting with Teachers

Karen Spear

To teach writing with response groups, you have to start with teachers rather than teaching. This book is about both, but before it's about teaching, it's about the teachers who are continually inventing new ways to teach. By teaching writing as a collaborative process, teachers find themselves in new intellectual territory. Our cultural traditions don't prepare us very well for collaborative ways of teaching and learning, nor do our teacher preparation, our school systems, or our students' expectations. Response groups interfere with the roles teachers and students are accustomed to playing; they conflict with the identities we are comfortable with; and they don't offer familiar alternatives. Nevertheless, teachers are drawn to using response groups because in spite of the difficulties they present, response groups make sense as a way to teach writing.

Response groups also make sense as reference points for the kind of classroom life in which creating community and creating knowledge are closely related. Teaching writing in this kind of collaborative context is teaching on the edge. We tiptoe there, wobbling a good deal, trying to maintain a balance between the known and the unknown, but always trying to take that next step over the edge into more inclusive understandings of writing and writers. Beyond imparting skills in syntax, organization, or revision, this kind of teaching takes teachers to the edges of what writing means in our culture and within the self and how it can transform writers and the classrooms in which they write. In using response groups, teachers express their yearning for an authentic voice that makes itself heard just outside of traditional classroom practice. Such teachers operate as what Donald Schon calls "reflective practitioners," professionals who are guided by "reflection-in-action" and whose work is characterized

3

not simply by high levels of knowledge about their work, but more importantly by the exercise of qualities like wisdom, intuition, judgment—in a word, by artistry.

This book tells the stories of nine English teachers—nine reflective practitioners—whose best instincts take them daily to the frontier of writing instruction as they experiment with their teaching and their students by teaching writing as a collaborative process. This sort of experimentation goes beyond strategy and methods; it touches our professional identities and shakes up our definitions of ourselves and our ways of relating with colleagues and friends. Metaphors of the edge arose repeatedly during the many authors' sessions, letters, and telephone conversations through which this book was planned and written. All of the contributors work in secondary schools as teachers and/or as teacher-consultants. Describing their teaching, they talk about helping students discover writing as an authentic activity—as a center of knowing and learning. Rarely do they talk about writing as skill-building, in spite of the continued dominance of such language and the mechanistic assumptions behind it in the curricular materials of secondary instruction. Rather, they talk about themselves and their students in the process of becoming effective users of language, and they define language in its most comprehensive social context of discovering, expressing, and negotiating meaning and relationships.

Equally important, these teachers describe their own needs for genuine uses of language in their classrooms and with their colleagues. They describe their teaching as a kind of journey—or in more modern terms, as an ongoing collaborative experiment with their students. Much of their conversation with students is conversation about the students' learning. These are teachers who engage students as collaborators in the teaching/ learning process just as they attempt to engage students with each other. Our conversations over the last year and a half as authors of this book have expanded those individual classroom dialogues, surprising each of us with the similarity of our inquiries and the frustrations, shortcomings, and successes each of us experiences along the way. We discovered that genuine collaboration is open-ended and multifaceted, involving teachers collaborating with students, students with students, and teachers with teachers. Moreover, it is a process that demands continued renewal and reinvention—of ourselves, our classroom, and our teaching.

One of the most insistent themes in our discussions has been the theme of isolation. Our coming together to create this book has relieved a sense of isolation from our colleagues which each of us has experienced somewhat but which the public school contributors sense more acutely. Despite decades of justification, both theoretical and applied, for the essential social dimension of writing, it's clear that the use of response groups still raises the eyebrows of principals and risks the subtle censure of colleagues because students don't look acceptably busy and classroom activities are not proceeding in orderly, familiar ways. I suspect that the contributors here are not alone, either in their sense of isolation or in their stubborn determination to teach in ways that make sense, as their instincts, their experiences, and their research tell them to.

One of the oddest ironies of teaching is that what looks like a highly social activity is really among the most isolating of professions. What Paulo Freire termed "the banking model" of teaching isolates teachers from students, students from students, and teachers from teachers. Knowledge is something to be deposited, stored, and withdrawn on demand. It exists outside us—objective, impersonal, and analytic—and in learning we try to take it in. Accordingly, one's interests in students are as holders of knowledge, possessors of skills. Students, too, define themselves in terms of the banking metaphor, and it becomes increasingly controlling as they move through secondary school and into college. Think about the lively conversations that precede a teacher's arrival in class. Although students' lives are richly social out of school, learning according to the banking metaphor makes it a solitary and isolating activity.

In much the same way, the banking metaphor describes teachers' isolation from each other. Educational philosopher Parker Palmer wrote a gem of an essay called "Community, Conflict, and Ways of Knowing: Ways to Deepen Our Educational Agenda." In it, he traces the effects of a "pedagogy that stresses the individual as the prime agent of knowing" and as "the focus for teaching and learning," and concludes that what results is "the competitive individualism of the classroom" (1987, 25). Palmer argues that how we know dictates how we live. By teaching as if knowledge is something objective, external, analytic, and impersonal, we invite students to live in "a world out there somewhere apart from them, divorced from their personal lives" (1987, 22). To the extent that we live as we teach, I would add that we tend to view our fellow professionals as holders of knowledge. You will hear that perspective voiced with brutally wrenching honesty in Heather Brunjes's account of an extended collaboration with a struggling teacher who confesses to Heather, "You were my teacher, I was ready to kiss your feet . . . I was willing to turn the class over to you totally." Perhaps this is why so many of our conversations about teaching are little more than "recipe swapping," to use Ann Berthoff's term. "Without the soft virtues of community," Palmer concludes, "the hard virtues of cognitive teaching and learning will be absent as well" (1987, 25).

As much as our assumptions about knowing, the daily realities of teaching work against community. Staggering course loads and the management of 150–200 students a term make it difficult for even the most experienced teachers to look beyond day-to-day survival and to cultivate the "capacity for relatedness within the individual" that Palmer identifies as the hallmark of community. There is simply no time for reflectiveness or sharing. Beginning teachers are inevitably socialized into the same kind of professional isolation. They are typically assigned the most demanding and marginal classes of basic or remedial students—the classes their more senior colleagues didn't want to teach in the first place, let alone talk about now that they are free. And of course teachers and students alike have difficulty resisting definitions of knowledge as something outside and apart from us, in the face of the public's and the educational system's preoccupation with standardized testing and other approaches to assessment that are themselves an embodiment of the banking model.

Teachers' isolation from other teachers extends beyond the individual school. Professional meetings, journals, books like this one, local and regional workshops, all provide opportunities for teachers to connect with each other. But so long as teachers view these resources as repositories of knowledge rather than as sources of community, they do little to relieve the isolation of teaching and hence are of limited success in offering alternative ways to define teaching or to interact with other teachers or students. Teacher networks like those fostered by the National Writing Project are, in both senses of the word, exceptional.

What emerges at all levels of education is an impoverished discourse about teaching. The exchange of tidbits keeps us at arm's length from our students, and eventually we move on to complaining about administrators, gossiping about students and colleagues, griping about students' rudeness, their laziness, their lack of preparation, their TV watching, or their latest haircuts. If there's community building going on here, it's a community of the oppressed, and it probably serves to keep at a distance the really hard work of thinking about ourselves, changing our practice, questioning our institutions or challenging the systems that sustain them. This sort of scrutiny is risky, particularly in a system that not only does not invite it, but that passively if not actively discourages it. The seemingly endless state of educational crisis and the unrelenting flood of school criticism simply sustains our isolation. Teachers increasingly feel under siege, like social pariahs who are asked to bear full responsibility for the ills of our present and the fate of our future. Everyone in our society seems to know better than classroom teachers how to make education work. This is not a climate that encourages risk taking and innovation. The impulse instead is to crawl in a hole and pull it in behind us.

When teachers work in isolation from each other, they soon become isolated from themselves. At its most extreme, isolation becomes a form of insulation. When others don't value our work or help us sustain intellectual excitement and curiosity about what we're doing, we can't easily go it alone. Alone, it's hard to tell whether our ideas are good or not, whether we're accomplishing what we want to or not, whether there are better ways to teach, better books to read, better assignments to make. Easier to go through the motions of teaching, to treat one's work as a job rather than a profession, to direct one's real energies away from school, toward one's family, church, neighborhood, recreation, or TV sports.

The school culture of "competitive individualism" further reinforces the isolating character of learning. Students compete for grades, for their teachers' attention, for scholarships, for test scores, for memberships on teams, in clubs, or in peer groups. Rather than competing against themselves for the intrinsic rewards of self-improvement, like a downhill skier or a long-distance runner would do, they target each other. Ironically, despite the near-deification of athletics in high schools and colleges, the fact that team sports are a complex blend of collaboration *and* competition has escaped notice. The mumbled homilies of the post game show in which the hero gives credit to his teammates get lost in the euphoria that one team beat another or that one player distinguished herself from the rest. Our culture is one that valorizes the individual to the point of ignoring—or not even perceiving—the group. Recent works such as *Habits of the Heart* by Robert Bellah et. al. (1985), and, more recently, Bellah's *The Good Society* (1991), argue forcefully that our romance with the individual has obscured and even denigrated the importance of community in American culture. As a society, Bellah argues, we have reached a point of paralysis in our inability to look beyond the individual claims of this person or that interest group and to think instead about the common good. By the time they reach middle school, American students have been well socialized into honoring competition and individuality. Witness the transformation of the willing collaboration of elementary students into the competitive insecurities of adolescence.

The culture of competition is embedded in our lives as teachers, too. We pit our classes against our colleagues' on standardized tests. We compete for merit pay or higher positions on career ladders. We compete to have our school better recognized in the community or better funded by the state. We compete for the good will and compassion of our supervisors. Competition goes hand in hand with isolation. We believe that we succeed by virtue of our own intelligence, imagination, strength, courage, or even luck; but we believe that we do so as individuals, and we define ourselves in terms of our separateness: me versus them, self versus other. The point here is not to decry achievement but to argue that we've defined achievement as an individual virtue by overlooking the equally strong element of collaboration. Good schools are also good because of the shared vision and energies that make them that way. Good teachers (and students) are good because they work out of a context of mutual respect, encouragement, and nurturance from colleagues, families, and communities.

> interchanges lead to ways of knowing that enable individuals to enter
> into the social and intellectual life of their community. Without them,
> individuals remain isolated from others; and without tools for represent-
> ing their experiences, people also remain isolated from the self. (25-26)

The women in Belenky's research report that they learn best first by overcoming silence and then by believing new ideas, by inserting themselves
into possibilities, trying them on for size, and seeing what it is like to live
in them. Connected knowing works for them experientially rather than
abstractly. To a separate knower, this looks naive, emotional, and uncritical. Women, on the other hand, report that they feel uncomfortable,
even resistant to the separate modes of inquiry long privileged in schools:
critical thinking as traditionally defined, debate, playing devil's advocate.
More meaningful are collaborative exchanges through which meaning is
constructed socially and attempts are made to incorporate everyone's
point of view. (See Figure 1 for an illustration of the contrasts between
separate and connected knowing.)

What's important here is not to substitute one way of knowing over
another, or to argue for the superiority of one over another, or to propose
that men just naturally think one way and women another. Instead, by
focusing on difference, we have a more complete understanding of what
it means to know and how knowledge and social context are so richly
intertwined. Psychologist Michael Basseches (whose work I return to in
the last chapter) portrays mature adult reasoning as a dialectical process
consisting mostly of looking for what has been left out of existing explanations and trying to come up with more inclusive understandings. If our
experiences in schools, both as students and teachers, have been largely
characterized by isolation and competition, collaboration and connection
offer the missing half of the dialectic. From a purely instrumental standpoint, collaborative learning—learning that values its social and personal
context—is empowering for students and teachers alike who don't feel at
home in the adversarial arena of separate knowing. This is one of the reasons that peer response groups make sense to so many writing teachers.
But arguing for collaborative learning purely from this instrumental perspective not only misses the larger issue, it also leaves us at the same point
of dead-end relativism that makes other arguments in education, such as
the need to accommodate various learning styles, so unconvincing. The
real point is that students and teachers must become adept at both separate and connected knowing because to engage in only one is to be incom-
plete, half alive. Writing provides a good example of the rhythmic interplay of solitary contemplation and doubting on the one hand and social
exploration and validation on the other. Or, to be equally accurate,
between social contemplation and doubting on the one hand and solitary

Figure 1-1
Separate and Connected Knowing

Separate Knowing	Connected Knowing
Individualistic: Self anticipates reciprocal relations with others	Empathic: Self anticipates responding to others on their own terms
Procedural: Discovery of truth and morality governed by rules	Interpersonal: Ethic of care and responsibility; truth is interpersonal
Truth is outside of self, waiting to be discovered	Truth is inside, mutually created
Abstract (knowing grounded in concepts, principles, ideas)	Concrete (knowing grounded in shared personal experience)
Centrality of doubt as a way of testing knowledge	Centrality of belief as a way of testing knowledge
Objective	Subjective
Exclusive: search for errors, inconsistencies, omissions	Inclusive: search for possibilities, connections, "fit"
Suspicious	Accepting
Disinterested, dispassionate	Engaged, involved
Argument is central to testing knowledge	Discussions and relations are central to knowing
Disagreements viewed as between principles, competing ideas	Disagreements viewed as interpersonal
Hierarchical: knowledge derived from authorities	Collaborative: knowledge negotiated, mutually constructed
Competitive, adversarial: best idea wins	Non-judgmental: goal is to share perspectives
Orientation to rights	Orientation to responsibility

exploration and validation on the other. We create language both as individuals and as members of a group, and we use it for both social and private purposes.

Most writing teachers experiment with response groups, sometimes as a result of attending a workshop or seminar, sometimes because the enthusiasm of a newly converted colleague spills next door. But before too long, both the convert and the colleague have gone back to more familiar ways of teaching. The legacy of classical rhetoric through which most college and secondary English teachers are schooled is difficult to put aside, and it is intimately connected with the banking model of knowledge and the qualities of competition and isolation that are associated with it. Thus, teachers have difficulty managing response groups in part because they are trying to work out of two inconsistent rhetorical traditions, the classical and the modern. Karen Burke LeFevre, in her monograph, *Invention as a Social Act* (1987), points out that you can't just "'add people and stir' to transform traditional writing instruction to a pedagogy based on social interaction" (49). In *Rhetorical Traditions and the Teaching of Writing* (1984), Knoblauch and Brannon, likewise, show how the old patterns of teaching writing by searching for the Ideal Assignment, assigning The Topic, and evaluating it according to the standards of The Ideal Essay often remain in place, even though teachers add a workshop component. These writers are reflecting the teaching of writing in colleges and universities, but their observations are perhaps more potent for secondary English teachers because of the strong influence of higher education values on secondary schools. For instance, in the following excerpt, Knoblauch and Brannon describe the traditional college writing class—the class that most of us took—and their description illustrates the close ties between traditional writing instruction and the tradition of separate knowing:

> Teachers often believe that the specialized knowledge they possess about composing —a conscious grasp of grammar rules as well as logical and grammatical structures —must be conveyed to novice writers, who obviously don't possess it, before maturation can take place. Teachers readily accept the burden such a belief places on them to give students "what they need," realizing at the same time that the way to offer people complicated information they don't yet understand is to transmit it in as clear and orderly a fashion as possible. Hence, they design syllabi which "cover" all the relevant principles of writing in a logical way, progressing systematically from "the basics"—grammar, word usage, punctuation—to advanced skills—paragraph patterns, rhetorical modes, professional genres. They control class business because they know the principles, emphasizing lecture, drilling, and testing to insure that students come to know precisely what they know. (100–101)

Teaching writing in this way, as a content course, and evaluating it according to formal or seemingly objective standards, makes writing look consistent with other subject areas. Parents are happy, principals are happy, testing agencies are happy. And at least to the extent that the students have remained relatively unbothered by the process, they are happy, too. For them, school life stays comfortably separate from the more compelling concerns of their hearts and minds.

The training that English teachers receive in colleges and universities may also make collaboration troublesome. LeFevre observes that "while collaboration is more common in some areas of science, medicine, and engineering, English professors are uneasy about dealing with the issues collaborative invention raises" (124). These issues include questions about the integrity of co-authorship: does it signal the ability to cooperate or the need to offset weaknesses by pulling in someone else; questions about how to credit the author: who did more work; and questions about ownership of ideas: in acknowledging others' assistance, is the author just being thorough or is she unduly dependent on other people's thinking? "Underlying such questions," LeFevre asserts, " is a persisting suspicion that if a person were *really* inventive, she would be entirely self-sufficient. The prevailing view of the atomistic inventor [read: writer] makes it difficult to develop new ways of understanding, acknowledging, and judging a wide range of collaborative efforts. It seems likely that teachers in the humanities, knowing consciously or unconsciously that collaboration is suspect, either avoid it or downplay its effects on their efforts as individuals" (124). Students learn the same skepticism quickly. You hear it every time they worry about how credit should be awarded for team projects or when one covertly complains to the teacher that she really did all the work.

Teachers who embrace collaboration feel all these traditions tugging at their conscience and nagging at their confidence. Nevertheless, they are drawn by a larger vision of literacy that a collaborative classroom seems to offer. In *Writing Groups: History, Theory, and Implications* (1987), Ann Ruggles Gere points out the unique contributions of writing groups to literacy. "If citizens are to become members of intellectual and social communities beyond those into which they are born, they are likely to do so in English classes. Defining literacy as membership in a given community means identifying one of literacy's central purposes as prescribing the terms by which individuals enter certain communities. Accordingly, composition instructors, in particular, face the task of initiating students into communities of educated people. . . . Writing groups offer a means for individuals, both inside and outside of school, to enter literate communities. The collaboration and language development inherent in writing groups insure that participants will begin to develop the cognitive abilities essential to literacy in the broad sense" (120–121). These are the values that beckon English teachers to reinvent themselves, their students, and their schools by teaching writing as collaboration.

Moving From Theory to Practice

Persuaded as teachers may be by the logic of this definition of literacy, they, like their students, find it challenging to carry out in practice. All of the contributors to this book agree that they would not have undertaken such major changes in teaching writing if they had not been members of response groups themselves. Here is where the absence of collaborative experiences in their teacher training and professional lives is most acutely felt. For some, collaboration came through a Writing Project summer institute; for others, a district-sponsored program; for still others, through the sustained conversations over a master's thesis subsequently revised for publication or a university writing course. What happens in all these experiences is subtle but profound. First, collaborative writing experiences turn nonwriters into writers—a significant redefinition of the self. A writer is a public figure, a person with a voice who engages other voices, other selves. A writer has grown beyond silence. Mutuality and responsibility are both involved here. The public character of writing "authorizes" the writer—gives her authority but demands a continued stewardship over ideas. A writer does not labor like a tenant farmer— silently, privately, defensively—in a field that is largely owned by an absentee landlord, whether that field is a classroom or a piece of writing.

Second, the authority one achieves through writing grants a place in the ongoing conversations of other writers. Summer after summer, writing project directors see teachers transformed. Even their most personal writing grows from tentative self-centeredness to a responsive interplay of ideas and experiences with other readers and other writers. As writers, they read in different ways—as participants rather than observers. James Reither and Douglas Vipond in "Writing as Collaboration" argue that while co-authoring and workshopping are valuable practices for understanding the collaborative nature of writing, they are not absolutely essential. What is essential is what they call "knowledge making": "All of us who write must ground our language in the knowing of those who have preceded us. We make our meanings not alone, but in relation to others' meanings, which we come to know through reading, talk, and writing" (862).

Third, by becoming makers of knowledge, teacher/authors begin to overcome what Garth Boomer in his contribution to *Reclaiming the Classroom* (1987) termed "the problem of elsewhereness." This is really the tradition of separate knowing: of locating the origins and responsibility for knowledge outside the self, outside the classroom, in universities where research questions for education are determined, in textbooks, in curriculum guides, in district administrators, in legislators, and in testing agencies. The problem of elsewhereness explains as much about teachers' disengagement from learning as it does students'. Without ownership of knowledge it is difficult for teachers to be more than transmitters or students to be more than receivers. Through writing, teacher/authors learn to redefine their classrooms as centers for inquiry. They allow their experience to mean something. Their expectations of themselves and their expectations of students change dramatically. Nancy Martin in "On the Move: Teacher-Researchers" (1987) puts it this way: "Generally, teachers have been trained as doers of other peoples' directions. They have carried out research directed from university projects, or worked to guidelines set by superintendents, and have seldom seen themselves as initiators" (22). Martin entertains a possibility that the writers here make explicit: "Perhaps, an early step may be for teachers to learn from their own writings" (28).

Finally, when teachers write in a workshop, they inevitably become highly self-conscious about what they are saying, which is to say, they become learners. This transformation from teacher to learner redefines classroom life. Writing and talking about writing become activities that teachers share with students. It becomes the essential medium for learning. Having been in response groups themselves, teachers develop a language for talking about writing and an emotional vocabulary for sharing it. As Kristi Kraemer observers in her chapter, the response group experience makes it clear that we are not really teaching writing; we are teaching writers. As the following chapters illustrate, the first writers we teach are ourselves; in teaching ourselves we begin to teach our students.

What You Can Look Forward To

Throughout these chapters, we have tried to offer what anthropologists would call "thick descriptions" not just of classrooms and teaching practices but also of the teachers' and students' experiences that lead to these various experiments in collaborative learning and what resulted from them. The chapters are richly illustrated with transcripts of students in response groups, teacher conferences with students and with other teachers, log entries from teachers and students, and drafts and revisions of student writing. Our goal is to invite you into each of these classrooms, to live in them as we have, and to be honest about our successes as well as our failures and uncertainties. There are lots of recipes to swap here, but we believe that no recipe is worth much without the right atmosphere and without being prepared and served in an appropriate environment.

In the next chapter, "The Delicate Fabric of Collaboration," Heather Brunjes probes the many complex layers and facets of teaching with response groups. This is a case study of Heather's collaboration with a high school teacher colleague to help her friend become more successful with response groups. As much as it is a model of how to read students' difficulties and devise new ways of working with them, the study is also an examination of how teacher-consultants and teachers can work together to yield deeper and more honest understandings of what it means to change and grow professionally. Heather's chapter concludes with a number of unresolved questions about writing, collaboration, and teacher change: questions concerning the kinds and intensity of support teachers need to succeed; similar questions about the kinds and degrees of support students need to give and receive useful feedback and questions about the possible extent of democratization in secondary classrooms, given the constraints of student number and time on the one hand and students' developmental levels on the other.

Next, I follow up on the theoretical context we've tried to establish by providing some concrete ways to think about designing assignments to foster collaboration. All the chapters in this collection show that writing assignments are really extended projects that painstakingly weave together instruction in reading, inquiring, sharing, analysing, and synthesizing as the stuff of drafting and revising. This chapter attempts to provide a global perspective on the writing assignment as the pivot around which writing classrooms revolve.

In "Friends First! Well Maybe Not!" Becky Reimer traces her seventh graders through the early stages of becoming effective readers of each other's work. She shows how she cultivates a climate for collaboration, guiding her students into increasingly discriminating readings of drafts and teaching them how the rely on each other to solve problems in communication. Following two groups through a response session, Becky shows that students can learn from being in polite, well-structured, "textbook" groups, as well as from groups in which members argue and fight with each other.

Marjorie Coombs starts with three successful groups of eighth graders and then retraces the steps she took to help them reach that point in "With a Little Help from Your Friends." The chapter shows how a well designed computer lab can make response groups a natural, almost inevitable feature of the English class. Writing becomes "a community project" and the class "a giant response group" as the students keep track of how everyone else's project is evolving. Here, composing and responding are inseparable.

Kristi Kraemer's chapter, "Revising Responding," is also an account of "decentering" the classroom away from the teacher. Kristi offers an unusual way of helping her tenth graders figure out for themselves what makes good writing rather than relying on Kristi for criteria or detailed response sheets. Liberated from depending on her as the guardian of standards, her students also become freer and more responsible for selecting their own topics and pursuing their own purposes for writing. Equally important, Kristi's standards of evaluation have changed. She freed herself from the all-purpose checklist of standards we teachers carry around in our heads and try to apply uniformly to student writing in ways we never would to "real writing," and she began reading her students' work as genuine pieces of communication. The result is that students learn to write their own texts, not Kristi's. She has taught them to be better writers, rather than just settling for better writing.

Becky Laney recounts a similar journey of decentering with her tenth grade students in "Letting Go." She contrasts a floundering group with a successful one and analyses the conditions that contribute to students' (and teachers') difficulties with response groups, focusing on the crucial question of how teachers can begin to share power with their students. Becky concludes that teachers' expectations of their students powerfully influence their performance, and that we communicate negative, distrustful expectations as clearly as we do positive, empowering ones. In return for the trust Becky places in them, her students play an important role in helping determine what works and how to accomplish their goals.

In her chapter on "The Writing Workshop," Cheri Ause continues this theme of teacher expectations. While her workshop methodology looks like the most structured and complex in this collection, it derives from a set of expectations modeled on graduate-level writing seminars that communicates standards of professionalism to her eleventh graders. This chapter connects the literature curriculum with writing to illustrate a seamless English program. You can see the serious professional context Cheri creates in her workshop and how it is mirrored in her students' detailed responses to each other's writing and their patient drafting and revising over repeated trials.

Beth Johnson's chapter, "Discovery: An Essential Outcome of Response Groups," explores connections between response group participation and students' discoveries of ideas and the value of writing about them. Modeled on James Moffett's cognitive and rhetorical hierarchies, Beth's writing program for twelfth graders puts her students in multiple reader-writer relationships and helps them build a final piece from the bricks and mortar of small, incremental activities.

Next, Nolyn Hardy takes on one of the sacred cows of senior English, the research paper. The opening vignette captures the cynicism with which students regard this assignment. Nolyn's project was to find a way to breathe life into this moribund requirement by helping students experience the real meaning of research as an active, expansive, intuition-laden process of investigation, culminating in the creative interpretation of findings. Working with already seasoned response groups, Nolyn tells the story of how she "stripped down to her theories" and plunged into the potentially hot waters of what came to be called instead, the "researched paper."

In a co-authored chapter with student Trudy Griffin, Bill Strong carries the developmental story we have been telling into a college classroom.

On one hand, Trudy's story affirms that learning to write is a continuing enterprise, particularly after high school and college experiences that tacitly encourage students to fake it. But on the other hand, as a college senior and prospective teacher, Trudy brings us full circle to the beginnings of the professional biographies that her more senior colleagues tell in these pages. Hers, too, is the story of how good teaching and learning entail the "Breakthrough" of looking inside oneself to see what's really underneath the facade and opening oneself to the possibility of change. The chapter raises the discomforting prospect that we have all probably wasted countless hours responding to fake writing with equally fake readings, but it also serves as a parable to share with our classes about the combination of personal commitment and multiple sources of collaboration that create a climate for more authentic acts of writing and learning.

Finally, in "Spiraling Toward Maturity," I try to illustrate the spiraling, recursive journey through which intellectual and social development crisscross. Like all the contributors here, I want to suggest that writing sits at the center of this spiraling progression. This chapter compares the writing and collaboration of college freshmen and advanced undergraduates. I've included it here to give teachers a preview of their own college-bound students some years hence—not so much to show how different they will become, even though they certainly will change considerably, but, paradoxically, to show how much they remain the same.

You'll find a great deal of consistency in the stories told here and you'll also find disagreements and uncertainties. Imagine, though, what it would be like to have a class full of seniors, or for Bill and me, of college freshmen, who had already had as teachers say, a Becky Reimer in the seventh grade, a Marj Coombs in the eighth, a Heather Brunjes in the ninth, a Kristi Kraemer in the tenth, a Cheri Ause in the eleventh, and a Nolyn Hardy in the twelfth. What was that about a literacy crisis?

Works Cited

Basseches, M. (1984). *Dialectical Thinking and Adult Development*. Norwood, NJ: Ablex.

Belenky, M. et al. (1986). *Women's Ways of Knowing: The Development of Self, Voice, and Mind*. New York: Basic Books.

Bellah, R. et al. (1985). *Habits of the Heart: Individualism and Commitment in American Life*. New York: Harper and Row.

———. (1991). *The Good Society*. New York: Alfred Knopf.

Boomer, G. (1987). "Addressing the Problem of Elsewhereness: A Case for Action Research in the Schools." In D. Goswami and P. Stillman (Eds.), *Reclaiming the Classroom. Portsmouth, NH: Boynton/Cook.*

Gere, A. R. (1987). *Writing Groups: History, Theory, and Implications*. Carbondale, IL: Southern Illinois University.

Gilligan, C. (1982). *In a Different Voice: Psychological Theory and Women's Development*. Cambridge: Harvard University Press.

Knoblauch, C. H. and Brannon, L. (1984). *Rhetorical Traditions and the Teaching of Writing*. Portsmouth, NH: Boynton/Cook.

LeFevre, K. B. (1987). *Invention as a Social Act*. Carbondale, IL: Southern Illinois University.

Martin, N. (1987). "On the Move: Teacher-Researchers." In D. Goswami and P. Stillman (Eds.), *Reclaiming the Classroom*. Portsmouth, NH: Boynton/Cook.

Minnich, E. (1990). *Transforming Knowledge*. Philadelphia: Temple University Press.

Palmer, P. (1987). "Community, Conflict, and Ways of Knowing: Ways to Deepen our Educational Agenda," *Change,* (September/October): 20–25.

Reither, J. and Vipond, D. (1989). "Writing as Collaboration," *College English* 51 (12), 855–867.

Schon, D. (1987). *Educating the Reflective Practitioner: Toward a New Design for Teaching and Learning in the Professions*. San Francisco: Jossey Bass.

2

The Delicate Fabric of Collaboration

Heather E. B. Brunjes

It may be that the most difficult thing writing teachers do is implement peer response groups. Response groups require that teachers weave together multiple threads in order to design a strong fabric of learning through collaboration. Shuttled into the tapestry are knotty textures of social interaction, a rainbow of student egos and insecurities, and a pattern which balances the geometrics of knowledge construction against the free form of shared authority and control. Successful peer response groups take a lot of time, energy, and artful intuition to design and create. Excesses of these are scarce in the world of school.

Most public secondary school teachers teach six fifty-minute periods each day. They are responsible for 150 or more new students each year. In addition to teaching composition, a typical English teacher runs ragged trying to cover literature, research strategies, study skills, vocabulary development, speaking, and usage in a very short time. Often, the thought of teaching writing at all, much less collaborative processes and peer response under such constraints, is enough to daunt even the most creative and committed teachers.

As Spear points out in *Sharing Writing*, teachers often "regard group work with anything from mild reservation to outright frustration" (1988, preface). It is no wonder. Group work is time-consuming and sharing authority with students can be frightening. Historically, teachers have been exonerated or condemned for their ability to control students; and teachers have been expected to pour ready-made, pre-packaged knowledge into their students, not to create it collectively. Additionally, teachers who risk incorporating peer response groups in their classrooms usually do so alone. They try to implement collaborative processes without the benefit of collaboration themselves—collaboration which might give them insight into the complexity of social interaction, the fragility of

20

human egos, the enigma of knowledge construction and the balance of classroom authority and independence which confounds collaborative work. A teacher who experiments with response groups may flounder, fail, or succeed in isolation. By herself, she may experience ostracism if she is not moving as quickly as her colleagues expect. Alone, she may be chastised because her classroom is too noisy for her administrator's liking. Every time she fails, everyone on her hall knows about it. Without the collaboration of a supportive other, no one is ever with her to acknowledge the successes of her experiments.

Why would anyone undertake such a project? One reason is to create a classroom environment based on the assumption that literacy is acquired as readers and writers engage in composing meaningful texts for functional and relevant purposes. With this as a goal, giving students opportunities to receive a variety of response to their writing makes good theoretical and pedagogical sense. Secondly, peer collaboration is the norm by which knowledge is constructed in most social and work communities (Lunsford & Ede, 1990), even though it has been noticeably absent from work in the classroom—a suspiciously missing component considering the power of peer influence in adolescent relationships and behavior.

Finally, as writing teachers and researchers have shifted attention away from products to the processes of writing, they have attended to research that suggests the significance of writers' awareness of audience in planning a piece (Flower & Hayes, 1979). Response groups help students develop a keener sense of communicating their meaning effectively. They allow writers to determine what a reader may need to know in order to comprehend and be intrigued by the writing (DiPardo & Freedman, 1987).

In an attempt to help writing teachers develop in their students an awareness of audience concerns, much literature and a host of teacher-consultants urge the use of collaborative learning through peer response groups. To sell the idea, they promise writing teachers that response groups will improve the students' writing, make their teaching easier, make learning more enjoyable, and reduce the paper load. Those are big promises (e.g., Elbow, 1973, 1981; Britton, et al., 1975; Healy, 1980; Gere, 1987; Spear, 1988).

Writing teachers are often persuaded by the commonplace logic that supports the promises of collaborative work in the writing classroom: If students are provided with the opportunity to receive response on their writing, they may be apt to revise and improve it. Sharing the work of response and revision with the students may reduce the workload. Since students are naturally social and often pay more attention to each other than to the teacher, collaborative learning ought to engage and interest them, and they may learn to become more successful writers. When students take more responsibility for their own learning, the learning may be more meaningful to them.

However, the commonplace logic of these promises does not hint at the deeper epistemological and political concerns underlying collaboration in the writing classroom. These promises leave unmentioned and unexamined the foundational issues undergirding knowledge construction and democratic practices in a collaborative classroom. Response group work is presented and accepted reductively, as a time-saving technique teachers can employ to eliminate stress and increase efficacy in a product-centered classroom. Viewed this way response groups may do more harm than good. Process pedagogy cannot be practiced successfully under authoritarian, product-centered conditions. Foundational conceptions about teaching and learning must be addressed if a process orientation to the curriculum is to be successful (Gere, 1987).

The tendency in the literature and by teacher-consultants to present response group processes as simply another teaching technique to apply in the writing classroom does not direct teachers to notice the finely printed warning label of the promising advertisement. Unaware that successful response groups take an incredible amount of reflectivity, time, and effort, teachers may attempt them without a clear sense of what the work will entail. Although any writing teacher often meets with failure or frustration on her first attempt at collaborative groups, a response group novice may conclude prematurely that she is somewhat less than adequate when groups don't seem to deliver what was promised, or that they are just a waste of precious time. Many of these teachers give up in frustration. If asked, they may say with a hint of bitterness, "I tried response groups once. They don't work." And they become reluctant ever to try them again. The promises fail and a door which may lead to teacher and student empowerment is forcefully closed.

Those persistent teachers, who continue to nurture fledgling groups in their writing classroom generally work alone to cope with their achievements, mistakes, and uncertainties. What they most need is a clear sense of direction about where they are heading and support to guide their efforts. These are rarely available. If teachers initially were made aware that the implications of group work include restructuring epistemological authority, in addition to the pragmatic promises they find so attractive, they may be more willing to tolerate the process of ongoing self-appraisal and struggle to find the balance between successes and failures. They may be more willing to persist until they actually reap both the promised and unpromised rewards of collaborative interaction. What writing teachers may need most to implement response groups successfully is the benefit of collaboration themselves.

This chapter tells the story of one teacher's solitary attempts to implement peer response groups in a secondary English classroom. It describes how she became convinced that response groups were a tool that would solve all the problems her students faced, and how she continued to try response groups and failed to make them work. She was one who believed in response groups and said to herself, "This year I'll make them work!" But every year she found herself concluding,

> I tried it knowing from the outset that they would fail, and they did. The attempt, although failed, helped me to assuage my guilt at not having implemented response groups. I figured, "Well, at least I tried. Groups just don't work for me." (interview, February 26, 1991)

Hers is a story of the uncertainty and self-deprecation that unfolded when things didn't work quite as she expected. But it's also a story about her ultimate success with response groups through collaborative intervention with a writing teacher-consultant/researcher.

The chapter is also a case study of a teacher's struggle to overcome reluctance, her own and her students', in using response groups. Like any narrative, the plot here has rising and falling action, but not necessarily in that order. Unlike many stories, this one's plot is muddled; it leaves the reader with several questions to ponder: How do teachers help students to trust and work with their peers when students rely on teachers for a grade? How do teachers justify the amount of time eaten up by peer response when they must cover so much content? Do teachers tamper with the nature of the peer relationship when they teach students how to read and respond critically to each other's writing?

The narrative has several subplots. It tells my story as well. It details my transition from writing teacher to teacher educator and writing researcher. Mine is also a story of overcoming reluctance, not in implementing response groups, but in becoming a teacher of teachers, and in learning to meet the challenges of someone else's classroom with authentic context-based responses rather than hypothetical gimmicks from my consultant's bag of tricks.

Also woven through this thickening plot is the students' story. Theirs is a story of resistance and reluctance toward peer response groups. In many cases the resistance and reluctance are overcome, and the students learn with their teacher to value response groups. However, some of the students never seem to experience success in their group work. The story is not fiction, and real life doesn't always have clearly happy endings. Together these narratives tell of our collaborative efforts to succeed with peer response groups. For writing teachers, this story is never ending.

Case Study

Background

In the summer of 1985, returning to teaching after a hiatus of several years, Kathryn enrolled in a satellite institute of the National Writing Project that Spear and I directed. Kathryn reminisces:

I had taught high school history for five years and then taken fifteen years off to raise a family. When I came back to teaching I was offered the choice of teaching history or English. I'd had an English minor in college. I decided to try and teach English on a whim. I really didn't know anything about it. I'd never done any writing, even in college, and I wasn't really prepared, but that's the job I took. I was really desperate to know what to do so I borrowed that red book (*Handbook for Planning an Effective Writing Program Grades K-12*, Smith, 1983) and read it cover to cover. That's when I decided to apply for the Writing Project as a way of finding out more about teaching writing. (interview, February 26, 1991)

Through the course of the writing project a special collaborative relationship developed between Kathryn and me because we were both to be teaching in a magnet program for at-risk gifted and talented students in the same urban school district. Students from my classroom in the middle school would graduate to enroll in classes taught by Kathryn in the secondary school. By sharing the same students, we began to create a common bond.

Through the years, we used the occasions of program, district, and state-sponsored meetings to keep tabs on students and to exchange teaching ideas. We brainstormed, problem solved, and offered one another support. We shared the successes we experienced in our respective writing classrooms and tried to iron out the toughest wrinkles. We found our exchanges to be helpful and rejuvenating. However, a ripple in our relationship occurred when some of our more precocious students began returning to tell me that Kathryn was not using response groups to help them work on their writing. They had been involved in very successful response group experiences in my classroom and missed being able to work with their peers to develop their writing pieces. I encouraged them to relay their desire to Kathryn, as I knew she had been exposed to response groups during the course of the summer institute. I assumed she would be happy to incorporate groups in her classes if she knew students wanted them. This did not occur. Each year some of my former students would return and express their regret that Kathryn was not using response groups. I didn't want to bring the subject up with her because I had been her teacher and was concerned that she would see my question as marking her failure. It didn't dawn on me that perhaps she was struggling with response groups and needed support for her efforts.

I finally approached the subject with her one evening when we bumped into each other at a poetry reading. By this time I was teaching at the university. I thought that my question would appear less as a criticism and more of a curiosity. What unfolded in the course of the conversation served as a basis for our ongoing collaborative research project on the implementation of peer response groups in the writing classroom.

I learned that Kathryn didn't know the students had missed response group work. They never told her. She recalls,

> They never mentioned it. If they had, I am sure I would have tried harder to make them work. It would have been important to me if it was important to them. (interview, February 26, 1991)

I also learned that Kathryn had tried to implement response groups each year, now five since she had participated in the summer institute, and that the groups had been a miserable failure in her estimation. She remembers her first year of attempting response groups following her participation in the summer institute,

> I was a new teacher. The thought of putting anything that wasn't completely under my control up for the students to mess around with was out of the question for me at the time. I wasn't about to entertain any notions that implied I wouldn't have complete control. My experience in the project helped me to realize I was a good responder and the modeling I saw of student response groups and the other adult groups helped me to realize what response groups were all about. I returned to school in the fall excited to try all the new things I had learned in the summer institute. I set out to implement response groups in my classroom. I told the kids what a response group was . . . and set them loose to respond to each others' papers. It didn't work and I gave myself permission not to try it again. (interview, February 26, 1991)

Kathryn had other stories to tell about each year's troublesome attempts, many sounding much like the first.

Since my university position offered more flexibility, I offered to come in and teach a composition unit in her classroom to demonstrate how I might incorporate group work. She was thrilled at the prospect of collaboration and we began immediately.

Method

We designed this project to explore the multifold nature of collaborative processes in the writing classroom. We entertained many preliminary assumptions that influenced the development of the project design and its development. Although the experience changed our perceptions in many ways, initial assumptions were pivotal to the ways in which we progressed. In order to follow our foundational line of reasoning, those assumptions are detailed here.

The project centered on Kathryn's work. Kathryn is a secondary English teacher, who is well known throughout her school district as a successful writing teacher. She had read extensively about the value of peer group work. Through reading and participating in several writing workshops, she initially believed response groups were a teaching technique that would serve to solve her students' writing problems. After several failed attempts using peer response groups, she began to question her own efficacy and the underlying assumptions of collaboration. Kathryn entered the project hoping to receive some instructional cues and solutions to the problems she had been experiencing. She did not view herself as a knowledgeable authority on response groups and anticipated receiving answers from the researcher, who she perceived to be more expert than herself.

As the researcher in this project, my role initially was to assume the position of supportive other while collecting data. I had successfully used response groups in my middle school writing classes for several years. I was convinced that response groups were an effective teaching technique for improving student writing. Additionally, I had a somewhat notorious reputation as the "response group guru" in our public school writing community. For some time, I had been featuring my students in response group demonstrations around the state. Now as a university researcher, I hoped to wed my experiential understanding of classroom practice with theoretically informed assumptions about collaborative processes.

Through collaboration with Kathryn, who had struggled and failed with response groups, I expected to use my perceived expertise "to share the benefits of my knowledge" while helping her to achieve success with response groups. We thought that success with the students would mean they would be able to pinpoint areas of concern in each other's writing, interact energetically, and improve their writing by learning to communicate their intentions more effectively. I thought that collaborative success with Kathryn would mean she would be able to identify successful strategies that worked with her students, examine her own instructional assumptions and practice to see areas that could use improvement, and begin to question the base of authority in her classroom.

Success for me would mean that I would write the story of our collaborative efforts. But, I also had a political agenda I wished to pursue. Smoldering beneath the surface of a desire to find successful classroom techniques was a challenge to explore the political and epistemological groundings of collaborative learning as they directly influence classroom practice. My experiences with collaborative interaction in the writing classroom had caused me to search more deeply into the nature of power relations in the classroom and the school. Years of watching my students grow as authoritative readers and writers through hands-on literate practice in a collaborative environment had helped us to reclaim a sense of power that commercially published materials and district-authorized curricula had usurped. Our co-constructed literate authority had made learning more functional, relevant, and meaningful. I wanted to know more about sharing authority, co-constructing knowledge, and creating democratic classrooms. I intended to address through this project my questions about the interconnections of power, authority, and literacy.

Although I hoped to demonstrate how response groups could work successfully in the classroom, and lead one teacher to discover her own and her students' efficacy, I realized the issue of authority that traditionally bristles between university researchers and public school teachers could not go unchallenged if the project was to be truly collaborative. I supposed I could not sit unobtrusively in the back of the classroom in the traditional ethnographic way, observe the occurrences, and run back to my office in the Ivory Tower to analyze them. I wanted to "collaborate democratically" with the teacher and with the students. At the time that meant I would work at their sides teaching, writing, and responding along with them.

I hoped the project might offer some insights to other teachers and consultants who might be puzzling over some of the same problems. I also hoped that our collaborative project might shed a faint ray of light on the design of effective classroom research (I pulled from work on dialogic educative research discussed by Gitlin, 1990a, 1990b; and feminist research methods articulated by Lather, 1986a, 1986b).

These preliminary expectations influenced our working definition of collaboration as the project began. Basically we thought we would work together, have a good time, and try and solve some classroom concerns. Our most naive assumption was that we figured the project would last about ten weeks.

As a result of our presumptions about the nature of collaboration, Kathryn and I knew we wanted to proceed together as equals and to involve the students as equals in whatever way we could. We made some decisions about our roles, agreeing to fine tune and adjust our methods as we went along. We really had no idea where we were headed. We found this lack of foresight acceptably reflective of our hopes about exploring democratic practice as it unfolded to us along the way.

When Kathryn and I began our project, the students in her sophomore honors English classes were just about to begin a free choice literature unit. Kathryn had given the students an opportunity to vote for the "genre of their choice," and the majority ruled in favor of "adventure." Kathryn and I decided to take a reading/writing workshop approach (Calkins, 1986; Atwell, 1987) to the unit. The students would read several pieces of adventure literature and the connected writing workshop activities would focus on writing an adventure short story. We agreed that I would teach the second-period class while Kathryn observed, and then she would teach the fourth-period class and we would compare notes and discoveries.

I taught reading/writing workshop in Kathryn's second-period class, which met for ninety minutes every other day for the ten weeks of the adventure unit. We met once a week to discuss, evaluate, and refine our work, brainstorm new activities and procedures, and solve any difficulties we bumped into. Once the adventure unit had been completed, we distributed questionnaires to forty-five randomly selected students in both the second- and fourth-period classes to gauge their response group experiences. Thirty-five questionnaires were completed and returned to us.

Kathryn continued to work with peer response groups in her classes, and she and I met once every two weeks throughout the remainder of the year to discuss her progress and concerns. I formally interviewed Kathryn on five occasions. At the end of the year I interviewed ten randomly selected students from the two classes. Kathryn and I determined the student interview questions together. I asked the students what they felt they got out of response group work during the year, what they thought Kathryn might do to improve the quality of peer response, what they hoped to get from and were willing to give to response group work, and what advice they would offer next year's students.

What Happened

When I began to teach in Kathryn's class, the students had already completed one "writing workshop." During the workshop Kathryn had introduced the idea of peer response and had let the students respond to each other's writing by working with partners. Although she had encouraged them to give each other substantive response, she said their work together generally amounted to peer proofreading sessions at best, gossiping and fooling around at worst (planning discussion, October 1, 1990). When the students were writing and sharing, Kathryn was available to conduct in-depth conferences (Graves, 1983) any time a student requested it. She kept track of whom she had conferred with during the course of the unit and made certain that she invited any students to speak with her who had not volunteered on their own. Kathryn felt that the students weren't taking the peer response sessions seriously and that they depended on her for "real" response. Old patterns of student lethargy and inattentiveness that had daunted Kathryn in previous years were already beginning to emerge, and she was feeling frustrated (planning discussion, October 1, 1990).

At this point, I was optimistic. Response group work had always proceeded rather smoothly for me. I assumed that Kathryn simply was neglecting to teach some essential component of the process. I also had a hunch from some of our previous discussions that Kathryn's teaching style was more authoritarian than mine. I predicted that she was unwilling to relinquish some of her control of the class and that might be another component that contributed to her sense of failure with response groups.

I assumed that I would just go in and teach Kathryn's class how to respond to each other's writing the way I had taught my students; Kathryn would see how it might work when students are given greater control over their own learning, and consequently her students would see how useful response might be, and then beg, as mine had, for additional sessions to collaborate with each other on their writing. I saw myself as a visiting teacher-consultant who would be demonstrating model writing lessons.

The students at this point were willing to go along with whatever Kathryn and I asked them to do. We told them that we thought collaborative learning would provide them with an opportunity to learn from each other, and that it would be more fun. They seemed eager to be able to work with their friends (class log, October 3, 1990).

Demonstration Lessons

I began the unit with a discussion about the adventure genre. We brainstormed characteristics of adventure stories. We listed all the many, varied, and unusual ideas we would expect to encounter in reading adventure. The character "Indiana Jones" was a favorite model for the students. They were asked to look for these elements of adventure in the first story they read, "Leiningen Versus the Ants," by Carl Stephenson.

After our first discussion in which we talked about elements of adventure stories they could identify in the reading, we identified suspenseful sentences and paragraphs. We examined the techniques that the author had used to make a passage work as suspense. We discussed what the students had learned about writing adventure stories from the techniques they had seen the author use.

The first writing exercise the students completed was to think of a character from a movie, TV show, book, cartoon, or real life who struck them as being particularly adventurous. They clustered (Rico, 1983) an array of characteristics and were to write a "character sketch" when they felt they were ready to describe the character traits of the individual they had selected.

At the end of the writing exercise I asked students to read their writing aloud to a partner. I offered no specific guidelines for the sharing session, asking if anyone would like to read their character sketch aloud to the whole class. As students stood up to read, I listened for techniques they had used in the writing that were typical of adventure stories. I repeated successful images or phrases and talked about the way they illustrated a particular adventure technique. I then asked the students to do likewise as they responded to each other.

We settled into a routine of looking for specific adventure characteristics in the stories we were reading and then followed with writing exercises, sharing, and debriefing discussions. The pre-reading focus set a purpose for reading that identified a typical adventure story technique in the conventional elements of a narrative: characterization, setting, plot, conflict, and theme. As the students read they were to look at techniques the authors used. Following the reading, they wrote exercises that developed the same technique.

Through the progression of the lessons the sharing sessions became more and more directed. I asked the students to look for suspenseful descriptions, vivid actions, and magnified moments that created a sense of tension, and to try to reconstruct the author's technique. In our debriefing sessions, I pointed out particularly successful constructions.

Kathryn and I wanted the students to write an adventure short story as the culminating project. The written exercises I had been using as post-reading/pre-writing activities began to consume less time. The students could select any of the exercises as a departure point for a finished adventure story, or they could develop a totally new idea. We gave them more class time for drafting their final product. After about four weeks, we decided to move into more formal response sessions.

Kathryn divided the students into groups. She tried to balance the groups according to gender, writing ability, and neighborhood affiliation. The large urban school where Kathryn teaches serves students from diverse socioeconomic backgrounds. Often the students' interactions and friendships cluster around neighborhood affiliations. It is taboo to cross over socioeconomic boundaries. Kathryn wanted to break down some of these barriers that were mirrored in her classes. Her criteria for group selection was based on wanting the students to meet and learn to collaborate with people they may not already know or choose to work with, and to create heterogeneous groups according to differences in background and ability.

We began the first formal response session with an open discussion about responses that the students thought were helpful. They didn't like it when kids didn't listen, or said things like, "That's really good, Diane. You read yours, now, Leon" (class log, November 2, 1990). They said they wanted specific feedback on "how to make the writing better" (class log, November 92, 1990). I asked for four volunteers to participate in a role-playing situation. Kathryn read a draft of an adventure story she was writing and each of the volunteers played a given response part. Each volunteer received a card which told them how to behave in the mock response demonstration. One student was asked to "Be a little obnoxious. Don't totally ruin it." I asked another to "Gush (praise everything)." Another student was to "Give specific suggestions (refer to the writing)." A fourth student was asked to "Act bored (disinterested)." We modeled the response session for approximately ten minutes, then followed it with a debriefing. The other students were quick to identify the most useful type of response and those that were unhelpful.

In the session that followed, I asked the students to begin with a five-minute freewrite activity (Elbow, 1973) to articulate what they were trying to accomplish in the writing, what they thought was working well, and what areas still seemed weak to them. They broke into response sessions that operated according to the following procedures:

1. Decide the order in which you will read your work.
2. The writer speaks first and shares the content of the freewrite activity with the group members.
3. The writer reads the draft out loud. Other members of the group should take notes in response to the writer's requests (#2).
4. Peer responders should share strengths first and then offer suggestions to help the writer to improve the weak spots the writer has already identified.

To encourage students to follow the guidelines, Kathryn gave them credit points for their response group notes. They wrote down what they said about each writer's piece and their suggestions to the writer. During response sessions I walked around the room and eavesdropped on the students. Kathryn sat in on several groups and modeled types of response students might give.

> I am not sure what you are trying to accomplish here, Ashley. I am confused when the man is chasing you in the dark alley. Did he catch you or did you just keep running? I think I need more clarification about that so I can understand more clearly. (Kathryn, class log, November 9, 1991)

Kathryn bribed the students to give thorough response by awarding them credit points for their response sheet records. I bribed them by passing out M & Ms and giving specific verbal recognition in praise of successful response comments:

> Luanne, I think the way you pointed out the fact that Angela might consider adding more detail, construct a "magnified moment," in the section on page 3 where she is running from the police was helpful and specific response. (Heather, class log, October 31, 1991)

We followed each response session with a debriefing. I passed 3 x 5 inch notecards out and asked the students to describe what worked and didn't work in that day's session. They turned these in anonymously and I shared the comments with the class. We made a list of things to work on for the next time, and began the next session attending to those issues. This was the standard protocol for each response session that followed throughout the unit. Students met three times to respond to developing drafts of the final story.

What We Discovered

All of the participants—Kathryn, the students, and I—experienced mixed reactions to work in response groups. We celebrated our successes and worried about our struggles. Overall, we thought the group work had proceeded well and that the students' writing improved in fluency and authenticity. We thought the students became much more adept at noticing qualities in the writing that contributed to the success or failure of a piece. Kathryn felt much more confident about group work in her classroom. The participants were asked to reflect on the purpose of response groups, the advantages and disadvantages they experienced through the implementation process, the quality of the response, and their commitment to continuing collaborative work.

Kathryn's Perceptions

Kathryn reports that her view of the purpose of response groups is to write for an audience, and to allow students the chance to test the communicative success of their writing through authentic social interactions. She says,

> The purpose of writing is to communicate. Response groups set up a writer/reader transaction for the purpose of improving the communicative nature of the writing. Response groups help to improve the writing by showing the writer how his or her writing is communicating to a reader. . . . The social transaction is really between the writer and his peers. I can give response from my perspective but it is not as valid as what they hear from each other . . . The students are the ones who take each other most seriously as writers. I have things to say but my comments are according to my measuring stick. This is not as valid as what the students have to say to each other . . . I think it is the writer's peers who are better at saying what shapes a particular piece. They are much better at it than the teacher. (interview, February 26, 1991)

Kathryn also realized the importance of sharing authority with her students in order to accomplish the writer/reader transaction.

> The teacher thing changes you know. . . . Kids can communicate very moving ideas, very important ideas all on their own. That has nothing to do with me. I have to step back and let it happen. I see my job as teaching them the tools to complete the transaction . . . It's just that the teacher voice is different from a peer voice—even though you can try to be a human being instead of a teacher, you are always the teacher. With the kids each writer gets a peer voice, the question that gets answered is "Does this communicate to me?" (interviews, February 26, 1991; March 5, 1991)

Kathryn was keenly aware of both the advantages and disadvantages of response group work. Collaboration gave the students a chance to see themselves as a community of writers and readers. This contributed to their commitment and improved their writing. Yet she felt time was a crucial factor in whether or not response groups would succeed in the writing classroom. There was never enough of it. Kathryn had always felt the pressure of time in trying to accomplish everything expected of her as an English teacher. She constantly struggled with the tension pulling her between knowing just how much time writing takes and just how little time she has with her classes:

> The writing workshop takes so much time and I am really nervous about neglecting literature. The students I am teaching are honors students and need to read around twenty-five pieces of literature in order to be prepared for the AP exam, and I feel obligated to prepare them adequately. I don't think I can spend all that time, be so extravagant in my expenditure of time in writing workshop and response groups and end up neglecting literature. (interview, February 26, 1991)

She was continually vexed when the students seemed to be wasting time in response groups. This problem had always impeded her progress in the past, and before had caused her to abandon the use of response groups altogether. This year she was committed to seeing it through, partly because she had committed to me, but mostly because of her growing commitment to the response group process. All year she vacillated back and forth between installing inflexible rules for response group procedure to keep the students from wasting time, and removing almost every restriction in order to provide students a more flexible setting in which to respond. This was an issue which we discussed again and again.

> You know after last time, when we talked about the way I was structuring the lesson, I was—I became really aware that I was not happy with the inflexible rules I had installed to keep the kids from wasting time. I knew that their best writing would come if they were able to respond when they were ready instead of when I told them to. (interview, March 5, 1991)

There was a growing determination on Kathryn's part to continue with response groups in spite of her struggles. She realized her commitment to their success. She was less daunted by the struggles she encountered and more aware of all it takes to implement peer response.

> I think that eventually, through years of responding, through reminders and rereminders [the students] will learn not only to give holistic response, "That's good, this is bad," but also specific suggestions. My job as teacher is to give lots of lessons on how to do response. . . . The kids are still not giving very specific detailed response, but I still do it [response groups] and it's still helpful. (interview, March 5, 1991)

Kathryn articulates the quality of the students' response. Although she is keenly aware that they are not giving each other very specific response, she concludes that what the students are able to accomplish in groups is fundamental to their development as writers. In her estimation it makes the struggle worth the effort:

> They can see that the paper is off topic. That it doesn't have a good lead or it skips around. They may be able to say, "You got off topic here, you start talking about what a good guy he was then move into this beer thing and talk about his having a drinking problem. It just doesn't seem finished." Now that is a different comment from "It doesn't seem finished because you bring up three new ideas in the last paragraph. Why don't you think this is finished?"(interview, March 5, 1991)

Kathryn realized that the first comment describes what is wrong with the writing. It demonstrates a fairly sophisticated kind of response that most of her students were eventually able to do. The second response is more metacognitive and shows not only an awareness of the problem in the writing, but demonstrates an ability to identify the strategies which could be employed to remedy the difficulty. It turns the writing back to the author with a question. Kathryn thought that students must be able to accomplish the first type of response before moving into the second type.

> I can't see them making those kinds of responses to each other. . . . That's a teacher voice. . . . I can get away with that, they can't. . . . What I want to do is each time we go into response groups, each time they meet with each other, I want to add one more way to be an effective responder. This would give them a series of process lessons over time on how to be effective in responding to writing. (interview, March 5, 1991)

Although Kathryn could see progress in the students' ability to read critically and give specific feedback to each other's writing, she continued to be troubled by how quickly the students finished in response group work. They seemed to rush through each other's pieces and then fritter their time away. They would speed right through each piece, make vacuous remarks, such as, "That's good," and move on. If she didn't hover over them and require response sheets to be turned in, they often did little. Frequently drafts were returned to Kathryn without much revision, and this frustrated her (conference notes, April 29, 1991). However, rather than throw in the towel, as she may have done in the past, Kathryn intended to focus in on these problems early in the next year, trying to see a way over the hurdles.

Kathryn was able to talk about the many factors that led over time to her growing confidence in her ability to implement response groups. Experience was crucial. So was having adequate space. The year Kathryn was given a bigger room to teach in, it made mountains of difference. Additionally, Kathryn was now receiving outside acknowledgment from her administrator and from parents that really helped to build her confidence (interview, February 26, 1991).

Kathryn was able to pinpoint two pivotal factors that led her to believe that her response groups were finally succeeding. In the fall, just after we had begun our collaborative project, she attended an in-service session on response groups given by some of the best writing teacher-consultants in our state at the NCTE (National Council of Teachers of English) Southwest Regional Conference in Park City, Utah (1990). Kathryn had felt obliged to make response groups work since we were going to be working together, and she wanted to see what other successful writing teachers were doing with response (interview, February 26, 1991). The teachers demonstrated a mock response session with some of their students. Kathryn reports:

> I saw the teachers demonstrate a response group with their students. I thought there were a lot of things wrong with their group. The kids were unkind with each other and I didn't think they gave very good response. I thought, "My kids do better than this." That helped to give me a more realistic perspective of what my response groups should be expected to accomplish. I realized that my own groups were better than I had thought. (interview, February 26, 1991)

Secondly, Kathryn determined through our collaborative efforts that the component she had been neglecting during all her attempts was the need for ongoing training and support of groups. Her realization came as a result of the demonstration lessons.

> This year the collaboration with you has helped me to learn about training. I can see that that was a missing link. You've shown me how to train kids for response. Your modeling really helped me to see what I can do. The things you've shown me specifically are how to train kids, that I don't have to have really high expectations. I have become much more satisfied with a less sophisticated level of response. You are so relaxed working with the kids, time is not an issue for you. I have learned to relax and be less formal in my approach to groups. (interview, February 26, 1991)

The collaborative relationship we shared influenced her growth significantly. She reports,

> I was working in total isolation trying to figure out how to do this. It is like trying to figure out how to do a difficult math problem without someone showing you the steps. Other than our summer institute I had no other modeling and no one to talk to. . . . Even though group work is really being pushed, no other English teachers (in my building) use groups in their classes. . . . People need to work with people. They need a buddy, they need a support group. It is too risky to do on your own.

You are bucking the traditional way things are done in the classroom. . . . People working together can help support each other's
change. They can show each other how they solve problems, make things
work, what they do when things go haywire. Support gives us permission
to take risks and make mistakes. We lower our expectations and feel
safer in trying new things out. (interview, March 5, 1991)

The Students' Perceptions

The students seemed very clear about the purpose served by response
groups. As a result of the student questionnaires distributed at the end of
the adventure unit, we discovered that over fifty-seven percent of the students reported that response groups gave them the opportunity to get
other opinions about and feedback on their writing, and to learn to work
with other students. More than twenty-five percent of those responding
reported response groups were for improving writing and learning better
editing techniques and techniques for responding to their friends' writing. Individual students also mentioned that response groups helped
them to learn better communication skills, how to take criticism from
others, how to identify their mistakes and learn from them, and how to
become aware of the needs and interests of one's audience.

All respondants reported that the opportunity to give and receive
specific feedback on the writing was advantageous and did improve their
writing, in their estimation. In terms of disadvantages, twenty percent of
the students reported that the groups were occasionally unproductive and
wasted their time. Twenty-two percent of the respondants mentioned
that some students were unwilling to cooperate. Seventeen percent said it
was sometimes difficult to concentrate and stay on task. Five percent of
the students mentioned that response groups often became the site of
interpersonal conflict and then it was difficult to accomplish the goals of
the group.

Even with their open disclosure of the disadvantages encountered in
response groups, more than seventy-five percent of the students were
favorably disposed to continuing to participate in groups not only in
English but in other classes. Fifty percent of the students reported that
they would like to participate in response groups in other classes because
they thought groups would help them to learn more and to better understand the content. Several students specifically mentioned biology, math,
and foreign language. An additional twenty-eight percent of the respondants wanted to participate in response groups in English, but did not
wish to participate in response groups in other classes reporting that
response groups may not be valuable because not much writing was
required. Twenty-two percent would not like to participate in response
groups again. Half of those students reported that response groups were

a waste of time, the other half indicated a lack of ease in sharing their writing with others.

The student interviews shed light on the students' perceptions of the problems of working in response groups. One hundred percent of the students interviewed reported that response groups were beneficial when they worked and frustrating when they didn't. For example one student says,

> . . .when they work it helps my writing a lot because they give me good feedback, but usually what's been happening is my group will just say, "O.K., that's good." So I haven't really been getting anything and usually my draft turns out to be my final copy and nothing is added to it at all. (Rasha, student interview, May 9, 1991)

Factors cited as inhibiting the success of the groups include "laziness," lack of comfort with group members, lack of confidence in knowing how to respond specifically to the writing, and anxiety around interpersonal interactions. One student sums up,

> We kinda waste our response group time . . . We just don't know what's good and what's not really good. I mean, I don't know what's good and what's not really good. I try to know and I try to listen to their papers and see what I think is good but maybe they don't think that's quite so good or other people do. Everybody has different views . . . I just feel like maybe that's a good part and I'm afraid of saying anything about a part that maybe no one else thinks is bad. (Michele, student interview, May 2, 1991)

One hundred percent of the students hoped for more specific feedback from their group. All felt when they received specific feedback it helped to improve the writing.

In spite of their perceptions that they weren't confident of their ability to give advice that would help their peers, many of the students spoke fluently about strategies writers use to improve the text. They seem adept at pinpointing areas of concern and able to offer suggestions for improving trouble spots:

> . . . when we do respond within our group, I think it really helps to add detail and to take out unnecessary details and to rearrange wordings, the way you put your diction down because, um, it makes the sentence flow better. (Sharon, student interview May 9, 1991)
>
> I like certain words, dialogue, words that I can relate to. I mean, if you put words that . . . are eloquent, if you use high words, words that are not really boring . . . big words I can relate to, that are really cool words, [they] are more interesting than words that are dull. (Dylan, student interview, May 2, 1991)

> [I look for] if it makes sense, if it sounds good like sometimes they will write a sentence and put a word in there that's a totally different style. You should point that out. (Roberto, student interview May 5. 1991)
>
> I want them to say, "On this part—magnify the moment." [When I'm responding] I listen for the funny parts, the really funny parts, and the happy parts and the sexy parts and the grody parts, it makes the writing more exciting . . . those are the good things I guess . . . sex and violence . . . I tell em, this could use a little more detail or something. (Michele, student interview May 2, 1991)

Additionally, records of the students' response group notes demonstrate the ability to respond specifically and provide supporting evidence from the text. The students do not seem to be at a loss in providing response feedback to their peers. Examples of the response group notes written by students on October 23, 1990, follow. Sharon writes Justin:

> Good plot. Your description of the actions of the soldiers gave good input to the storie, "the angle of their guns," etc. Your first statment catches the readers attention. Danny isn't very developed, and being the main character—he needs to be. You need to describe the area, the town, etc., a lot more. [sic]

Brynne writes Fiona:

> need ending, beleivable climax. I can feel her pain really well, I was suffering w/ her. for your ending, make sure we feel confusion w/ her. For the ending, you might want to make Ms. Blair reappear again somehow. You could use a better word/phrase for "numb," very forward. could make Ms. Blair more mysterious don't describe other residents in great detail, keep it with you feeling alone with no Ms. Blair. [sic]

Turaj makes one list for Branson:

Good

- Parents instructions
- Cookie jar with Michele
- Emotion of child

Improve

- To factual, seems a little like a documentary
- Dialogue, use words other than "said"
- Sometimes you use the same word twice in a sentence

And another for Susie:

Good

- Description of view and accomplishment of climbing the mountain
- Very "to the point"
- Stuck to her subject

Improve

- To many figures and numerals when explaining the time
- More on climb up mountains
- (Only half of story)

The majority of the students interviewed asked that their teacher impose more structure on the response group experience in order to make it work the way they hoped it could. They wanted to make their writing communicate better, and although they felt their peers could tell them when a piece of writing did or didn't accomplish a communicative function, they viewed the teacher, not their peers, as key in teaching them how to make the writing work. Several students requested more modeling of group procedure and direction on strategies that may be used to improve the writing during response sessions:

> [I want the teacher to] play a little bit more role in the response groups instead of just telling the groups to respond and just sitting there listening [in each group]. (Dylan, student interview, May 2, 1991)

> [I think she should] maybe go through [the groups] not just asking how it's going but going around and telling them what they should be looking for and maybe she could go through it and tell what she liked about it and what she didn't like about it and we could agree or disagree or tell 'em what we thought or I don't know, yeah, I kinda feel better when she's there cause then I feel better about saying stuff. (Michele, student interview, May 2, 1991)

Students suggested that Kathryn take a more aggressive role in disciplining students who came to response sessions unprepared. They also wanted her to be "more aware" of whether groups were on task or not. They wished she could somehow prevent students from shrugging off the response sessions as unessential. Many thought a solution might be found in having to continue to keep response sheet records throughout the year. They felt Kathryn weaned them from that structure too soon.

Every student identified that the most useful response sessions were ones in which everyone gave specific response. For the most part, they reported that they knew enough about responding to the writing to tell specifically when they understood or didn't understand a piece. But many expressed anxiety that being more direct with their feedback could cause interpersonal complications. They expressed concern that others' feelings might be hurt or they might be laughed at. This made them reluctant to share their writing in groups.

All the students expressed support of Kathryn and said she was an "excellent teacher." They were struggling to overcome the frustrations of complex peer interactions, and they weren't sure Kathryn could aide them in their struggle. They wanted to improve their writing, saw the advantage response groups might play in achieving that goal, but were not quite willing to give response groups the energy they knew they required. When it was pointed out to the students that their professed intellectual goal to produce better writing conflicted with their lack of willingness to give the type of response which profferred the potential to meet their goal, no one could clearly articulate the reason for the contradiction. They claimed factors such as laziness, boredom, not wanting to hurt others' feelings, not wanting their feelings hurt, and lack of confidence in knowing what to say to other writers. Contrary to their assessment, observation of the students indicated they were hard working, involved, cautious to frame comments in ways that would not hurt others, and certainly well versed in providing direct response. They looked to each other for approval and recognition, and to Kathryn for guidance and support in dealing with intellectual and management concerns.

> I really don't think that the teacher can do anything to play out the role [of responding]. It's really up to the students . . . I would like the teacher to help us to make the groups more comfortable and productive though. (Amber, student interview, May 6, 1991)

> I think she should assign response groups or else friends will just like go off and something like that or mess around. Especially with a lot of boys in our class nothing ever happens, like even during the time she gives us to write. I mean, no one ever writes. Well, some people write, but not really. (Rasha, student interview, May 5, 1991)

Heather's Reflections

I agree fully with Kathryn's articulation of the purpose of response as providing students with an opportunity to write for an authentic audience of their peers. I think response sessions improve the writing because the experience teaches students how to be critical readers, how to recognize and experiment with successful authorial techniques, and how to be in control of their writing process. I also think the purpose of response groups is to shake up authoritarian hierarchies and create student-centered environments. I think the learning is richer and more meaningful, functional, and relevant when it is directed by the learner herself. However, I became painfully aware through this project that the structure of educational institutions will never afford us the privilege of truly being equal with our students—of creating liberating democratic classrooms. But I think providing students with the opportunity to find their own authority and voice through collaborative work in response groups is the closest we may come to narrowing the power gap between teachers and students.

Having spent most of my years in the public schools teaching middle grade students, I had never experienced the frustrations caused by lack of time that created such a disadvantage in response group work in a secondary classroom. Elementary school teachers are afforded the luxury of working with the same students all day long. In my middle grade classes we could take all the time we wanted to make groups work successfully. Working under the constraints of time in Kathryn's classes was a new experience for me. Nonetheless, I approached response groups as I always had—in a relaxed fashion. I took a great deal of time modeling response sessions for the students. I wanted them to have adequate opportunity to gain a sense of security and camaraderie. Kathryn was often urging me to move on. Had she not done that, we may never have completed the unit on schedule. I found this to be a great disadvantage. I sensed the students needed more opportunities to feel safe in their groups. I thought they needed more support and direction in learning how to give specific response. The clock did not permit us that opportunity. Once I was no longer modeling response sessions, Kathryn had to pick up her struggle against the clock. She was unable to allow herself the luxury I had privileged myself with. She could not be as repetitive and thorough as I had been in modeling response sessions, and I think this frustrated her and ultimately the students.

Another complicating factor I struggled with was the nature of the adolescent experience. Kathryn's students seemed to wrestle all year with finding a comfort zone in their response sessions. Their experiences seemed to be colored by the ambivalence of adolescent insecurity. Many of the students were forever worried about hurting their own or others feelings. Female students were more likely to come right out and say they were not comfortable in their groups. Male anxiety can only be surmised from comments such as Michael's, "I can do it myself, I don't need any help." Gere (1987) points out that one of the major keys to success in response groups is establishing trust and safety in the response environment. Adolescents typically have a very difficult time feeling comfortable with or trusting anyone.

Kathryn's students were clearly able to provide in-depth response to the writing and give textual support to their comments, but they also seemed to hang back from pursuing rigorous response with each other more often than not. They expressed a desire to grow as writers who could communicate successfully with their peers. Kathryn let her students choose their own topics for writing, but they still viewed much of their writing as simply meeting a school assignment. They were apt to value efficient means for completing their work, rather than improving the communicative function of the writing.

Prior to this project, I had assumed Kathryn's struggles in implementing response groups were due to having a more controlling teaching style. I was wrong. Kathryn established structure in order to cope with the constraints of time. She created an organizational structure—the establishment of formal rules for behavior and daily academic routines, stiff assignment deadlines, mountains of record-keeping strategies—in order to survive. It seemed clear to me as a result of our collaborative project that the high school experience, with its segmented day and brief allotments of time for each class, contributes more to the precariousness of response group work than any other factor. The students and the teacher are multiply constrained and influenced by the time and scheduling limits placed on them.

I also gained difficult insights about being a teacher and a teacher educator through this collaborative project. When I volunteered to work in Kathryn's class, in addition to a sincere desire to support her, I had two less noble motives. I wanted to strut my teaching stuff and to collect some research data. Kathryn and I discussed the events that unfolded. I told Kathryn:

> When I came in, I was trying to be the teacher to the kids. I just figured that if I showed you what I did as a teacher in a classroom, you would be able to do what I did. I figured what had worked for me would work for you. But I never was their teacher, I was always an outsider.

This was a difficult and traumatic realization for me. I identified myself as a writing teacher and teacher-consultant. I felt like a failure because I had been unable to take over Kathryn's class and achieve immediate success. She replied:

> It was interesting when we got started. You were my teacher, I was ready to kiss your feet and give you anything you wanted. I was willing to turn the class over to you totally. But the kids weren't willing to give their loyalty to you the way I was. It became clear that you were here for me and not for them. (interview, March 5, 1991)

I realized during the course of the project that I was there for Kathryn, not for the students or to validate myself. If I was to be effective, I had to establish myself in her environment and work within her boundaries. I had to muddle around with her and try to find practical solutions to her very real problems and not just respond with a vagary of theoretical platitudes or exotic gimmicks. If our experience together was to be cooperatively educative and not just a showcase, I had to learn to see her classroom through her eyes. It was difficult for me to let go of the demonstration teaching role, but in order for me to be helpful to Kathryn, that was what I needed to do. I had to practice the democratic teacher/student relationship I preached. Creating that relationship is a never-ending process. Ultimately, we all learned from the experience that we each have our roles to play and it is impossible to erase the boundaries which delimit our spheres of participation. Kathryn sums up:

> The kids were relieved when I took the class back. They enjoyed having you, you have charisma and you work very well with kids, and for that they tolerated you, but they were always looking to me for the last word. I realized after the third or fourth time you were here, that they weren't going to turn their loyalty to me over to you, and that kind of surprised me. When you were out of the demonstration phase, they were glad to have done it, thought they'd had a very attractive substitute, but ready to get on with what I had planned. And that let me trust them a bit more. . . . All this collaboration has let me trust myself and them more, just by having someone else to talk to. (interview, March 5, 1991)

What Might This Mean?

Kathryn initially had tried to use response groups in her classroom and failed, but not because she didn't have the tools to make them work. She was stymied by a complex array of factors. When Kathryn was just beginning to try response groups, she felt that she didn't have the knowledge or the authority to experiment with a process as unpredictable as that of peer response. She was under a great deal of pressure to cover specific content and to do so in a very short amount of time. She had not yet gained the acknowledgment of her administrator or the community and that caused her to proceed with caution, not wanting to upset the institutional order of things.

The in-service training Kathryn had received in the Writing Project served both to help and hinder her success. She had seen experienced groups of students model peer response. She had participated in a successful adult response group with other Writing Project participants. She read writing process literature that promised her students would emerge from response groups as accomplished writers. She believed the promise. But when she returned to her classroom and response groups did not proceed as smoothly as the models, Kathryn began to doubt her ability to succeed. She measured the success of her groups against the yardstick of experience and maturity, and came up short every time.

The turning point for Kathryn came through collaborative involvement with people she viewed as more knowledgeable and experienced. It is not important to ascertain the validity of that assumption. It was what

Kathryn believed to be true. When she saw the tribulations experienced by highly respected teachers who publicly modeled peer response groups at a professional conference, she began to surmise that her expectations for groups may have been too high. That, in combination with the assurance she received in watching the struggles I had in working with her class, gave her the confidence to recognize her strengths and take additional risks.

Kathryn says that the collaborative process made her a different teacher. Before, she had focused on response with only one eye open, afraid to see the consequences. Having other eyes watching in her classroom caused her to examine closely what was going on. She evaluated herself along with the researcher who was there analyzing success and failure with her. Kathryn appreciated the specific feedback she received and learned to value the process of modeling collaborative processes. The modeling process helped her make a grand shift from operating out of a product-centered to a process-centered pedagogy. The process models provided her with a new menu of choices that allowed her to expand her teaching repertoire. She finds herself looking forward with new plans, ready to fine tune her expectations (interview, August 18, 1991).

Through open disclosure of the realities of conflict inherent in response group work by experienced teacher-consultants and the support of a collaborative other, one teacher was able to persist in succeeding with response groups. The experience of supportive collaboration gave a struggling teacher permission to relax unreasonable expectations and work developmentally at response groups, one step at a time. It gave her permission to accept the struggle as a stepping stone toward progress rather than a benchmark of failure.

In an analysis of the broader implications of this study on the process of collaboration, several factors are illuminated. In keeping with what Freedman discovered in a case study of response groups in two ninth-grade classrooms (1987a), the students in this study were reluctant to endorse the process of peer response, not so much perhaps because they were unable to do it because they were resistant to assume a role which might complicate peer relations. Freedman reports that "students cannot and do not want to play the role of teacher. They see the role as inappropriate for them both socially and intellectually" (1987a, p. 26).

However, something about Freedman's conclusions denies the ways in which Kathryn's students remained committed to the collaborative process as a means for helping them become more effective writers and readers. Kathryn's students wanted to receive direct and specific response to their writing, but limited their response sessions to what they deemed was a peer-appropriate level of holistic reassurance and demonstrative appreciation. They were puzzled by their simultaneous realization that although this type of feedback was reassuring, it wasn't what they needed to improve their writing. Ultimately they rejected it as counterfeit tender, wanting something more legitimate. They longed for more specific and direct response from their peers, but were unable to succeed in consistently giving it to one another. In spite of these complications, they continued to endorse the response process in the hope that it might succeed in helping them to become better writers and readers. Peer response in this instance seems to create an unresolved conflict between students' perceived social needs and their intellectual aspirations.

It is interesting to note, however, that some of the tension is erased when the students respond to their peers in writing rather than through oral response sessions. Students seem to be less hesitant to respond when providing written criticism to the writing of their peers. They give specific and direct feedback supported with textual references. This would tend to confound Freedman's findings that students feel the instructive role required in collaboration is inappropriate. We did find that students seem to have greater difficulty negotiating face-to-face critique. Perhaps this is because the nature of adolescent interaction is determined in a primarily oral domain and governed by an unwritten code of conduct that shuns openly confrontive behaviors which may brand one as an outcast. But written response may provide adolescent students with enough distance between speaker and audience to transcend the code of conduct that seems to limit adolescent interactions in oral response sessions to feigned despondence and inane vacuities.

Another point to notice is the difference between the teacher's and the students' perceptions of conduct appropriate for student interaction in response groups. The teacher resolved to provide less structure and more indirect methods of teaching as an indication of her commitment to the benefits of collaborative learning, and her trust in her students. The students, on the other hand, requested more structure and direct instruction in order that they might perform the task of response more successfully and efficiently in the academic setting. The teacher seems most interested in focusing on the social nature of knowledge construction, and meeting intellectual needs in the process. The students are most concerned about school activities focusing on the cognitive aspects of their intellectual growth. The students may perceive their involvement in response group work, which requires pedantic as well as social interaction, to constitute role reversal, but it does not cause them to reject the process altogether.

Perhaps the students resist active participation in response groups because they want to maintain control in their social realm, protecting it from the foreign assault of institutional infringement, embodied by the teacher. This is a troublesome conflict of interest which cannot be easily resolved. How might the teacher in a democratic classroom respond? She determines that a balance of power and authority evolves in an environment in which students have the freedom to make curricular and procedural decisions. The class environment operates informally and students have the opportunity to work at their own pace, with peers of their choosing. The students, on the other hand, reject this freedom. They want the teacher to be more directive, police them more so they don't have to take responsibility for managing interactions with their peers which may create unequal relations of power between them—assuming a hierarchy with which they are uncomfortable. The teacher is trying to loosen some of the oppressive restrictions limiting the students' full participation in their own literacy development. The students want the teacher to take more control of their literacy learning within the boundaries of school. What's the appropriate response?

Although Freedman is on the right track in pointing out the social entanglements that confound the intellectual process of collaboration, what we see illuminated in this project is that students do not unilaterally reject collaboration. They are simply asking for greater assistance in negotiating their way across a nettled path. Their call for more structure may be interpreted as a healthy one—a call for support through the process, not retreat from the process. The students seem to be asking for assistance in regulating their social interactions in the classroom because they see interpersonal control as within the teacher's legitimate domain, not theirs. If the teacher will assist them in monitoring social interactions in their classroom environment, they will not be encumbered with complicating peer relations, which for adolescents are already tenuous enough, leaving them free to learn to do the literacy work they really want to do.

In our growing understanding of the collaborative process, we became aware that teacher-researcher-student hierarchies were inevitable. Being democratic did not make us equal. Although we tried to share authority and balance the power relations, what mainly occurred for us through collaboration was an articulation of the different and unequal roles each member of the team fulfilled. We learned to attempt to share power through negotiation. But the power balance was always heavily weighted on one or the other side. We tried to be open and honest and express our wants and needs in order to complete the work we were trying to accomplish, but our openness always was filtered through and constrained by the role we played. Often our goals conflicted with the ways we determined progress. We ultimately decided that we gained a tolerance for dissensus (Trimbur, 1989) through collaboration. We learned together that we each had realized the inevitability of our power to take control of our situation from others. In the multi-cultured world of our classroom, that was simultaneously unsettling and unsatisfying.

Where Do We Go From Here?

Implementation of peer response groups is not an easy task even for experienced writing teachers. Collaborative classrooms are never struggle-free. Teachers attempting peer response groups in their writing classrooms should set forth with the smallest expectations and the largest patience. It takes months of preparation to create supportive environments in which students may feel comfortable responding to one another. Students need ongoing demonstrations that model response group protocol and critical reading techniques. Responders need to be familiar with strategies for improving the communicative function of their writing. They need many opportunities to discuss response successes and failures. Successes ought to be celebrated and failures to be viewed as obstacles to negotiate around. All this takes time and support.

Teachers are rarely free to authorize use of time or decide appropriate curriculum in their classrooms. This is a considerable roadblock that impedes the pursuit of best practice. Even when teachers struggle to overcome the oppressing isolation and deskilling (Apple, 1986) conditions of their work, they continue to question their own efficacy. How might the secondary school be structured in a more humanizing way?

As teachers learn to support the collaborative efforts of their students, they need the support of collaboration themselves. Finding a colleague with whom to share the small successes and failures may make all the difference in whether a teacher is able to succeed with response groups in the writing classroom. The formation of peer support groups, buddying up with a colleague down the hall or a teacher in another school, and soliciting the district writing or language arts coordinator to make a series of observations, may give us the other pair of eyes through which we see ourselves and find the authority to control our work.

Demonstration in-service response sessions may be boon and bane to struggling writing teachers. Experienced teacher-consultants ought to think about ways in which they may spotlight not only the successes of peer response groups, but the struggles as well. Discuss the milestones and pitfalls of response group work. Think about asking teachers to bring a group of their own students to a response group in-service. Involve everyone, teachers and students alike, in a mock response demonstration. Spend lots of time in follow-up debriefing sessions. Address the epistemological and political implications of collaborative learning.

The ability to give useful response to writers is an art learned over time. When more teachers are providing their students with the opportunity to collaborate in peer response sessions, students will feel more at ease and become more adept with the process. It is worth the effort to provide support to teachers struggling to teach collaborative processes in their classrooms. When more teachers are incorporating response groups in the writing classroom, the endeavor will benefit us all.

However, none of this unknots the tangled threads still dangling from our delicate fabric of collaboration. We are left to negotiate among an array of student responses that range from, "Leave us alone!" to "We need more direction!" We are left to ponder the contradiction we uncovered—that providing students with the opportunity to respond to each other as collegial members of a community of readers and writers may inextricably change the nature of the peer relationship, the very thing we value. We don't know what to do with our realization that no matter how much we desire a democratic balance of power through collaboration, there is no such thing. Or that the humanizing process of democratic negotiation is not often comfortable. We also squirm with the realization that the most important thing for all of us, teachers, researchers, students, is to maintain equilibrium in our social interactions—that we often choose to be polite instead of honest. But these are the hard-edged results of working through collaborative processes. Even though our questions are unresolved, we have gained through collaboration insight into the problematic nature of our work, along with permission to keep trying to untie the knots.

This analysis fits for teachers and researchers alike. It may help us renegotiate the constraints under which we work. If collaborative processes are continually evolving, so are writing processes, and social and intellectual development. As teachers we must keep pushing on these things in our students and in ourselves rather than retreating to the comfort zone. Collaboration may play us the music to dance on the edges where we try so hard to live.

Works Cited

Apple, M. (1986). *Teachers and Texts*. New York: Routledge and Kegan Paul.

Atwell, N. (1987). *In the Middle*. Portsmouth, NH: Heinemann.

Bartholomae, D. (1985). Inventing the University. In M. Rose (Ed.), *When a Writer Can't Write: Studies in Writer's Block and Other Composing Problems*. New York: Guilford Press.

Berkenkotter, C. (1984). Student Writers and Their Sense of Authority Over Texts. *College Composition and Communication,* 34(3): 312–319.

Britton, J., et al. (1975). *The Development of Writing Abilities, K-12*. London: Macmillan Education Ltd.

Bruffee, K. (1973). Collaborative Learning: Some Practical Models. *College English,* 34(5): 579–586.

————. (1978). The Brooklyn Plan: Attaining Intelectual Growth Through Peer Group Tutoring. *Liberal Education*, 64: 447–468.

————. (1984). Peer Tutoring and the "Conversation of Mankind." *College English*, 46(7): 635–652.

Calkins, L.M. (1986). *The Art of Teaching Writing*. Portsmouth, NH: Heinemann.

DiPardo, A.S. & Freedman, S.W. (1987). *Historical Overview: Groups in the Writing Classroom* (Tech. Rep. No. 4). Berkeley: Center for the Study of Writing.

————. (1988). Peer Response Groups in the Writing Classroom: Theoretic Foundations and New Directions. *Review of Educational Research,* 58(2): 119–149.

Elbow, P. (1973). *Writing Without Teachers.* London: Oxford University Press.

————. (1981). *Writing with power.* London: Oxford University Press.

Flower, L. & Hayes, J.R. (1979). Writer-based Prose: A Cognitive Basis for Problems in Writing. *College English,* 4: 19–37.

Freedman, S.W. (1985a). *The Acquisition of Written Language: Response and Revision.* Norwood, NJ: Ablex.

————. (1985b). *The Role of Response in the Acquisition of Written Language.* Final report to the National Institute of Education, NIE–G–083–0067. Berkeley: University of California.

————. (1987a). *Peer Response in Two Ninth-Grade Classrooms.* (Tech. Rep. No. 12). Berkeley: University of California.

————. (1987b). *Response to Student Writing* (Research Report No. 23). Urbana, IL: National Council of Teachers of English.

Gere, A.R. (1987). *Writing groups: History, Theory and Implications.* Carbondale: Southern Illinois University Press.

Gitlin, A. (1990a). Educative Research, Voice and School Change. *Harvard Educational Review,* 60(4): 443–466.

————. (1990b). Understanding Teaching Dialogically. *Teachers College Record,* 91(4): 547–564.

Graves, D. (1983). *Writing: Teachers and Children at Work.* Portsmouth, NH: Heinemann.

Gray, J. (1986). University of California, Berkeley: The Bay Area Writing Project and the National Writing Project. *Carnegie Quarterly,* 27(2).

Guskey, T.R. (1986). Staff development. *Educational Researcher,* 15(15): 5–12.

Healy, M.K. (1980). *Using student writing response groups in the classroom.* Berkeley: Bay Area Writing Project.

Lather, P. (1986a). Issues of Validity in Openly Ideological Research: Between a Rock and a Soft Place. *Interchange,* 17(4): 63–84.

————. (1986b). Research as Praxis. *Harvard Educational Review,* 56 (3): 257–277.

McLaughlin, M.W. (1990). The Rand Change Agent Study Revisited: Macro Perspectives and Micro Realities. *Educational Researcher,* 19(9): 11–16.

Rico, G.L. (1983). *Writing the Natural Way.* Boston: Houghton Mifflin Co.

Spear, K. (1988). *Sharing Writing.* Portsmouth, NH: Boynton/Cook.

Smith, T.S. (1983). *Handbook for Planning an Effective Writing Program Grades K–12.* Sacramento: California State Department of Education.

Strong, W.S. (1988, May). Utah State University, Department of Secondary Education, Utah Writing Project Coordinator, Logan, Utah. Interview.

Trimbur, J. (1989). Consensus and Difference in Collaborative Learning. *College English,* 51(6): 602–616.

Vygotsky, L.S. (1962). *Thought and Language.* (E. Hanfmann & L. Vakan, trans.). Cambridge: MIT Press.

——— . (1978). *Mind in Society.* Cambridge: Harvard University Press.

3

Designing Assignments that Foster Collaboration

Karen Spear

There's nothing magical or even unusual about the kinds of writing students do in a collaborative writing class—except that they do a lot of it. The formal assignments themselves are typical: Heather's class writes an adventure story; Becky's class a series of letters; mine various types of analysis; Nolyn's THE RESEARCH PAPER. Students write journals; they write notes and letters; they write drafts and multiple revisions; they write comments on papers and suggestions to each other; they write to each other and they write to teachers.

What is distinctive about writing assignments in collaborative classes is the context. Writing, talking about the writing, and writing about the talking are what the class is all about. Writing is not just something held off for the final performance; it is woven into the fabric of daily activity and is integral to creating and sustaining the community life of the class. Although revised and polished pieces still signal the completion of one chunk of study and the beginning of another, the development of individual pieces of writing and the use of writing and talking to develop them are the regular business of the class.

Concerns for audience and purpose are central in classes like these, displacing more conventional preoccupations with form, length, or mode. This is no small shift for teachers to make. We have spent our professional lives surrounded by lists of one hundred sure-fire essay topics and we've probably yearned to be able to plug them in to our classes and achieve the success that's implied. These lists reinforce the notion that writing can exist out there somewhere and can simply drop in for the occasional visit when it's time for students to produce something. Such lists feed the myth that successful teaching is struggle-free.

For some years in writing workshops for faculty, I have asked participants to describe on an index card a writing assignment they had recently

51

given that they thought was "pretty good." The list below, synthesized from hundreds of teachers ranging from elementary to graduate school faculty, illustrates their notion of pretty good assignments. It also represents our students' experience of school writing:

Sample Writing Assignments, K–graduate

1. Research the life of Michelangelo or Leonardo da Vince and discuss the impact of the man's work on Renaissance art.

2. Discuss the relationship of "*x*" line of poetry to the rest of the poem, considering diction, imagery, tone, and structure.

3. Compare your initial reactions to the characters in the film *Pride and Prejudice* to your reactions at the end of the film.

4. Describe what you have learned in the last two terms.

5. Write up and present an oral report on some aspect of consumer education, such as the use and care of clothing.

6. Write an essay about some aspect of the future: what will happen in twenty, thirty, or three hundred years in one particular area such as education, dress, music?

7. Write an autobiography analyzing a childhood experience as a way of remembering childhood feelings.

8. Write about what you considered the most interesting chapter in the social studies text.

9. Write a critique of Shakespeare's *Othello*.

10. Tell me what you learned about _____ today; tell me why you think we talked about _____ today.

11. Choose a short story or poem from our recent unit that was especially meaningful and in an essay of at least three paragraphs, explain why it was so meaningful.

12. Choose a practice in your society that you find reprehensible and, based on your reading of *Candide*, write a satire in which you make your readers share your feelings about that practice.

13. Write an essay that answers the following questions as they are explained in "*x*" reading assignment.

14. Write an argumentative essay of five paragraphs in which you give three reasons to support your position on a controversial topic.

15. Answer in essay form, "How does Cervantes feel about Don Quixote?"

16. Explain the side effects of "*x*" common compound in several over-the-counter drugs.

17. Write a summary of our World Affairs forum.

18. Submit reading notes from four hours of reading _____ book.

19. Write a five-page theme paper dealing with one of the following issues: the social, political, and economic effects of the Black Death on Europe; the Shiite and Sunnite sects of the Moslem religion; the Renaissance; the Reformation.

20. Evaluate your progress in this course by examining your strengths and weaknesses, gains and losses achieved during the term.

21. Read a newspaper article and make up a quiz with questions on one side of the page and answers on the other.

22. Final exam: Compose an essay on the nature and function of literature: Why do we write it, read it, analyze it?

23. Compare English society before and after the Industrial Revolution.

24. Write the autobiography of your shoe.

25. Relate the following passage to the play as a whole.

26. Write a summary of the first three paragraphs of "*x*" article, which you have just read.

27. Compare creationism and evolution as examples of scientific explanation.

28. Write a one-page review of a fine arts event. Use one paragraph to give your reactions and a second that relates the event to class material.

29. Take a basic concept in American government such as freedom of speech and apply it to society today.

30. Trace a specific bill through Congress.

31. Pretend you are a foreign reporter and write a column predicting the outcome of a revolution occurring in the country where you are stationed.

32. Write about the concept of time in Western society.

33. Relate an incident in which you experienced intense anger, explaining how you resolved your feelings.

34. Write an evaluation of the teachers, administrators, custodians, cafeteria staff, and student government as you have observed them this school year.

35. Describe how you would handle the following situation: a group of your friends is being rude to a new student, and while you want to be part of the "in group," you believe the outsider is being treated unfairly.

36. Write a short story on the topic of your choice.

37. Describe a person you know, listing physical characteristics, interests, skills, hobbies, and dress. It should be three-quarters of a page long.

38. Write a letter of complaint.

39. Write a five hundred-word report on any state in the United States.

40. Write an essay describing the central conflict in Robert Frost's poem, "A Hillside Thaw."

41. Write a research paper (five hundred-word minimum) about something significant in your denominational history.

Faced with this list, workshop participants generally make these observations:

1. Preoccupations with form and length dominate school writing. (Small wonder that our students' first question is, "How long does it have to be?")

2. The assignments mostly seem generic, interchangeable, lacking any particular context.

3. A high proportion ask essentially for regurgitation of information—a way to certify that the student has mastered the necessary content.

4. Many of the assignments are so abstract that even workshop participants are at a loss about how to approach them.

5. Writing for an audience other than the teacher-as-examiner seems almost unheard of; writing for a purpose that approximates genuine communication is equally unusual.

6. A high proportion of the assignments sound as if an ideal version of them exists in the teacher's mind, and the students' job is to guess what the assignment is and write as close an approximation as they can.

7. Only a few assignments (like the autobiography of the shoe) are genuinely engaging or acknowledge a role for creative expression. Collectively, this group does not evoke much interest in writing, or in reading what's been written.

8. We have all written too many of these assignments in our own school careers; in fact assignments like these have probably shaped our notions of what a writing assignment ought to look like.

Flawed as my experimental design may be for eliciting these examples, the list calls forth nods and squirms of recognition from teachers who see their own practice reflected here. The point is that shorthand responses like these are common when writing is product- and teacher-centered. Teachers who organize their work around collaborative principles find it nearly impossible to reduce their assignments to a series of one-liners. I can hear Nolyn saying, "I assign the research paper, but . . ." or Becky Reimer saying, "They write letters to Navajo students in southern Utah because . . ." or Heather saying, "We wound up writing adventure short stories after . . ." Assignments in collaborative writing classes are, quite literally, "designed"—sculpted from the clay that's available in a particular classroom at a particular time and place, evolved collectively, and frequently chiseled or sanded even after the clay has dried and hardened into what was once thought to be a finished piece.

Or, to shift the metaphor, writing assignments in these classes are roadmaps designed to take students to a particular destination but also to point out the interesting sights along the way. They teach students to write by writing rather than asking the writing to demonstrate mastery of something that happened elsewhere in the life of the class. Each of the chapters in this book is, in one sense, a writing assignment, or more accurately a series of related assignments. Even stripped of the narrative and the examples, the assignments come with lots of material: brainstorming guides, lists of criteria, model texts, response guides for various stages of drafting and editing, evaluation guides, checklists, and debriefing materials.

If the assignments are the roadmaps, writing them is the journey. In fact, the road trip is a useful metaphor for thinking about designing and teaching collaborative writing assignments. In this chapter, I'd like to develop this metaphor fully as a way to think about designing assignments that foster collaboration, and then take you through one of my own assignments to show you how the process works.

As in any road trip, there are several events: Figuring Out the Destination, Packing, Checking the Map, Roadside Picnics and Other Unscheduled Stops, Getting Gas, The Last Miles, Unloading. First, no matter how many trips you take, you always start a journey at the beginning. While this may be obvious for travelling, teachers forget that the same truism holds for the road trip of writing: you always start at the beginning and the beginning is much the same for every trip. The chapters in this book follow different groups of students from seventh grade to their junior year in college. Nevertheless, each group of students starts at the beginning—every year, with every assignment—learning and relearning how to share their writing, how to respond, how to revise. My college students may be able to figure out where they're going or to pack more quickly than Becky Reimer's seventh graders, but all of them still have to go through the same processes of building community, establishing trust, adapting to the demands of new courses, new ideas and teachers. They still have to start at the beginning.

Figuring Out the Destination

Collaborative writing teachers involve students in deciding where they want to go and how to get there, but the process is far from unstructured. You can see from the chapters that each teacher has a clear idea of what she wants the assignment to accomplish, and each one takes a highly directive role in helping students map the course. The chapters model an array of approaches. Collecting a writing autobiography is a helpful way to start the year because students write to a teacher-as-reader rather than teacher-as-examiner, and teachers get a glimpse of students' assumptions about writing and learning. Collectively devising a list of criteria or characteristics for the sort of writing students will be doing is another way of figuring out the destination and making sure everyone is preparing for the same trip. Developing a group portrait of the audience, as in the case of Becky Reimer's letters to the Navajo students, teaches students about their ability to work together to create something fuller than anyone could create alone. Giving students a chance to talk about what they already know about the topic or the particular form of writing sets the collaborative process in motion and also helps them see the personal roots of knowing. Many teachers organize students in groups for these initial activities and ask each group to report their findings—listing their ideas on the board or an easel, selecting their best idea, identifying the hardest part—all to engage students in solving problems collaboratively, to draw on prior knowledge, and to be accountable to the rest of the class for their work. Each group's work in these early stages contributes to what the class is doing as a whole. Thus, all these activities are ways of anchoring writing in students' interactions and of building community around students' contributions.

In a study of peer review in a college anthropology course, Anne Herrington and Deborah Cadman conclude that the peer review is a product of the teacher's effective balance of structure and autonomy, particularly the exercise of student autonomy within the collaboration. Their closing observations characterize the sort of context-setting that is part of assignment design for successful collaborative teachers:

> The kind of learning that develops confidence and authority in students, independent decision-making and an ability to present themselves effectively to others can be accomplished with peer review. Whether it does will in large part depend on teachers. It means that the primary concern when initiating peer review in a class is not to teach students how to critique written drafts—that's secondary; it is first to create a classroom

environment where we give students the gift of having some responsibility—some authority for their own learning. To do that means first believing that students can exercise that responsibility productively. They can (Herrington and Cadman, 1991, 197).

Herrington and Cadman are suggesting here that students aren't the only ones who need to figure out the destination. Teachers, too, need to develop a clear sense of what they want their role to be and to communicate to students what they can expect. Heather Brunjes's account of her colleague's hesitation in plunging into response groups and Becky Laney's account of her early flounderings portray what can happen when teachers try to embark on one kind of journey while trying to keep one foot planted back at home.

Packing

When you pack for a trip, you assemble all the stuff you think you might need; you find containers that will hold it, and you organize it so that when you unpack, everything will come out pretty much as it went in. Collaborative writing classes help students pack together. They may break up into groups to discuss specific questions about a text that will guide their writing. They may form research teams along the lines that James Reither and Douglas Vipond describe in "Writing as Collaboration", (1991) with each team member responsible for collecting information on one aspect of the topic. They may list everything they know and then work with a partner who tries to draw out more material or help to focus what's there. Whatever the activity, collaborative writing teachers show students how to do it, sometimes by demonstrating, sometimes by having students model the process, sometimes by asking students to figure out what will work. Marj Coombs helps students pack for their trip by having them read transcripts from other students in a response group to analyze the strengths and weaknesses of writing groups. Collaborative writing teachers help students master the process, describe what worked and what didn't, talk about what they need or what they did well. They see these activities as central to the assignment, not peripheral, because each individual assignment is part of a larger journey toward competence as readers, writers, and collaborators.

Checking the Map

In any journey, you need to pause periodically to see if you are where you think you ought to be—or if you like where you've found yourself and where you are heading. After all, drafts, like maps, are only rough approximations of the road itself, and to read one well you need to be able to fill in the gaps by imagining how the representation corresponds to the real thing—and whether you really want to go where the map is pointing you. This is where some of the inherent difficulties in peer response make themselves felt. As novice writers look at drafts, they often don't know where they are and don't know quite how to find themselves. Teachers and students alike complain that they "get off track" or that they don't know enough about writing to say when it's good or bad.

Collaborative writing assignments provide some natural stopping points to check the map and teach students how to read it. Equally important, they build in opportunities for students to teach each other. The variety of response guides in these chapters shows that responding to a draft is not a generic process, but that teachers are trying to develop specific skills or to add a new dimension to the ways students talk with one another. Beth Johnson's chapter shows how she convenes groups to look at some very specific elements of writing, while Becky Reimer illustrates how she works with students to shape very specific kinds of responses to each other's work. These teachers also help to structure students' discussions to keep them from wandering, usually by asking students to do something that pulls their conversation together: making notes or suggestions, free writing, turning something in that makes students accountable for their time. The teachers assume a role I frequently describe in my own classes as a spy: They drift from group to group, listening to what's going on, exerting a subtle pressure on students to stay focused, conducting impromptu conferences, underscoring for the class as a whole both problems and successes, keeping tight time limits that push students to get the job done.

Roadside Picnics and Other Unscheduled Stops

One of the real pleasures of road trips is taking time to enjoy what you see along the way. Effective writing assignments likewise emphasize to students what they are learning by taking the trip and invite them to savor what they encounter by sharing it. In many of these chapters, you get a sense of playfulness—that the trip is as rewarding as the destination. You can see this in Kristi Kramer's chapter as her students use writing to discover themselves, in Beth Johnson's student, Mike, who realizes after starting one draft that he didn't have much to say, in Marj Coombs's writing samples from her eighth graders, and in Bill Strong's co-author, Trudy Griffin, who discovers through the writing workshop that writing can be an authentic activity after all. In fact, one of the most remarkable unscheduled stops reported in many of the stories here, teachers' and students' alike, is the realization that writing in a collaborative setting helps people begin to experience themselves more honestly, to appropriate learning for their own ends, and to take off the masks they have learned to wear before their teachers or peers. Collaborative writing assignments have enough structure to achieve the ends teachers desire, to provide writers some heuristic guidance, and to give students a common basis for peer review, but they also have enough flexibility to let students adapt the assignment to their own needs—to make their own unscheduled stops.

Getting Gas

In *Active Voice* (1981), James Moffett called this phase of the journey "mid-writing." Novice writers need to learn what experienced writers encounter all the time—that writing generates new ideas and new questions, and that writers need to stop periodically to re-think or to re-search. In other words, they need to refuel to follow the directions that emerge from their preliminary work. For students, the difficulty is to suspend closure on their thinking and to remain open and receptive to new insights. Many of the chapters here illustrate how teachers can keep writing alive as a process by delaying the point at which their students review each other's work as emerging product. Cheri Ause's case study of Aron traces the development of his story about an encounter with a train through successive drafts, each becoming increasingly detailed, while she suspends the final editing until he has reached his destination. The research project that I discuss below also shows how an assignment might unfold to point writers toward more sophisticated levels of analysis.

In both these examples, conversations among peers keep the thinking process open. These mid-point conversations are structured to promote question-asking and idea generation, in Cheri's case through directions she provides to give students new perspectives on their work, and in my case through the complexity of the inquiry and the natural stages of investigation that are built in. Role playing gives students a way to look at each other's work from new perspectives and to understand that to offer advice or ask questions is a form of coaching rather than criticism. For instance, teaching students the differences between separate and connected knowing gives them new ways of thinking about unfinished writing and legitimizes the dialectic between doubting and believing, between challenging what's there and supporting it by expanding it. Thus students might take on the roles of doubting and believing, by assigning roles to different students in a group or by asking all students to play the roles of believers for one period and doubters for another. This sort of role playing helps them respond to drafts with lessened anxiety and self-consciousness about hurting feelings or being overly presumptuous.

What's important in all these examples is that the students have assumed ownership of their work, and what helps them assume ownership is the regular return to response groups for a new infusion of ideas or a new set of questions, along with the implicit expectation that the writing should be changing and growing. The examples from students' conversations and their writing itself suggest that they are not simply completing an assignment; they are working out ideas that have become meaningful to them and that they want to communicate to others. The assignments are structured to keep students' levels of attention and energy high.

The Last Miles

Process-oriented writing teachers and writing workshops are often criticized for failing to reach completion. Faculty writing workshops are littered with brilliant but unfinished work, and writing teachers who are resistant to sidetracking writing instruction with too much emphasis on grammar and mechanics often come under fire from parents and administrators for the errors in their students' "finished" work. Collaborative writing classes offer a wealth of possibilities for traveling these last miles of correcting and polishing. Gerald Camp's fine monograph, *A Success Curriculum for Remedial Students* (1982), published by the National Writing Project, illustrates how remedial students can become "expert" in various grammar and mechanics problems and teach their peers how to correct and edit their work. Editing groups can spot errors in a novice writer's work more quickly than the writer herself when a final editing session is part of the trip. Aron's final paper offers a strong statement of what happens when the assignment is unequivocal about a final, perfected product and when the teacher organizes the class so that such products can emerge.

Unloading

Unloading the car symbolizes the end of any road trip. For collaborative writing assignments, the unloading can occur in two ways: First, students often share their final pieces, not as a speciman of writing but as a legitimate mode of self-expression and communication. Nolyn's class, for instance, publishes the work of each response group in a magazine and shares it with each other and audiences out of class. Becky Reimer's class sends the letters they have written and follows them up with an actual visit to their Navajo neighbors. Unloading after a trip has that fatigued feeling of accomplishment. No less so with writing.

Equally important for these classes is another facet of unloading—debriefing about the experience itself. These teachers insist that students reflect on what they've learned from the journey, particularly what they've learned about how to read and nurture each other's writing. The journals and learning logs that are so prominent in these classes are one way to help students become self-reflective. The letters to teachers are another. Heather's and Kathryn's class is full of opportunities for students' to talk freely about what they have learned, and Becky Reimer's careful attention to techniques of responding keeps students reflective and questioning. Marj Coombs's invitation to her students to tell her who in the class they think would make a good response partner is another way in which students are encouraged to plan for the next journey as soon as the present one is complete. The student talk that you hear throughout these chapters emphasizes the centrality of students' voices to the collaborative process.

The Journey in Miniature—An Illustration

Let me illustrate this road trip by taking you on a journey I developed for my own writing courses. This particular version is for a writing course on nuclear weapons, but the features of the assignment are generic enough that it can be adapted to many topics and levels. In this course I am interested in engaging students with an issue that affects their everyday life, politically and economically, and that may well affect their very existence. Whatever the topic of the course, I use this type of assignment to help students connect what we're studying with their lives outside the classroom and with the lives of members of their community. I am asking them to collect and analyze information through interviews and thus to see research in more inclusive terms than the obligatory hours in the library and the mechanics of footnoting and citing sources.

This assignment occurs about a third of the way through my course. Students have been working in response groups and writing personal narratives and some other brief, "objective" assignments such as a precis and some analyses of simple statistics. The assignment is a highly collaborative one that involves interviewing a number of people in the community, sharing interview notes, analyzing the data these notes present, and writing up the analysis. We call it our "Public Perceptions Survey." The goal is not just to find out what people in the community think about nuclear weapons, but to come to some deeper level of understanding about what they really know and what their attitudes reveal about them.

The first step is to decide what we want to know—in other words, to figure out a destination. The class takes a day to brainstorm questions while I write them on the board. Either I or a volunteer from the class writes up our preliminary questions as a handout for the next class, when our task is to refine and narrow down our questions and decide on a population to interview. These are lively sessions with lots of debate and negotiation about the clarity or appropriateness of our ideas, the reliability of the information we will gather, the desirable scope of our questions, and who we will interview. As with any genuine research, the class anticipates the outcome and works to develop a survey that will get them there. They begin to see that research is not a matter of filling empty vessels or writing on blank slates, that real researchers have a pretty good idea where they are going before they set out. Obviously, the class must call upon what they have already read in ways that deepen their understanding and ability to use what they have previously studied.

My classes have typically decided not to interview people their own age since our own attitudes and experiences have become pretty clear by this point in the term. Generally, they decide to interview an older population, sometimes people their parents' age, sometimes people who fought in the Second World War, sometimes a split population such as men and women or people in the military and people not in the military to see how their attitudes compare. They realize that some demographic information will be necessary as a way to characterize individual respondents. Figure 3-1 gives an example of the questionnaire that a class of college freshmen developed.

Once our survey questions are complete, we spend some time talking about how to collect the data. This is the packing phase of our trip. The plan is for each student to interview one person and to write up interview notes as a one-page handout for the rest of the class. We talk about what we need from the notes to make them useful as a basis for the analysis, and it becomes clear, among other things, that paraphrasing, quoting, and the issues of selectivity that are involved in these skills will be essential—which comes as something of a pleasant surprise since previous assignments such as precis writing have emphasized just those activities. My own goal is to set up a collaboration that places the students' notes at the center of their task. Students find themselves relying on each other's writing—depending on it, in fact—to develop their analysis.

Younger students need to spend some time practicing interviewing. By having them interview each other in class and then debrief, I find that I can continue to validate role playing as a way of learning, teach them how to ask open-ended questions, and defuse the prospect of "criticizing" each other since the goal at this point is to coach and troubleshoot for each other. Here, too, the public nature of the practice continues to emphasize the collaborative character of the class. No one wants to be embarrassed by turning in poor interview notes to the rest of the class.

Next, I ask two students to volunteer to do their interviews early as a pilot test of our survey. The class is typically grateful for their help, and since their role is so clearly experimental, the rest of the class feels free to discuss the pilot interview notes as a way to get the bugs out of the process for themselves. We usually find that some of our questions don't make sense to our subjects and need to be modified. The student volunteers are also useful resources for advice on how to conduct the interview, how to get answers of some depth, what to do and what not to do, what

Figure 3-1
Interview Questions for the Public Perceptions Survey

Demographics:
> Age
> Occupation
> Education
> Income $0-$15,000
> > $15,000-$35,000
> > $35,000 or higher

Questions:

What are your feelings about the dropping of the atomic bomb
> a) at the time of World War II?
> b) presently?

How likely is a nuclear war during your lifetime?

Do you believe you and your family are likely to survive a nuclear war?

What do you know about the effects of nuclear explosions on the environment and on humans?

What do you think is the best solution to the arms race?

Do you believe the United States and the Soviet Union are making any significant progress in controlling nuclear weapons?

Who do you believe is the more aggressive party in the arms race today: the United States or the Soviet Union?

Why do you believe the United States has insisted on retaining a first strike option in its use of nuclear weapons?

Is it necessary to retain nuclear weapons for possible use against terrorism?

Can disarmament or arms reductions agreements be trusted?

How do you think the Soviet people feel about nuclear war? Where do they get their information?

Are the American people subject to propaganda regarding nuclear weapons and nuclear war from their government?

In the event of an international incident such as the Cuban Missile Crisis, can the American government be trusted to make decisions that will prevent further escalation?

difficulties they ran into when compiling their notes. What is particularly interesting in this phase of the assignment is seeing authority shift to the student volunteers, and thus implicitly to the students themselves. Figure 3–2 is an example of one student's interview notes from a class conducted at the time of the Persian Gulf War.

Once the interviews are finished and the notes are distributed, students assemble in small groups to read and make initial observations on what they are seeing. They have a lot of material to sort through: a class of twenty-two students, for instance, means twenty-two pages of notes for each person. I periodically call the whole class together and ask them to share their observations and to begin making some interpretations and anticipating problems. Early on, students will see that the data are messy, that conclusions are not immediately apparent, that this doesn't look as neat as a workbook exercise. Students undergo a period of considerable frustration at this point because they can't make blanket statements about the data. They discover that they need to identify strategies for organizing the data in order to analyze it at all, strategies such as making their own notes question by question and beginning to categorize different sorts of responses. Their attention to the process of making knowledge becomes highly self-conscious: it's the only way to make sense of an otherwise bewildering array of material. Much of the conversation in class has to do with how one analyses the notes, and students come to value their peers' ingenuity. Some employ statistical analyses ranging from the primitive to the sophisticated, with means, percentages, and frequencies; others look for conceptual or thematic linkages. They all realize that just staring at the notes won't generate much meaning; they have to do something with the material to get it to make sense.

Nevertheless, once they have had a chance to make preliminary observations in class, they begin drafting more thorough independent analyses using some of the strategies the class has discovered, and they return with more complete notes to share and eventually with a first draft. Once they begin working on the draft, a new set of difficulties opens up. By now they are confronted with important questions about how to justify observations that are only partially true, how to separate fact from opinion (and whether it's possible to do so at all), how to decide what to pay attention to and what to leave out, whether to rely more heavily on some respondents, why some seem more reliable than others, how to select examples, the value of the extended example, how to justify omitting some material, and so on. These discussions are the important side trips of the journey because they move students away from a naive faith that answers are either right or wrong and help them instead to consider how to make a convincing case for their interpretation of the material. During this phase of the writing, the response groups hum with these questions,

Figure 3-2

A Student's Interview Notes from a Class Conducted at the Time of the
Persian Gulf War

Demographic Information:

    Age 53

    Sex M

    Educational Background 2 Years College

    Residence Loveland Colorado

    Two Nephews in the Gulf

    1 war-Vietnam, Lebanon and Cuba crisis

    25 years U.S Navy Ret. Capt.

He felt that the U.S should not use nuclear weapons in the Gulf because too many lives would be lost. Other surrounding countries would too suffer the effects of the weapon. But he stated under some circumstances a nuclear weapon should be used, as retaliation for the use of a nuclear attack against us. If the war was lasting to long and service men were dying at an alarming rate. Last if Iraqi-sponsored terrorist activities involving nuclear weapons and used then against us. He felt that if Chemical weapons or Biological weapons were used we should use the same "Eye for an Eye". As for the environment he felt that it would be total Chaos, no growth of vegetation what so ever for years, people being massively deformed "Mutated", unbelievable burning of human flesh and environment. In general the environment would be unlivable, "The place would be Desolate". "Look at Japan" he said "People are still living the after math of a nuclear weapon—that was a little one compared to the ones we have today". It would take years for the earth to clear up, but in time it will.

"Third World Countries would most likely use a nuclear weapon." He felt that they (Third world Leaders) really don't have anything to lose, so they don't look into the future and think differently then the U.S. U.S and Super Power leaders tend to look at the long range effect of the weapon and know what the weapon does.

With concerning disarmament he felt that it could be done "Yes, not make them". As for reducing them it is impossible because other countries will lie, "Look at the U.S Navy." The United States said they will cut back on military build up and reduce the number of ships. They then Moth Balled the ships and continued to stock up on the ammunition they used. Any new weapon developed was made to adapt to the old Battle Ships like the U.S.S Wisconsin now serving in the Gulf. So we would say that we would cut back but in reality would not, like any other country would". It is desirable for disarmament but every country is afraid of one another and will not commit to disarmament. Nuclear weapons play no part in the decision in today politics. "It's a weapon like any other weapon but used as a last resort. First Conventional, Chemical-Biological then at last resort Nuclear, but doesn't play any role in going to war.

and though the students feel that they are about to crumble under the weight of the cognitive overload they are experiencing, they are neverthe-less caught up in a process of making meaning out of their own materials.

Once into their second draft, I begin nudging students to do less reporting of the data and more interpreting. Many students have diffi-culty really making this transition, and many (as I illustrate in the final chapter) will continue to have difficulty well into their college careers—not surprisingly, since this is one of the most challenging intellectual tasks of education, yet one of the most central. I try, however, to open up the possibility that one way to resolve some of their nagging questions about how to strengthen what they think the interview data are saying is to incorporate some of their readings as outside sources of authority. The most successful papers, as you can see in Kevin's example below, are those that place their analysis of the interviews in the larger conversation about nuclear weapons. More typical are papers like Helena's—a well organized, thoughtful analysis that is reaching for a larger context for her observations but that doesn't quite find it. (See Figures 3-3 and 3-4.)

This is obviously a long, complicated, and difficult assignment. I don't disguise the fact that it asks a great deal of the class; in fact I believe it is the most intellectually challenging work they do all term. Other than making it the final assignment instead of a middle of the term project, I haven't yet found a way to cope with the letdown that inevitably follows its completion. The destination of this journey is the collection of interpretations about what all the material we've collected means. Students recognize that the road wasn't the same for everybody and that everyone ended up in a slightly different place even though they all took the same trip. Equally important, of course, is the sustained collaboration that is essential to all phases of this assignment—a collaboration that is different in kind and intensity from simply offering feedback on someone's draft.

One of the most satisfying outcomes of this project is the students' discovery that what they have learned is indeed significant. At this point in the course, they have read about the development of nuclear weapons, they know what led up to the decision to bomb Hiroshima and Nagasaki and the controversies that still surround that decision; they have mas-tered much nuclear terminology and have plowed through explanations of throw weights, MIRV's, and megatonnage vs. kilotonnage, and so on. But they still know this stuff in isolation, the way students learn much of what they study in school. After interviewing people they presumed were more knowledgeable and authoritative then they and finding them rela-tively uninformed and uninterested in the problem of nuclear weapons, they come away feeling confirmed in their knowledge—and just a little bit superior. I think they've earned it.

Figure 3–3
Kevin's Paper on Nuclear Weapons

Through a recent survey conducted on public perception of the nuclear arms race, I will explore the reasons why people behave in a self-contradictory manner. Most people agree that an all-out nuclear exchange would be devastating for all nations involved; however, these same people favor policies that steadily develop nuclear arms and increase the likelihood of it occurring. This contradiction in opinions is shown in the fact that of seventeen people polled, sixteen initially favored the use of nuclear weapons on Japan. Yet, when asked about the probability of a nuclear war during their lifetime, sixteen of seventeen people felt it was unlikely. In short, people were in favor of using nuclear weapons on Japan, but don't think a nuclear bomb could be dropped on them in their lifetime. With the exception of the remaining survivors of Hiroshima and Nagasaki who witnessed the devastating effect of a nuclear bomb, and a few who have actually witnessed an outdoor nuclear test, most people don't have firsthand knowledge of the awesome power. For the majority of people, nuclear weapons in distant countries can't be seen, heard or touched, therefore, we must use our imaginations to keep in mind the threat of annihilation. This probably explains why some Americans, who have never experienced the catastrophic effects of any conventional weapon on American soil, let alone a nuclear bomb, speak so calmly about a limited nuclear war.

Behind the public's perception of nuclear weapons lies human traits shared with all social animals: fear and mistrust by members of a group of another (Rival) group. In his essay, "Psychological Causes of the Nuclear Arms Race," Jerome Frank uses the concept of the "enemy image," which is defined as the competition between humans for the same goal, causing distrust to deteriorate into the "enemy image," forming language like, "us against them." This distrust of the members of another group (Russian) showed up in the Public Perception Survey where 82% of the people polled felt that the Soviet Union could not be trusted in an arms reduction agreement. And when asked who they felt was the more aggressive party in the arms race today, only four out of seventeen answered the Soviet Union, even though it was the United States who has been the only nation to use the nuclear bomb against another nation. According to Frank, the enemy image acts like a sieve, filtering out information that confirms it, and lets contrary information run through. Thus, each side propagandizes incidents of hostilities and cruelties by the enemy, and overlooks incidents of humanitarian or honorable behavior. You can see how the enemy image has distorted our view of the Russians in these brief quotations taken from the Public Perception Survey: In response to the question of the United States retaining a first strike option, some of the people surveyed answered, "Because you never know what they (Russians) have up their sleeves. This way we can get the first hit." "We need it to ward off any possible move by the Soviet Union."

To better understand people's perception of war in relation to how they answer the questions of the Public Perception Survey, we must look back at how war was viewed before the invention of nuclear weapons. Before nuclear power, weapons from spears and clubs to bombs and shells have shown strength both in appearance and in reality. The image of strength projected by nonnuclear weapons was based on numbers. Thus, the more weapons a nation controlled, the stronger and more stable that nation was. This caused people to try to outarm their rivals in the hope of deterring an attack or in defending themselves in the event of an attack.

continued

Figure 3–3
continued

Opinions in the Public Perception Survey showed that attitude of the people polled followed the pre-nuclear view of war. In response to the question which asked for the best solution to the arms race, one person replied: "I feel that the only solution to the arms race is to fight power with power, because it's the only thing the Russians will listen to." But, nuclear weapons have forever separated the connection between strength and the amount of weapons possessed by a country. We have long since reached the amount of nuclear arms necessary to defend and deter against attacks. The accumulation of more powerful and advanced nuclear weapons has increased the number of people that control or have access to these weapons. This, in turn, has increased the possibility of one being fired accidentally or out of malice. If we continue to handle nuclear weapons with methods that have worked in the past with conventional weapons (stockpile arms), we will further decrease stability in the world, and increase the likelihood of a nuclear war. But support for current policies is high. According to the Public Perception poll, almost 90% trust and support the government's policies.

In conclusion, the Public Perceptions Survey has shed a lot of light on how America's middle-aged citizens perceive the nuclear issue. It was interesting to see their point of view, having watched the nuclear bomb develop from infancy to where it is today. This generation possesses a lot of knowledge, but unfortunately they are also caught up in the old school thought about weapons and war and the Soviet Union. A solution for nuclear arms lies on the shoulders of this generation's children and their children.

Implications and Extensions

Although my example is from a college writing class, secondary and even elementary teachers have adapted this assignment to their own students and topics. One junior high teacher, for instance, constructed a similar survey around her literature unit on the hero. Her students developed a questionnaire that tried to probe their community's definitions of heroes, their attitudes toward heroes, and their experiences with them. An AP class did a survey on the uses of writing. Other topics include surveying colloquialisms in the local speech community, folk traditions, reading habits, television viewing, and so on.

This sort of assignment derives from the assumption that students can create meaningful texts in English classes and not just consume the writing of "experts." The process of developing such texts is no different from professional practice. Experienced writers don't set out to write research papers; they set out to answer questions or solve problems, and research is one way to achieve those ends. The process is messy and open-ended; it proceeds piece by piece, idea by idea; it is seldom conducted in isolation. Considerations of form and style take a back seat to the driving issues of meaning and discovery and the experience of being challenged and stretched. But whether the project involves collecting data as in the

Figure 3-4
Helena's Paper on Nuclear Weapons

How does the average middle age American view nuclear war? Who would start it? Would we survive? These are just a sampling of the survey questions posed to adults age thirty-five to forty-five with varying educational and occupational backgrounds. My observation, after carefully studying the data, is that many were either generally misinformed, lacked knowledge of this subject, or held self-contradictory attitudes and opinions about most of the nuclear issues.

Survival

There were a wide variety of responses to the question about survival. I found it most interesting to understand why they answered in the way in which they did. One woman stated that she would survive a nuclear war, "because of the area in which she lived," while two men believe that they would not survive because of the area in which they lived. All of the respondents live in the same general area in Utah. So, there seems to be some confusion as to what exactly would be targeted, military installation or large civilian populations. Most studies reveal that military targets tend to be more attractive targets, although history tells us quite a different story. Utah does have an air force base as well as military related industries, although it is difficult to tell if this area would be a definite target.

Effects of Nuclear War

Those interviewed knew little about the effects of a nuclear blast. Radiation was the most commonly sighted effect. Only two of the people referred to the below freezing temperatures of a "nuclear winter." Another mentioned that his only knowledge of the effects came from the television movie "The Day After." I find this lack of knowledge astonishing, considering that a good number of interviewees were college graduates. Granted, a person cannot be an expert in every field, but I still find it interesting that so little is known about a subject which is constantly in the media.

Conventional War or Nuclear War?

Only three out of the twenty-two people believed that if the super powers went to war it would be a non-nuclear war. A woman thought that chemical warfare would be chosen over any other kind in order to keep the U.S. from being totally destroyed. Her reasoning was that the U.S.S.R. would not want to take over a country which needed to be rebuilt. The majority, however, think that even though a war might start out conventionally, escalation to nuclear war is inevitable. If one of the countries involved fears losing, there is no reason why that country would not resort to its most powerful systems. There was some confusion about where escalation would lead. I get the impression that most poeple interpret escalation as meaning full blown war in which most of our population would be killed. Escalating from conventional to nuclear weapons does not necessarily have to imply this. Herman Kahn, founder of the RAND Institute believes that a distinction can be made between "small, controlled attacks on limited targets" with nuclear weapons and large attacks on cities. Limited nuclear warfare would be difficult to control and maintain and maybe this is why people do not automatically consider this as an option.

continued

Figure 3–4
continued

Effectiveness of International Agreements

The survey revealed that there were the same number of people who believed nuclear arms agreements to be effective as there were those who did not see them as effective. Two common responses were, "very effective, it keeps awareness levels up," and "according to the papers, it is all effective, but what do we know about what's really going on behind the scene." Who might be the one to violate agreements? Interestingly enough, not all of the people answered the Soviet Union. Many believe that both are guilty of violations and would be prone to do so in the future. Some see the Soviet Union as being more likely to because of their "character" or because "we cannot trust the Soviets." Trust is the key factor in maintaining arms agreements. One stated that "neither side would block or violate agreements unless they thought that the other side was doing the same." Agreements are successful and are maintained as long as both sides are feeling invulnerable. As soon as feelings of inferiority or vulnerability arise agreements tend to be disregarded.

Defense Spending and Continue Research and Development

This is the area in which I found people contradicting themselves, not just each other. Quite a few of those who were surveyed do not believe that current defense spending is justified. At the same time they also think that the U.S. should continue research and development of nuclear arms in order to keep up with the Soviets. Furthermore, these same people do not believe in using these weapons which our government is researching and developing. I am sure that many are unaware of this contradiction of opinion.

Who Would Be Most Likely to Start a Nuclear War?

A large percentage see a third world country starting a war instead of one of the superpowers. An unstable Middle Eastern country could "draw the two super powers into conflict." Smaller powers such as Iran might feel that there is not much to lose by engaging in some sort of nuclear conflict. Also, Iran is a religiously fanatical country and its people believe that their actions are somehow sanctioned by God. Every day we hear about problems in the Middle East, so it is not surprising that people fear that a Middle Eastern nation will initiate a conflict. This was one area in which those interviewed seemed to be most focused on and least confused. They were aware that the Middle East is an important concern today and might be the source of problems in the future.

Conclusion

This age group ranging from thirty-five to forty-five has only been exposed to conventional warfare, as seen in Vietnam and Korea. They are too young to have been a part of the generation which experienced the devastation of Hiroshima first hand. Yet, they cannot be included in the younger generation today which seems to be more actively involved and interested in learning more about this subject. The psychology surrounding nuclear war and related issues, such as strategies and weaponry, is much different than that of conventional war. This might partially explain the lack of clarity among those surveyed pertaining to nuclear issues.

Public Perceptions Survey or writing an adventure story, the collaborative writing class is a setting in which students rely on each other through the life of the assignment to create and convey meaning.

Works Cited

Camp, G. (1982). *A Success Curriculum for Remedial Writers*. San Francisco: National Writing Project.

Herrington, A. and Cadman, D. (1991). "Peer Review in an Anthropology Course: Lessons for Learning," *College Composition and Communication* 42 (5): 184–199.

Moffett, J. (1981). *Active Voice: A Writing Program Across the Curriculum*. Portsmouth, NH: Boynton/Cook.

Reither, J. and Vipond, D. (1991). "Writing as Collaboration," *College English* 51 (12): 855–867.

Part II

Response Groups in Junior High

4

Friends First!
Well, Maybe Not!

Becky L. Reimer

Seventh graders are social. Rarely can I find a silent mouth or still body in the class. They travel in pairs or packs down the hall, outside to play, and through the narrow classroom doors. It would seem to be a ready set for collaboration. It is, if collaborative talk about real dudes, boss girls, rad movies, or the newest jeans is the focus of the curriculum. Seventh graders are into themselves as individuals and their culture as nouveau teens. They readily argue, seeking to practice newly acquired cognitive skills.

My work, as a facilitator of productive group interaction, is never finished nor is my students' learning about productive ways to communicate. Middle school students can find themselves embroiled in multiple power struggles. They can easily lock horns with parents over independence and privacy, friends over misuse of power and trust, and the opposite gender over intimate relationships. I use peer response groups in writing and reading situations all throughout the school year. They not only facilitate the growth of the writer/reader but also the growth of the communicator.

In this chapter, I present a snapshot portfolio of the progression of writing response groups in my classroom last year. I have divided this portfolio into three parts. In part one I discuss the planned peer response activities in which I purposefully engage my students. These activities, albeit at times awkward and unnatural, do help the students be aware of important communication skills needed in peer response activities. In part two, I present snapshot moments of my classroom in which students have identified communication problems and work together, as a class, to solve them. In the final part, I present peer response groups in action so that the reader may see the dynamic interchange among the students.

Part One: Practicing Peer Response to Writing: Teacher-Directed Lessons

Creating a Context for Collaborative Work

It was an exciting year for our middle school. We spent three days in Monument Valley, Utah, the home of the Dineh nation (Navajo Nation). Each of our students spent one night with a Navajo host family. The summer reading prior to the year and the first six weeks of middle school curriculum were related to the native peoples of Utah. Most of the first quarter's work was related to our trip. During the remainder of the year, the assignments were related to functional writing activities and thematic units I established. My intent was to provide content and activities that were meaningful to my students.

I use small-group problem-solving projects at the beginning of the year as one step in our journey toward productive writing response groups. This past year, the group projects focused on the book which all my students were required to read during the summer, Tony Hillerman's *A Thief of Time*. My colleagues and I chose this book as a way to introduce our students gently to the Dineh culture and prepare them for a three-day visit to the Navajo Nation in southern Utah. Groups of four students were assigned to represent something unique about the book on poster board.

It is during the making of this project that my students and I learn about being together as a productive group. Daily we brainstorm all the problems and/or questions we have as well as solutions:

1. What are some unique ideas we might explore for our project?

2. How can the work and possible expense be shared equally among the group?

3. How can the project be worked on both inside and outside the school context?

4. How can the group complete the project on time?

One group made a poster of the significant clues found in each chapter, representing each by a picture. Another represented the significant settings in the book by drawing them on a poster board and writing a short sentence of explanation for each. While the groups work in class, I allow myself to stand back and watch the individual members. I take note of the students who say little or nothing, those who find it difficult to follow the conversations of the other group members, those who boss, those who continually argue, those who are "helpers," the group that socializes but forgets about the task at hand, and the creative problem solvers. I rarely intrude in this project because I want to send them the message that they need to handle this project on their own and to do so by working with each other.

I chuckle at the varied interactions among the students. They play-act as they plan their posters. Tom stood up from the floor and awkwardly walked across the room as he declared himself to be an old man. Tom was part of the group studying the significant characters. They laugh at their less-than-artistic abilities. Sam leaned back on his haunches, gazed at his piece of scenery drawing and declared himself to be a "renowned artist." They also accept and celebrate the strengths of the different group members. "Wow, what a great idea!" Kay complimented Ann on her idea for representing a significant clue.

At the end of each period, we discuss what problems they had and how they tried to solve them. We also listen to each other's plans for the next day. Group projects like this allow the students to brainstorm freely and share ideas as they create their product—a behavior I want transferred to writing response groups at a later time.

Writing and Response: Awkward First Lessons

Within the first two weeks of the school year, I announce the first formal writing assignment. This generally evolves from an immediate writing need I see. This year it was the writing of book-lending contracts. Some of the avid Hillerman mystery reading fans were willing to loan their books to other students in the class but weren't sure that they could trust the borrower with their books. Through discussion, we agreed on acceptable rules for lending and consequences for infractions of the agreement and decided to write book-lending contracts to be signed by both the borrower and the lender. We brainstormed a list of what should be included in such a contract. Each student then created his or her own contract with art work.

The following day the students exchanged book contracts and evaluated, using the previous day's list, whether the writer included all necessary information. Response to writing, albeit structured, controlled, mechanical, ritualistic, and somewhat unnatural, has begun. The contract writers revised their writing and returned the next day with final copies. Book lending began immediately and contracts were put to their test.

As the borrowers began to complete their contracts, many reported missing or confusing information. The book contracts were used a few times during the next two weeks. The major problems in book lending were solved and no longer was the written contract necessary. The students had each received both formal and informal response to their first piece of writing: the formal from a peer who pretended to be the real audience and judged whether parts of the document were indeed in the contract, and informal from a peer who, as the real audience, physically used the contract and spontaneously spouted forth the missing or confusing parts.

For the next writing assignment, I purposely search for a task which will involve an audience outside the school walls. Since my students would be visiting middle school students at Monument Valley High School, I assigned them to write a letter of introduction and/or inquiry to a Dineh student. Before we wrote these letters, we generated a list of what we knew about the audience for the letter, what the audience might expect to see in the letter and also what the students' varied purposes were for writing it.

My students know very little about the culture of the Dineh teen, a lack of knowledge that is reflected in the whole-class brainstorming session. The next day, I ask students to quickly read over their letter and on the back side, list what they liked and what needed to be added or changed. (The lists are rarely specific and sport the expected—make longer, watch punctuation.) This is their first lesson in declaring ownership of their writing.

Because I want to help them think from the perspective of their audience, I ask my students to exchange their letters with another student in class, someone they haven't worked with before. I ask each student to write a letter of response as a Navajo student, then I ask them to explain the purpose of this activity. They can quickly tell me this will help the writer detect problems in his letter, such as rude statements, incorrect spelling, confusing remarks, even cases of bragging.

Unfortunately, this doesn't usually carry over into their written work. They write responses, playing with stereotypes, using greetings of "How!" and signatures of "Little Red Chief," not unlike the cowboy-and-Indian games they have played for years. Some, though, take this task seriously and try to write a response from that perspective. They all anxiously await the return of their letter, giggling and chuckling as they read their responses.

When I announce that I need a final draft from them in two days so that I may send the letters, some panic. "How can we possibly send these letters? We don't really know what to even ask or say." They are right. To write to an audience, one must know more than stereotypical information. For others, they anxiously begin to list a few of the items they will change in their letters; telling why they like Bon Jovi, describing their school in more detail, and telling more about their families.

These intial first lessons are like play practice to the students. They go through the motions, discussing every item on the checklists, nodding approval of the writing, and occasionally asking a pre-practiced question. Independent thought rarely occurs, however. That comes much later.

Part Two: Doing Peer Response

I initially structure writing response groups. I place students in groups and I also help students generate lists of what makes a piece of writing good. I sometimes even hand them a prepared checklist. After these first awkward lessons, I allow the students to plan and execute a response session. They need to discover fluid ways to communicate in a group situation about each other's writing. As with all discovery learning, problems occur from which students learn.

Student Identified Problems

Usually, after the second or third student formulated response group, someone politely says, "Mrs. Reimer, I don't mean to be critical, but we don't feel that we get any help with our writing from our response groups. I'd rather that you give me feedback." This begins a discussion about why the response groups don't work.

I could come to the rescue by becoming the major respondent to their writing, saving them from grappling with a communication problem. Instead, I turn the problem back to them and ask, "Why don't you feel response groups work?" After some gentle prodding, several issues arise: "I don't want to be rude to my friend." "My response partners don't care about my writing." "People in my group just want to hurry and finish it so they can talk about their social life." "Responses to my writing weren't helpful." It is at this time that I can, through my own demonstration of active listening, parrot back what I sense are the problems. I generally reiterate the following: members in the group find it difficult to send messages which might be misinterpreted, and members in the group don't all feel equal in participatory roles.

I tackle the first problem—sending clear messages to the writer.[1] I ask for some examples of unhelpful messages students have received to their writing from before. I quickly write down the first ten on the board and then I draw a Likert scale on the board. Under the numeral one, I write *not helpful* and under the numeral five, *helpful*. I take the first *not helpful* response (It's good.) and invite students to help remake the comment into a helpful response. Along the way we talk about why, as a writer, that comment isn't helpful. "It doesn't tell me what was good." "It makes me feel like he really didn't pay attention to what my piece was about." "She doesn't care about it."

Through such talk we generate a more helpful response. "Your second paragraph was good." I assign that response a three and the students

1. My students are also fortuante in that they receive communication strategies in their Ethics class which is taught by our school counselor.

wonder why it doesn't receive a five. Someone usually comes up with the idea that the statement needs to be specific about what counts as good. "That second paragraph is good because you described the fishing off the boat." To this comment, I write a four. I then remake the level four statement into "I liked the second paragraph because I found myself very interested in your description of the fishing off the side of the boat." I don't have to justify the importance of "I" statements because my students have been practicing them in their Ethics class.

We do the same with the second *not helpful* response on the board. I assign responses to pairs of students to remake and write their remake on the board. As a class, we discuss and evaluate the remakes. The next day, the students meet in their response groups and practice giving helpful responses. A great deal of side chatter occurs on that day about the helpfulness of the remarks. As I near a response group, I hear an exaggerated "I-I-I-I" from a member of the group, their signal to me that they are practicing "I" statements. On this day, the writing is secondary because the focus is more on practicing responses.

Occasionally, I'll hear someone rejecting an "I" statement with "Well, that's your problem if you're confused. Everyone else understood it." This serves as another point in communicating in a response group and the role of the writer. We make a chart which represents what the respective roles of the writer and reader are in a response group.[2] The primary purpose of a response group is to make the writing the best that it can be and also that the writer has the final say in all revisions. That chart is then placed on my classroom wall.

Some time later, we tackle the second problem—members not responding or participating. I do this by asking the students at the end of a response group session to list each member's name and the strengths of each response partner. At the same time, I ask them to list any particular problems they ran into and how they solved or attempted to solve them. In helping each member identify each other's strength, group acceptance is built as well as individual accountability. Such comments occur as "Sam, you didn't say anything to me about my piece. What do you think? I want to know what you think." Individual students begin to hold each other responsible for participation.

The Reading Angle: Encouraging Questioning Behaviors with Written Texts

The first critical reading assignment I make is one that I use for my own diagnostic purposes. I ask my students to read a short story silently in class. I have prepared it with a wide right margin and Xeroxed it for each student. I ask my students to do their thinking aloud in that margin, to

---

2. I adapted this chart from Bill Strong, Director of the Utah Writing Project.

write a three- to four- sentence summary and record any surprises they noticed while reading the story. From this in-class activity I can judge whether the student understood the text as demonstrated in their summary, and whether the student asks questions, seeks clarification, notices incongruities, and offers comments while reading.

A few days after my students do this assignment, I ask them to compare their reading of the story with mine. I provide each student with a Xeroxed copy of my marginal notes and summary. From their comparison and associated discussion, we generate a list of what an active reader does. From this list, each student picks two as reading goals for the next few weeks.

I continue to promote active reading of their texts in varied assignments during the first semester. Even on free reading days, which occur weekly, I ask that my students during the last ten minutes of class record in their reading journal surprises, confusions, new words and/or concepts, and a brief summary. Students spontaneously share their thoughts about their reading with each other. Occasionally, I will collect their journals and read their thinking. I applaud their questioning and search for understanding with my own marginal notes. These reading behaviors are the ones I want them to apply to the writing response groups.

I also extend the active reader concept by teaching about perspective or role-taking with a story. When we start the short story unit, I assign my students to groups of four. Each person has a different role, one a question asker, one a new word detector, one a summarizer and one an interpreter. As they co-read their first short story, I ask them to stop at varied points and each present their data from the point of view of their assigned role. The titles of the roles change as we progress through the year. One day I might have the detection roles of character action, character motive, character description, and character dialogue. On another day, I might have the detection roles of setting, theme, plot, and characterization. I also ask them to take on the role of teacher as reader of the story. These are some of the varied perspectives I expect them to adopt during the writing and response to writing activities in class.

Of course, while we read short stories, we also write them. In story writing, the students spontaneously share what they do. They help each other brainstorm believable plots, characters, and settings. They diligently work on great beginnings. They laugh not only at humor in stories but at the ridiculous sections they have written. The writing of their short stories, albeit an individual project, always turns into a group problem-solving event.

Part Three: A Well-Practiced Routine or Is It?

By midyear, when I ask my students to prepare for writing response groups, most bring multiple copies of their writing. We begin response days by brainstorming a list of important focusing questions for the day. They usually generate specific questions about what counts for whatever genre they are writing (How well is the setting described? What has the author done with characterization? What appears to be the theme?), specific suggestions to guide the giving of response (Underline what you liked and what you don't understand.), and specific questions to provide helpful revision hints (Where might the story be cut? The questions I have are:). The list of focusing questions remains on the board for the class period while my students read aloud and discuss their writing. Response on these days is not at all like the creating phase. The students are focused and to the point with their responses, nothing like the wild, untamed brainstorming of possibilities during the writing.

I still play an important part in setting up formal response to writing. I ask my students to predict the qualities of a good piece of writing before they go to response group, brainstorm important focusing questions for the day's study, reflect on what worked and what didn't in the day's response group, and problem-solve difficult group situations or writing dilemmas.

In February of this last year, my students and I engaged in a letter-writing unit which I carefully designed so each assignment built upon the previous one. During the last letter assignment this year, a letter to an editor, I tape-recorded the response groups in one of my classes. I present transcripts from two groups, one a helpful, supportive group and the other not. In human interactions, nothing is static. Groups change from productive to nonproductive and back again. I've learned to expect the unexpected, celebrate the successes, and encourage clear communication in writing and among students.

A Group of Friends

In this first group of four female students, all four work together quite well. They search for incongruities, ask for clarification, and help the writer reconceptualize and rewrite the text. Since the writer brought only one copy of a draft to response group, they all sat closely together, carefully reading the paper as well as listening to the writer read the contents. They have worked together on several projects. They are friends outside the classroom. In the past, their friendship has led to silliness and off-track discussions. One of the problems they were working on as a group was how to stay focused and accomplish their purposes for the day's work. They refer to this problem in their letters of reflection to me.

The group is quite interactive and bubbly, many times overlapping each other's speech. They help Tammy, the writer, solve her conclusion problem and further clarify the issue for her and her responders. At the end of the response cycle, the group talks about the formatting of the letter and return to the first paragraph. This group, as interactive response groups do, cycles and recycles through the letter addressing issues of meaning, format, spelling, and punctuation.

Tammy is very aware of her control over her piece of writing, a letter to the editor on a proposed abortion law pending before the state legislature (see Figure 4-1). She begins the response sequence by directly stating to her group where she feels she needs help. Alice and Karen restate Tammy's needs in order to insure common understanding.

Tammy: This is what I need help with is my last line. This is all I have right now—"Utah may have a problem with" and I need to know how to say . . .

Alice: Like a summary?

Tammy: kind of

Karen: to end it up, you know!

Tammy: to finish it up. Well, like, should I say, "May have a problem with all the above?"

Alice: Yeah, No. No. I think "Utah" then give your solution.

Tammy offers an idea, and the others continue to brainstorm a possible ending sentence. Along the way they entertain simplistic solutions such as deleting the sentence and complex ones which evolve from their discussion of what is the nature and extent of the problem as well as who has the problem. They discuss the needs of the audience, as well.

Tammy: That is my solution, to educate them.

Alice: Then take the whole sentence out.

Tammy: Then put what in to fix it?

Alice: to let them get pregnant, period.

Tammy: "For if we enforce this. If our children do not have access to ways of not getting pregnant."

Alice: Yeah.

Tammy: No. Ahhhh. "Utah may have a problem with this new law."

Alice: No. with, ahm, like, if you can't prevent it in any way then there's going to be a lot of pregnancies and it's gonna . . .

Tammy: Yeah and it will cause a lot of problems.

Karen: Yeah. Yeah.

Alice: It's the law.

Figure 4–1
Tammy's Letter to the Editor, Rough Draft

Salt Lake Tribune

Dear Editor,

~~I~~ I am writing this letter ~~To you in hopes~~
~~that you will publish it in your newspaper.~~ This
letter concerns the abortion Bill passed last month.
This letter contains my concerns and solutions
about this Bill.

The abortion bill has caused many mixed
feelings. I personally think it should be
the woman's choice. If we are to pass
this bill many problems may follow. Since
Utah does not make it easy to purchase
birth control devices many women could
get pregnant so many times that it will
be harmful to their health. Some teenagers
may be forced to get 'back alley' abortions
which ~~can kill them~~ may lead to their death.

A simple solution to solving this
potential problem is to educate adolescents about sex and birth control
devices. For if we enforce this with our
children not having access to ~~preventing~~
getting pregnant Utah may have a problem
with teenage pregnancy.

Sincerely
Tammy

Tammy: Or poverty rates might go up because teenagers can't support the children.

Karen: Yeah, right.

Alice: No.

Tammy: We have a problem with teenage pregnancies.

Alice: No. It's not just teenagers in this law, it will change . . .

Nancy: It's mostly teenagers because teenagers might not want to tell their parents.

Karen: Because they go out . . .

Nancy: They don't have money. They don't have jobs.

Tammy: Store people won't sell birth control devices to teenagers.

Alice: Why not?

Tammy: Because they don't . . .

Alice: They think, "Goodness me, that horny little child."

Tammy: Well, the thing is . . . but the thing is we need to educate them about how not to get pregnant.

Alice: Yeah, okay, okay. Then keep this.

Tammy: Okay.

Alice and Karen help Tammy solve her conclusion problem and further clarify the issue for the writer and her responders. Tammy signals the end of the session by verifying the end of her letter.

Tammy: Then, "Sincerely, Tammy."

This group, as interactive response groups do, recycles through the letter addressing issues of meaning, format, spelling, and punctuation. Alice begins by pointing out problems in the formatting of the letter.

Alice: But you don't have things lined up.

Tammy: Okay. I'm going to line them up.

Alice: And the zip code has to come up to this line, and, and, and, and,

Tammy: When I type it, it will all . . .

Karen: This should all be on this line.

Alice: It should be this line, this line and a new line.

Karen: You should put "The Public Forum" here.

Tammy: Should I say, "Dear Public Forum?"

Karen: Yeah.

Alice: No. No. Just keep it that way.

Tammy: Alright.

Alice again begins the next segment of discussion by introducing a question regarding the audience and the expectations they may have as they read the first paragraph.

Alice: In this first paragraph, it tells you what you are going to read.

Tammy: Well, that's like my beginning. Look at this letter. [Tammy points to a model of a letter she has been using.]

Alice: But if he reads that, then he'll say, "I know what's going to happen in this letter. She is going to tell me that she hopes to read it."

Karen: Yeah, don't put, "I'm writing in hopes that this letter will be published and she hopes that the abortion bill will change."

Alice: Yeah. Don't put that line in, just say, "I am writing to discuss the abortion law."

Tammy: Wait. Okay. Start with this, maybe. "This letter contains my concerns and solutions to the abortion law."

Alice: Yeah. That's good. Leave that in.

Tammy: Okay. Thank you.

The group helps her change her introductory paragraph so that she more carefully addresses the readers' needs and by doing so keeps their attention. Tammy feels she is finished discussing her letter but again Alice finds other topics to discuss:

Alice: No. We're not done.

Tammy: What else is there?

Karen: Just have it checked for spelling.

Alice: There's another thing down here. Okay. "Some teenagers may be forced to get back alley abortions which may kill them." Which may lead to their death or something like that? Which may kill them?

Karen: It sounds funny when Alice says it.

Tammy: Do you know what back alley abortions are?

Alice: Yeah, they take a hanger and do this. [demonstrates]

Nancy: Take a what?

Alice: Never mind.

Tammy's revisions in her typed copy reflect the discussions from her response group (see Figure 4–2). Several major problems still exist in the final draft Tammy assembled. She is not yet an adult writer. She has four and a half years of writing instruction before her in our school and then more in college. She is also writing about an issue of which she will become more aware as she and her friends mature.

At the end of this formal response group, I asked each of my students to write me a letter and tell me what was helpful and not helpful in group work. I also asked them to report what each member's strengths were in response group. Here is Tammy's letter:

> Dear Mrs. Reimer,
> My group was very helpful to me in my letter. I needed to change the beginning. I needed to rephrase some of the things I said.
> Alice was not helpful because she got off track sometimes. But most of the time, she was helpful by thinking of things to put in our letters.
> People in my group and what they did well:
> Alice = was best at rephrasing things
> Nancy = kept us on track
> Karen = punctuation, form

Tammy's initial assessment of Alice, that she got off track sometimes, doesn't seem true from the transcription. This remark reflects past history the girls have had with Alice. During the writing of their mystery stories, this group never finished peer response to their drafts because Alice entertained them with her antics. Tammy also lists Nancy as helpful at "keeping the group on track." Something the audio tape does not record is the nonverbal interactions that occur among the members. Nancy was the group recorder for the day, listing comments, questions, and problems for the group. Nancy would guide the group through her gaze. She would shift the talk and topic by shifting her gaze to another member of the group.

Alice makes comments similar to Tammy's.

> Dear Mrs Reimer,
> I think we achieved alot today, more than usual. We had alot of unclear and strange sounding sentences that we cleared up. We didn't do much on spelling and punctuation errors, even though Karen said to make sure everything was correct in form and spelling. Nancy kept us all on track and Karen helped with spelling and form and Tammy and I gave suggestions. I feel that Tammy summarized by repeating and clearing things.
> Sincerely,
> Alice

Alice is perceptive. She is able to see the roles carried out by her response partners. She most insightfully describes an effective strategy used by Tammy.

Figure 4–2
Tammy's Letter to the Editor Final Draft

Salt Lake Tribune
P.O. Box 876, Salt Lake City, Ut. 84110

Dear Editor,
    This letter concerns the Abortion Bill passed last month. This letter
contains my concerns and solutions about the abortion bill.
    The Abortion Bill has caused many mixed feelings. I personally think
that it should be the woman's choice. If we are to pass this bill many
problems may follow. Since Utah does not make it easy to purchase birth
control devices many women or teenagers could get pregnant so many
times that it would be harmful to their health. Some women or teenagers
may be forced to get "back alley" abortions which can lead to their deaths.
    A simple solution to solving this problem is to educate adolescants
about sex and birth control devices. For if we enforce this bill with our
children not having access to ways of preventing getting pregnant Utah
may have a big problem with pregnancies.
                                            Sincerely,
                                            Tammy

This group is productive during formal peer response. They treat
Tammy's text with respect, helping her craft sentences which will communicate the meaning she desires. The next group does not operate in such
synchrony.

A Group of Individuals

In profiling this group, I'll start with their reflection letters.

Dear Mrs. Reimer,
    Arghhhh! I am exceptionally frustrated!
    Mark was so busy telling me I was wrong on my issue, I got few ways
I could improve my letter.
    Both Tom and Sue were pretty good about where I had used the
same word twice, repeated something etc. . .

Dear Mrs. Reimer,
    1. I really thought my peer response group helped me. They told me
how to put more info. & examples in my letter.

2. I felt though, on the other side it was destructive because Mary & Mark argued almost the whole time over one little thing, and I couldn't consintrate very well.

Sincerely,
Sue

Dear Mrs. Reimer,

My response group helped me clearify my letters points. It didn't help me by messing around.

Mark	Tom	Sue	Mary
subtle	quick	quiet	very dramatic

Sincerely,
Mark

Dear Mrs. Reimer

My peer response group didn't help me personally, at all. They just said, "Oh, that's just dandy," even after I kept asking them about it. This maybe because my letter was perfect (though I really doubt it) or because they were lazy. But other than that I thought they were helpful and gave good advice.

Mark was good at making sure the arguments were good. Mary was good at little mistakes. Sue was good at I don't know, and I was good at pointing out mistakes.

Sincerely,
Tom

This group had several problems during the class period. I had constructed the group so that the three strong writers would receive helpful feedback from each other and the one weaker writer might hear a different way to look at her writing. My ideas don't always work. I'm not always aware of all the social issues for each student. I intervened twice in their response group because of the loud statements being tossed back and forth between Mark and Mary . In their letters to me, each person wrote about the problems they had as a group.

The group started with Tom reading his rough draft aloud to the four. He received some response about what he did well in his letter. This group should have discovered the problems with run-on sentences, a few other mispelled words, and the ambiguity in his arguments (see Figure 4–3).

Mary: I liked it.

Mark: Ah, let me see.

Mary: I think you really covered the other person. Like, if someone was for censorship, I think you covered a lot of the arguments they would make.

Figure 4–3
Tom's Letter to the Editor, Rough Draft

Dear ~~Juh?aNVMpXXXX~~ Editor,

I am ¹²year old writing to complain about the issue of censorship in our music and art in general. I think, that in most instances, censorship is wrong. Many times I have seen "Explicit Lyrics" and "Parental Advisory" stickers which I have no problem with but it's ~~unless~~ the 17+ and No viewers under 17 labels and when I am told that I cannot buy a record or tape that really gets me.

I realize censorship restricts underaged viewers or listeners from seeing "unapropriate" material, but this is a free country and I think kids today are smart enough to choose what they listen to. And for the people who ~~this~~ material may be offensive to, hey, just don't buy it.

Censorship also restricts the artist from expressing his/her ideas or beliefs. The rock group Jane's Addiction's cover of "Ritual de lo Habitual" displaying 2 nude people in a clay sculpture in no terrible way is censored. I have seen many pictures like it in art museums or stores which have been dubbed "O.K.". 2 Live Crew, of course have been the victim of censorship. Almost every store I walk into has the clean version of 'Nasty as they wanna be, which is censored all over the place. I'm no rap fan and I can't really agree with 2 live Crew's message, but why shouldn't they be able to express what they believe in?

So Cmon guys let us say what we want. It is a free country.

Sincerely,

Tom

Mark: Yeah and I think you really did well with proving your point using examples.

Tom: Really? Okay.

Nancy: Sue, do you have anything to say?

Sue: No.

Tom received few helpful comments. He displays his frustration to his group.

Tom: This always happens. I don't get anything. I'll get like a C or something like that on this.

Mary: No you won't. It's good. Excellent form.

Tom finds one thing he needs to change and mentions it to the group. He again receives applause; the group does not meet his needs.

Tom: This sincerely needs to be over here.

Mary: You are just amazing.

Tom did not receive helpful response from his group. They were quite satisfied and impressed with his piece. The problem for Tom has always been that his classmates see him as an outstanding writer. They expect he will write well and accept each text he produces as a well-written text. They question little of what he produces. There are few differences between his rough draft and final copy (see Figure 4-4).

This group performs much differently for Mary. Mary took a position on the Olympics in Utah that was opposed to Mark's. They quarrel about who is right on the issue rather than question and clarify the persuasive argument that Mary wrote.

Mary: Mine is not a letter to the editor but it's a lot like a letter to the editor. And it is to Mayor DePaulis. [see Figure 4-5]

She reads the first paragraph and is interrupted by Tom. This is usually not accepted practice in formal response groups. The writer is always allowed to read the piece through once before discussion occurs.

Tom: You are a little repetitive. Yeah, don't have two of these issues.

Mary: Wait! What's wrong with it?

Again, she is interrupted by another student.

Mary: Shhh. Just a second.

Tom: I did a debate on this.

Figure 4-4
Tom's Letter to the Editor, Final Draft

Dear Editor,

    I am a 12 year old writing to complain about the issue of censorship in our music and art in general. I think, that in most instances, censorship is wrong. Many times I have seen "Explicit Lyrics" or "Parental Advisory" stickers which I have no problem with, but it's the "17+" and "No viewers under 17" labels and when I am told that I cannot buy a record or tape that really gets me.

    I realize censorship restricts underaged viewers or listeners from seeing "unappropriate" material, but this is a free country and I think kids today are smart enough to choose what they listen to or watch. And for the people who take offense to the material, hey just don't buy it.

    Censorship also restricts the artist from expressing his/her ideas or beliefs. The rock group Jane's Addiction's cover of "Ritual de lo Habitual" displaying a sculpture of three nude people in no terrible way is censored. I have seen many pictured like it in art museums or stores which have been dubbed "O.K.". 2 Live Crew, of course have been the victim of censorship. Almost every store I walk in to has the censored version of "Nasty as they Wanna Be", refusing to sell the uncensored one. I'm no rap fan and I can't say I agree with 2 Live Crew's message, but why shouldn't they be be able to say what they believe in?

    So c'mon, guys, let us say what we want. It is a free country, you know.

                                 Sincerely,

                                 Tom

Figure 4–5
Mary's Letter to the Mayor, Rough Draft

Mayor Palmer DePaulis
City and County Building

    Dear Mr. DePaulis,
        I am writing to address the Olympic issue. I respect many of your
    ~~decisions~~ decisions as Mayor but I think you need to consider the ~~issues~~. *facts*
        The Olympics are a very beuatiful tribute to peace and
    athletics, but Salt Lake and the surrounding area can not handle
    the enviornmental stress. Our precious enviornment can not be subjected
    to the pollution this event will leave in it's wake.
        Furthermore, aside from the enviornmental damage the economic damage
    would be overwhelming! Salt Lake is not prepared for the cost of a speed
    skating rink if we still can't afford uncrowded schools and competent teachers! *toxics*
        In conclusion, I ask you to reconsider the issue at hand *Money*
and advocate for a revote at the next election.
                        Sincerely,

                        Mary

Mary: Shh, be quiet.

Tom: I did a debate on this.

Tom tries to impose his expertise on her, discrediting hers. Mary's ownership of her piece is now in question. Tom seems to be controlling the
discussion.

Mary: Shh. So did I, so be quiet.

She continues to read her letter and finishes it. She notices Mark shaking
his head and anticipates his argument.

Mary: Everyone else has gone overbudget.

Mark: As soon as we do this, we'll get a bunch of money.

Mary: But no we won't.

Tom: Let's continue with this. I think you have good evidence.

Tom, despite his rude interruptions earlier, tries to redirect the group's energies to the written text, away from the personal issues between Mark and Mary. He says this while Mark and Mary continue to argue about the money.

Mark: No! Look, we have lots of money.

Tom: Shut up, Mark. I think I have . . .

Mary: That's why our schools still have thirty-six kids to a class. Way to go, Mark!

Mark: No! That, no! That's school board. That's government. That's screw up.

Tom: Shut up, Mark. I'm trying to talk.

Mary: They have a lot to do with this state!

Mark and Mary continue to argue the issue. Mary sticks by her argument and evidence. Again Tom tries to redirect the discussion to the letter, not to the rightness of the issue.

Tom: Okay. We will talk about Mary 's letter.

Mark: We are.

Mary: We are.

Tom: Okay. I think you have good evidence but the same thing is . . .

Mark: It's hard to talk about it, if you don't agree with it.

Mary to Mark: I'm not asking you to agree with me. I'm asking you about my letter.

Mary very clearly articulates what she expects of Mark in this peer response group. Mark explains why he can't do what she expects.

Mark: I know. I can't agree with it.

Tom: You 'd need more of what they'd say.

At this point, Tom struggles into the argument. Mary and Mark are locked into opposing positions, verbally hashing out an argument about who is on the right side of the issue.

Mary to Mark: It doesn't matter. I'm not asking you to.

Mary to Tom: They'd say okay.

Tom: I realize this would come as a great success to Salt Lake.

Tom offers an idea for the text to satisfy Mark's concerns, but Mary negates Tom's suggestion.

Mary: Okay. But it would not.

Mark: Yes, it would. It would!

Mary: It would not, you fool! You are such an idiot. Now listen. We don't have tons of money in this state. Otherwise we wouldn't be getting taxes.

Mark: As far as economy goes, we have the best economy in the whole . . .

Mary: Oh, boy. That's a big improvement and . . .

Mark: It would get even bigger if we build these facilities.

Mary: No, it wouldn't because in every other state, every other country that has had the Olympics, has gone underbudget and has ended up borrowing money to finance these things.

Mark: I can't agree with the economy part.

Mary: I don't care. I'm not asking you to agree with me. I'm asking you to judge my letter.

Mark: I am.

Mary: No, you're not.

Mark: I am.

Mary: You are judging my issues, not my letter!

Mary again tries to help Mark understand what he is doing in this response cycle. She wants him to listen to the letter rather than judge her according to the side of the issue on which she stands. Mark cannot separate his profound commitment to the issue from the statement of the argument.

Mark: Well, your letter has a lot to do with your issue.

Mary: Very good. I'm not asking you to debate my issue with me. I'm asking you to tell me how good my gosh dang letter is.

Mark: They're going to put out a lot of arguments.

Mary: I don't care.

Mark: Okay. It won't damage the economics.

Mary: Yes, it would.

Mark: Uh uh.

Mary: Every other . . . uugh. You're not listening to me.

Tom again tries to redirect the focus to the text. He does so by directing the discussion to the format of the text.

Tom: This should be lined up here.

Mark: It wouldn't.

Mary: It would. We'd end up underbudget.

Teacher: There's a problem here with the way this group is going. I hear loud voices. It sounds like it's a communication problem. Mark, what's your point you are making back to Mary?

Mark: She says it will be a big damage to economy and it won't.

Mary: He's debating my issue and not . . .

Tom: They're arguing the issue, they're arguing . . .

Mary: How good my letter is.

Teacher: You can debate your issue if it is pertinent to.

Mary: But it's not. He's just saying what he thinks.

Teacher: Mary, I was speaking. You interrupted me. You don't let anyone finish their point.

I intruded ineffectively. I entered the group with assumptions on my own part about what was occurring. It wasn't until I listened to the tape later that I discovered how Mary was rudely interrupted from the start and I failed to see the wonderful job she was doing with communicating.

Mary: I know. I can't help it.

Tom: The facts are good.

Mark: If you can consider them facts.

Mary: Shut the heck up.

Tom: You realize this is on tape?

Mary: Yes, I do. Okay. Don't say anything.

Mark: No, the part about the economy. You can't say that.

Mary: I will give statistics. I will. Are you happy about that?

Mary tries to appease Mark and agrees to give some facts.

Mark: No.

Mary: Good statistics. Okay. Go for it Sue.

Despite the war, quite a few concepts were covered in this discussion. In a heated issue, the writer or the debater has to anticipate the arguments from the opposing side. Mark strongly represented that audience and voiced the counterarguments loudly and stubbornly. Mary's commitment to her side of the issue helped maintain her ownership in the piece. Although Mark didn't send helpful responses as we defined them in class, Mary still listened to his information. She did major revisions to her draft. She didn't add statistics but she did cast the economy problem into concrete examples, as she had done with Mark (see Figure 4-6). Mary can survive tough arguments. Not all students can.

I think about what I need to do next for this group. I have several options at my disposal. I can reconstruct its membership, although that doesn't really help them learn about communication or problem-solving. I could ask them to write a response to their pieces from my perspective. "Put on Mrs. Reimer's glasses and write down what I might say about this piece of writing." Asking my students to adopt my perspective helps them generate a new list of questions and problems to solve in their writing that they may not automatically receive from their response partners. At the beginning of the next formal response session, I might ask this group to develop a set of guidelines they will use in conducting their response to writing as well as assign varied monitoring roles to each other such as problem-detector, leader, or summarizer.

As a teacher, I celebrate the successes of both groups. The synchronous first group has not always been synchronous, but they can be when they want and need to be. That's success to me. When they have problems again in the future, it will be easy to sit with them and ask them what they see as the problem and how they think they might solve it . With the second group, despite the warring, Mary did learn and grow from it because she owns her issues and her writing and knows she must defend them well. Good peer response is fluid and dynamic. There are few well-practiced routines.

Part Four: Reflections

It is now a year later. I am busy helping my students learn how to communicate in writing response groups. We are at the midway point in writing short stories and have all been involved in at least two formal response groups. Issues are similar—students complain about not receiving helpful feedback, students refuse to listen to feedback, and students don't notice problems in the writing. It would be easy for me to jump in and do my tried and true mini-lessons to "teach" my students how to communicate. Unfortunately, my years of experience with middle school students nag at me. Experience reminds me that my students have to discover and own the problems before they are ready to learn what to do about them. I have again turned the problems back to my students to solve with my support.

Not surprisingly, this year's students have developed different ways of solving their problems. I will be implementing one of their ideas after

Figure 4-6
Mary's Letter to the Mayor, Final Draft

```
Mayor Palmer DePaulis
City and County Building


    Dear Mayor DePaulis,
    I am writing to address the Olympic issue. Although the votes
have been cast, the debate continues. Many of Utah's enviormentally
and economically aware citizens are worried about the effect
on Utah once the flame has gone out.
    The Olympics have always been a beautiful event that has brought
nations and athletes together in a world wide celebration of
hope and the endless struggle to win. But many people are blinded
by the prestige of hosting the event and ignore the cold hard
facts such as this event will probably hurt our economy as it
has hurt many other hosts. What will we do with our expensive
facilities once the show is over? Few people will pay to use
a luge!
    And even if we build these domes and super domes, there is
no guarantee that we will receive the event. I don't see how
a state that still can't afford competent teachers and control
overcrowded schools can build a speed skating rink!
    But aside from this, there is the damage that will be done
to our allready strained enviornment. Even if you claim to protect
the enviornment by not holding the events in some of our more
sensitive canyons, you can't stop people exploring on their own,
which will inevitably lead to further pollution and exploitation
of your future grandchildren's world.
    So please call a revote or simply withdraw our bid altogether.
                Hopefully,

                    Mary
```

---

the holidays. We will have a blind reading of their stories. One class of students will read another class of students' short stories. The stories will not carry their author's names. Each student will be given a short story to read as if it were his or her own. Each student will have the job of representing the story in a formal response group and communicating back to the owner, via letter, the nature of the problems and recommendations for changing. All of my classes are excited about this. My students see the blind reading of stories as a way to be honest in their responses, to create mystery and suspense, and to have fun while doing response.

As a teacher, I'm not sure this will solve the communication problems among my students, but I'm willing to try new ideas that have been carefully thought about and planned. I trust my students' ideas. They know better how to combine play and work than I.

I'm anxious for the three days we will spend doing blind readings of the stories. I am most anxious to listen to the discussion of the questions—"How did blind reading work? What are the advantages and disadvantages?" I openly invite the next response adventure which may evolve from the discussion.

5

With a Little Help from Your Friends
Computers as a Catalyst for Collaboration in the Classroom

Marjorie Coombs

Wayne punched the tape recorder and began reading. "'The Dump,' by Wayne Pendleton," he announced.

> It doesn't smell that good
> With the aroma of old food
> Nonbiodegradable plastic full of toxic waste
> In the occasional sight of a dead cat
> The heaps of garbage going up to the sky and out to the horizon
> It goes on for miles where someone can surely get lost
> For the young child there are monsters waiting to eat people.
> The garbage man makes his daily rounds
> Dropping off hundreds of pounds of poor unwanted waste
> Nobody can speculate the amount of refuse
> Put into this lovely camping ground for the outcasts of human society
> But let us not forget the animal inhabitants of this noble estate
> Our friends, the seagulls.

"How'd you like that, guys?" Wayne asked.

Robert: That was great, man.

Dylan: I really liked how descriptive and all the big words you used.

Wayne: Like unbiodegradable? Boy, I had a hard time trying to spell that.

Robert: Is that a real word?

Wayne: Mm huh.

Robert: But when it says "the heaps of garbage going up to the sky and out to the horizon," it, um, sounds weird, it sounds strange.

Wayne: Oh, I got it. How about this? The heaps of garbage going up to the sky and on out to the horizon.

Robert: Yeah, that sounds good, that sounds better.

Wayne: What about this sentence?

Robert: "It goes on for miles where someone can surely get lost"— that doesn't sound like it makes any sense there.

Dylan: He's surely—

Wayne: He was a friend of mine—I lost him in a dump when we were young. We were playing around; he's gone now. Okay, um—

Dylan: There's not really much you could do with it.

Wayne: Just delete it. Let's see how it sounds without that sentence: the heaps of garbage going up to the sky and on out to the horizon for—nope, see, 'cause it has to have something that it symbolizes, or something.

Robert: Why don't you just say it goes on for miles and miles?

Wayne: No, the heaps of garbage going up to the sky and on out to the horizon for miles.

Robert: No, the horizon is like the end of it.

Dylan: All right, yeah. So—

Robert: Out for miles to the horizon, does that sound better?

Wayne: I know, it goes on for thousands of square acres—

Robert: Square miles, square feet, square centimeters—

Dylan: Okay, we got the point.

Wayne: I got it. The dump is a pile of refuse that could go on for miles and miles—Heaps of garbage going to the sky and on out to the horizon.

Dylan: Surely someone can get lost between the piles of refuse.

Wayne: Yeah, that's good, I like that.

Dylan: Did you hear that? I had a good idea.

Robert: That was a good idea.

Dylan: I know. What did you expect?

Wayne: Guys, we're being recorded, so don't goof off. "For the young child, there are monsters waiting to eat people."

Dylan: Okay, that sounds great.

Wayne: Okay. "The garbage man makes his daily rounds, dropping off hundreds of pounds of poor unwanted waste."

Robert: The "poor" sounds weird. It sounds like you're saying, "oh what poor—"

Dylan: Nobody can speculate the amount of refuse put into this lovely campground without casting a sight—

Robert: What if you said, "The garbage man, making his daily rounds, drops off hundreds of pounds of poor unwanted waste?"

Dylan: That's fixed, that's beautiful.

Wayne: Okay, thanks, guys.

Robert and Wayne and Dylan have become good friends. In the writing lab, they talk through their stories constantly as they write. In their response group, they insult each other frequently and joke as they talk, but each author in turn takes charge as the group discusses his piece of writing. As Wayne goes through his poem line by line, the others are willing to suggest different arrangements to help him with the meaning he wants. Parts of the discussion sound almost like an argument, with the boys trying out minor changes to see how the new wording changes the meaning and how it sounds. During the formal response, each of the three interjects humor: Wayne joking about a friend of his being buried in the garbage, Robert carrying the "square miles, square feet, square centimeters" to an extreme, and Dylan commenting sarcastically that he "had a good idea"; but each time, one of them brings the group back to the discussion of the poem. Wayne takes the lead in keeping the group on task, deciding when the session has ended, and choosing when to discuss the next piece of writing. He begins by announcing, "Next," and punching the tape recorder again.

"It's called 'The Dragon Killers,' and it's by me, Dylan Hansen."

"Is that your first name, me?" Wayne asks. Robert giggles, and Dylan begins reading his draft:

Centuries ago in the central plains of Ireland there was a group of thirty knights known merely as the dragon killers. These brave men were on an impossible quest to rid the world of all forms of dragons. We now move to the tent of the leaders as they plan their first attack. . . .

"Sir Riley, I still suggest that we take the more honorable approach and fight the dragons with only one man at a time."

"If we do as Sir O'Malley suggests, we stand a much greater chance of losing. I say that we fight in great numbers so that we are assured of victory."

"Listen, both of you, we will fight in pairs, to make it more fair for both sides of the battle."

Dylan: Something wrong, Wayne?

Wayne: Well, it—you make it sound like it's a game.

Dylan: It is.

Wayne: Well, what do you mean, I mean these guys have to kill dragons, okay—[Even as Wayne is talking, he understands Dylan's response and corrects his first impression in mid-sentence.]

Robert: Let him read the whole thing.

Wayne: Oh, for fun—oh, I thought that was like their job.

Dylan: No, no, no, they just want to do it to be like heroes and stuff.

Wayne: Oh, okay, I gotcha.

"But, Sir O'Henry."

"That's enough of that, I'm the leader and what I say goes!"

"There is a pair of dragons up on that hill, they will be our first victims."

"What type are they?"

"One is a red dragon and the other is black."

They chose a third man and made their way up the hill. Soon they saw the large hole in the hill that the dragons lived in.

"There it is!"

"Draw your weapons! You, prepare your bow!"

The dragons, hearing the noise, began to emerge from the cave.

"Here they come!"

The archer let go his arrow, it flew quickly and embedded itself in the side of the red dragon. Steaming blood splattered from the wound. The dragon seemed to take no notice as it opened its mouth and blew a cone of flame at the attackers. The knights hid behind their large shields and the flames passed around them. Unfortunately, the archer had no shield and the flames ripped his charred body into pieces.

"Forward, men!" O'Henry yelled.

They were close enough to use their swords. Sir Riley charged, but the black dragon's claw came down and ripped through his armor. Blood flew everywhere as the dragon's sharp claws sliced from his chest to his legs. He lay on the ground, his intestines strewn about, in a pool of his own blood.

The black dragon stepped forward preparing to attack, but Sir O'Malley thrust with his sword, leaving it protruding from the wound. Blood poured from around the sword. The dragon, opening its mouth, breathed a line of acid toward Sir O'Malley. Turning to flee, O'Malley tripped and the acid poured into his armor.

"Help, I need water!" O'Malley yelled, running for the river.

The loud sound of melting flesh filled the air. Skin dripped from his face as he made his way to the river. Unfortunately, he never made it; his arm dropped off from his body before he fell to the ground in a heap of steaming armor.

Wayne: I hate it when that happens. [Without missing a beat, Dylan responds quickly and continues to read.]

Dylan: So do I.

Sir O'Henry turned and ran into the woods. The dragon killers also fled, never to fight a dragon again.

Robert: Now, who got ripped apart?

Wayne: The names were kind of the same.

Dylan: Well, that's because they're all . . . Irish people.

Robert: Who got ripped apart here?

Dylan: Let's see—um, by what?

Robert: By the dragon claws.

Dylan: Sir Riley.

Robert: Sir Riley. And who got acided?

Dylan: Acided? Um, O'Malley, I believe. Yes.

Robert: And where was Sir O'Henry?

Dylan: He was just doin' his stuff before he ran.

Robert: What was he doing, though?

Dylan: I don't know, I'm not sure. I could make that up, I guess.

Wayne: You have to—what you've done is you've built up the dragon killers as the good guys—

Dylan: Yeah? What's the problem?

Wayne: And the dragons as the bad guys. Well, a good story—the good guys always win. Maybe you should take it—

Robert: It annoys me, too, when the good guys always win. I hate it.

Wayne: I mean, you should kind of start out how one Irishman didn't like it because it was cruel to the dragons, or something like that—just do it so that at the end of the story they don't feel completely sorry for the dragon killers and hate the dragons completely.

Dylan: Uh-hum.

Wayne: Maybe if you make it kind of midway like, when they are talking up there, have one of them say, "Well, I don't like this because it is kind of inhumane, because, you know, they don't have a chance," something to make whoever's reading it feel kind of sorry at the beginning. Then when the dragon killers are chased away, then they feel that they have kind of reached a compromise—those guys will be killed and the dragons won't be bothered.

Dylan: Right. Okay. I will make a note of that.

Robert: And then who says—it gets confusing with all these different things here—O'Riley, O'Henry, O'Malley, O'Hubert. It doesn't say who says each of these lines.

Dylan: Well, let's see. I only have three characters with names. So I guess I could change some names. Or I could do—well, so basically what we have to work on here is names, and then some sympathy for the dragons.

Robert: And then you need to say, at least for a few of these, who says what. It gets confusing.

Dylan: I guess it would help, yes. . . . Well, all right, those are very good ideas. Thank you, Wayne, thank you, Russ.

Though Dylan is interrupted twice in his reading, he responds quickly and then continues so as not to interrupt the effect of his story. Both Robert and Wayne have listened intently to the reading and are direct with their comments. Robert is insistent that Dylan identify the characters clearly. First, he wants the action in the fight to be clear, telling what happens to whom, and second, he wants Dylan to specify who is speaking at the beginning to avoid confusion. Wayne offers Dylan a strategy to make the story more appealing to its audience. The boys initiate alternatives and explore possibilities—techniques used by students who feel comfortable with each other—and they offer suggestions in an atmosphere of camaraderie such that their feelings aren't hurt if their suggestions are rejected. At first Dylan seems surprised at Wayne's suggestion to complicate the story, but he accepts it. Dylan concludes by summarizing his revision jobs. I can almost hear his voice as he thanks his group members for their good ideas.

Another response group begins with, "Okay, Annette, you read yours." The other girls see Annette as a good writer, and they expect her to read first. Annette is a fairly sophisticated critic of her own work; she sets the stage for her group members by telling them how she needs help before she reads her poem. She begins by saying, "This is called 'Lava.' One of the things I need help on is line breaks and stuff like that. Okay?" Then she reads.

> Boiling as hot as a teapot and ready to scream
> I gurgle
> flowing up and over the top
> of my mother
> riding the smooth rocky curves
> of my ancestors
> gently melting them
> to their old
> vitality
> as I slip away
>
> Someday I'll be like them
> able to cool
> farther spread from the rest
> able to see
> the outside world
> all year round
>
> Then I won't need to be
> such a nomad

Suzanne: I thought it was very interesting; I like it.

Eleanor: It's very creative.

Annette: What about this part that says "I slip away" and doesn't mean like disappeared? Do you think that that means I've disappeared or not?

Suzanne: I think it just means coming down the mountain.

Annette: Umm. What about this last phrase?

Eleanor: I like it, except not a lot of people know what nomads are.

Annette: Should I explain it?

Eleanor: No.

Annette: What about this ["to be"]? Should I break it up or put it all on one line?

Eleanor: Break it over here, and put "to be" on the next line.

Suzanne: Yeah.

Annette: So what about "vitality?" Should it be on the same line as this ["to their old"]?

Suzanne: I think it goes together.

Annette: Should I put it next to here?

Eleanor: Yes.

Annette: Ummm. Thanks.

When Annette finishes reading, she ignores Suzanne and Eleanor's praise and begins her questions. She has decided which lines might be ambiguous or confusing and asks specifically about them. First she wants to test their understanding of "slip away," and Suzanne verifies the response that Annette wants. Then she asks about their understanding of "nomads," and Eleanor agrees that Annette doesn't need to explain it. Maybe it is because the other two girls sense that Annette knows what she wants to say that they do not initiate any discussion of the poem. Annette continues by asking about the arrangement of the lines; then, when she has asked her questions, she ends the session. She seems to be completely in charge of the group.

I am pleased with what is happening today. My students have chosen a piece of writing from their folders which they are interested in rework- ing. Their discussions in the formal response settings are examples of the interaction that I hoped to see; the authors have directed the discussions, asked for response from the others in their group, and received help with their writing. The writing lab, too, has a comfortable feeling; it hums with purpose, yet there is joking and laughter. I hear students asking each other for advice on which pieces to rewrite, and there are some serious discussions of the work in revision as students go back to their computers from the response groups. I see a growing concern to make the writing match what they want to say as well as a much higher level of ease with each other.

But the tone of the class and the peer response, both formal and informal, has not always been like it is today. This class now is very differ- ent from the same group who walked into the writing lab at the end of January when the semester began. I don't think that my students then really understood what peer response could be. I do think that the physical arrangement of the lab contributed mightily to the changes which occurred as the semester progressed, both in the dynamics of the class and in the changes in my role, and that I was beginning to understand how the arrangement of the writing lab was a tool for changing behavior—something to work with, rather than against.

My first experience in designing a writing lab was six years ago, at Bryant Intermediate School in Salt Lake City. The principal and I had written a productivity grant and had received state funding for thirty-two Macintosh computers. All of our 650 seventh- and eighth-grade students would spend at least twenty percent of their English class time in the lab. Four English teachers, two of us teaching half-time, one Chapter I teacher, and one resource teacher would rotate our time in the writing lab. Our grant included funding for a full-time lab aide.

Our thirty student computers were arranged in groups of six at hexagonal tables with a raised platform in the middle for the printer. I had seen computer labs designed with rows of computers along the walls of a classroom where students sat with their backs to each other, a design which allowed the teacher to see each student's monitor and gave more control of the class. But this new design would support response groups in the classroom, for students would be able to talk as they wrote (Figure 5-1). In every class, the first week was filled with confusion. But as students learned more about the computers, they asked fewer questions about how to save and print, and we were able to spend more time with them on the content and organization of their writing.

Even though early research has suggested that computers do not change revision, ideas, or overall quality of writing, our expectations were realized that students would be more willing to write and would write longer pieces, they would spend more time "on task," they would revise more because it was easier to revise, they would learn punctuation, capitalization, and correct usage because we would be teaching those skills in context, and they would take pride in the neatness of the final product. At the end of a year, the number of our students' writing samples judged to be competent on a district holistic writing assessment had increased from 79.4 percent to 87.3 percent, and the number of student writing samples below acceptable quality had decreased from 20.6 percent to 12.7 percent.

When I moved to Rowland Hall-St. Mark's, an independent school, four years ago, part of my job was to design another writing lab. I tested several brands of computers and word processing programs, but because Macintosh computers were so easy for students to use, we purchased them. Again, I wanted an interactive configuration which promoted talk and sharing. Even though the size of the classes I taught would be nearly half that of the public school, the two writing labs would be similar in that both designs offered the same opportunities for informal response.

Figure 5–1
A Computer Lab Design with Hexagonal Tables

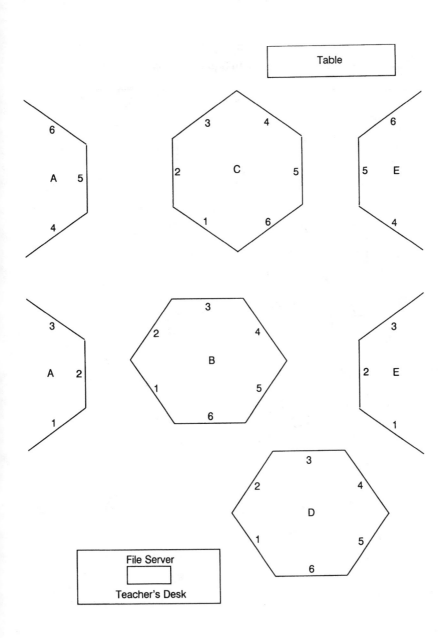

Groups of four students, each with a Macintosh computer, would sit on all four sides of low square tables, facing each other (Figure 5–2). The inner corner of each table would be cut off so that a short person such as I could reach the printers easily. I decided to network the lab with a file server for our word processing program. Unlike the writing lab program

Figure 5–2
A Computer Lab Design with Square Tables Facing Each Other

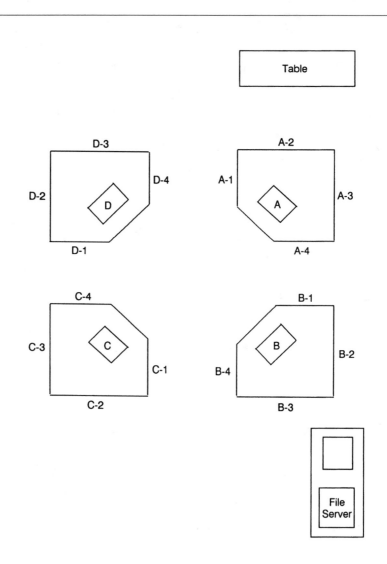

at Bryant, students would be scheduled into the writing lab at Rowland Hall-St. Mark's for one quarter of the year in addition to their English classes. Another major difference in the Rowland Hall program is that the class size ranges from fourteen to eighteen students, a number which is a luxury for teachers in Utah. I am able to confer with each student during a class period if I wish, or I might spend twenty minutes with one student, ten with another, and only a short time with the rest.

I was aware that I wanted to support peer response with the design of the computer writing labs. I knew that in many classroom settings, the computers aided learning in a variety of ways while the teacher's role was unchanged. I also knew that another exciting potential of computers was that they could be a catalyst to change the teacher's role from a teacher-directed to a teacher-assisted one, providing the mechanism for a transition to a more collaborative, student-centered classroom. Several years ago, I attended a workshop for teachers of gifted and talented students presented by Dr. Roger Taylor, at which he depicted various teacher interactions with students, contrasting "Sage on the Stage" to "Guide on the Side." I remembered the catchy phrases; now I saw them fitting into my writing lab situation.

Yet in the early stages of teaching in the lab, I was hesitant to allow much informal interaction. I was far more comfortable with the seventh graders, who were new to the lab and had a healthy respect for the new technology. They filed in, sat down at the computers, typed in a short paragraph, practiced their fingering, and thanked me when they left. At the beginning of each class, they expected me to give them the assignment for the day. They looked to me as their leader and treated the writing lab as a traditional classroom in terms of the teacher being the focal point. My role as their teacher was essentially unchanged from what I had been accustomed to after twenty years of teaching in a "traditional" classroom. I appreciated them.

I was uneasy with the eagerness of the eighth graders, who were familiar with the writing lab from the previous year and burst in, scoffed at taking a few minutes for a typing drill, and were enthusiastic about doing their own writing and experimenting with the features of the computers. In this second stage, students were excited about using the computers and not quite sure how to manage the freedom I wanted to give them to work on independent projects. The noise and seeming confusion bothered me. After the first few weeks, if I wanted to pull the class together at the beginning of the period, I had to put a note on the door to divert their attention. Otherwise, they were completely in command, coming into the lab, grabbing their disks from the table, turning on the computers, and beginning projects immediately. My eighth graders were responding to the new layout and moving toward the student-centered classroom I had envisioned, and I wasn't ready to move with them. In my attempts to manage the class and control the noise, I made assignments for everyone. At one point, I even held a class meeting to tell them of my unhappiness with their behavior and of my solution—to provide a more structured environment for them. On a conscious level, I knew that a more structured environment wasn't what I wanted. I did want to create a context that would allow peer response to occur naturally. I wanted students to have power and confidence and to be in charge of their writing, and I wanted their interests, rather than mine, to be central.

I knew that my job would be to change my role from director to facilitator, structuring talk in the classroom, encouraging students to help each other, and recognizing informal response. Subconsciously, though, I still felt I needed to be "the teacher"—to have control. The new role was a big change in my own self-concept—more than I ever thought it would be.

Giving Students Ownership—A Tough Proposition

Two conversations have nagged continually at my perspective about control. I will always remember an early class in the writing lab several years ago when I suggested to Annemarie that she read over a paragraph for possible changes, and her emphatic response was, "I like it the way it is." I wanted her to think about making it more detailed and specific, but those were my suggestions. Her words effectively ended our discussion. Perhaps she thought that I was asking her to make revisions which I designed, turning the piece of writing into something that I would write.

The other conversation occurred at the beginning of a term when I assigned a personal narrative. Mindi responded, "I don't have anything to write about. I haven't led a very interesting life." Phil, overhearing her, asked, "What about all those stories you tell in advisory?" and Mindi said, "Those are different." Perhaps Mindi was uncomfortable telling her stories in the new setting of the writing lab to an unfamiliar audience, or perhaps she thought that her stories didn't fit my assignments and my expectations. When I reflect on Annemarie's and Mindi's responses, I think that they were reacting to my role as teacher-director.

In previous years, my instructions to my classes to lead into peer response began with an assignment which had been particularly successful in the past: writing a narrative about an elementary school experience. After I read several models which had been written by students the previous year, students wrote about an experience of their own. We began with partner response with specific directions about how to respond, and then I split the class into groups of three for small-group response, for which I offered questions from a guide. I was surprised when groups of three students with three short pieces of writing were able to complete their responses in ten minutes.

GUIDE TO PEER RESPONSE (used for partners and small groups)

1. Tell one feature that you like about the writing.

2. If there are any parts that aren't clear—where you aren't sure what is happening—tell the author about those parts and offer suggestions about how they might be fixed.

3. If there are places where examples or more details would make the paper more interesting, tell the author what might be added.

The groups were supportive and complimentary about each other's writing, asked questions about clarity, and moved on quickly to the next piece. It surprised me that their responses were short and superficial. What I did not realize was that I had always given that particular assignment later in the school year. It was successful because students were accustomed to working with each other and were more comfortable about sharing their experiences.

Building a Writing Community of Trust

My students' performance should have been no surprise to me, because their experiences paralleled mine with my own writing response group. Since 1983, my first summer in the Utah Writing Project, I have participated in a monthly writing group. Grace, Charlotte, Rebecca, Alfene, Sandra, and I have shared letters to superintendents and news media, drafts of thesis chapters, poems and essays and stories, and memos to faculty and fellow teachers, whenever our schedules provided an opening—on Saturday mornings, over dinner, and during vacations over the past nine years.

Our common experience is that we teach, but none of us teaches at the same school, and we represent three different school districts. One of us teaches at the elementary level, four in middle school/junior high, and one in high school. In the beginning, we knew little about each other's background, experiences, and expertise in writing. Like my students, we began by being hesitant, apologetic, and tentative in our new situation. My students also have the same differences: they happen to be in the same class, but they know little about each other's backgrounds, experiences, and expertise in writing. I needed to provide some experiences to help them trust themselves and each other.

My early attempts at peer response in the classroom gave me experience and confidence, but I decided that my approach was too structured. I was limiting students to generic questions which could be used for all of their writing, and, in doing so, was taking away their control. In a way, I was supporting their insecurity by setting rules. Maybe the students didn't really feel like authors with my assignments.

And so, for this term, I held my breath and decided to try some new techniques. I would change my teaching in two ways: First, I would give my students choices. After several beginnings, students would choose pieces which they wished to work on. I hoped that that feeling of ownership would help them take charge of asking for response. Second, I would model response in as realistic a way as possible, to help them expand, define, and clarify their writing. I would not only ask for whole class response to a piece of first draft writing from one of last year's students, but I would also compare their responses to a transcript of a previous group responding to the same piece of writing so that they would have immediate corroboration of their own response. I would give students experience in playing the roles of responders in the response group. In retrospect, students seemed pleased to see the similarities between their feedback and that of the more experienced response group.

Just as we teachers don't require that students learn to name parts of a sentence before allowing them to write their own, I don't insist that students know how to operate a computer before they begin writing. On the first day in the writing lab, the eighth grade students turn on the computers (I say, "Reach around to the back left and turn on the switch," and some of them grope for it but everyone is soon successful), and I remind them about being careful to insert the disks correctly in the disk drive. I show them for the first and only time how to call up a blank screen, and then we are off and writing. Nor do I insist that students have a thorough knowledge of the keyboard and proper fingering before they begin. We have a five-minute typing drill to get the stiffness out of their fingers and help them remember the keyboard, and after that I keep an eye on their fingers as I walk around, reminding those who are using only two fingers about the correct fingering. On the second day, I see whether students can remember how to call up a blank screen by themselves. If they can't remember, I ask a neighbor to show them. That promotes the purposeful talk and atmosphere of helping each other that I want to see. Each day, I teach skills as they need them: using tabs to indent, centering a title, cutting and pasting, changing the font style and size, making columns, and double-spacing the text. I show them once; then I ask them to help each other. I want to build the idea of students teaching each other. It's back to the idea of coaching, in the sense of using the computers to help change my role. I am finally willing to be the coach rather than the director.

There are always students who know far more than I do about the computer's functions; they become valuable aides in helping other students. For those who need typing practice, we have several typing programs which students may choose to use. They include practice on home keys for the beginner as well as races for speed drills at all levels of proficiency. Sometime during the first two weeks in the lab everyone works on the typing program for one day; after that, students have the option of choosing to work on their typing skills for as many days as they'd like.

Most of our writing is done in class on the computers. I tell students what we will be working on the next day, and sometimes I ask them to make a list of possible ideas for writing. Many eighth graders appreciate some preparation and thinking time, and it is especially helpful for them to crystallize and organize their ideas ahead of time if I expect them to finish a piece of writing in one class period.

On the first day of class, I asked for a letter from the eighth graders, outlining their goals in writing and telling me what kind of writing projects they'd like to work on over the semester. For ideas, I provided two lists. The first was a list of writing activities taken from Marge Frank's *If You're Trying to Teach How Kids to Write, You've Gotta Have This Book*! (1979), including soap operas, fantasies, cereal box texts, bumper stickers, party invitations, ransom notes, movie reviews, and horoscopes. The second list was made up of writing goals adapted from Nancie Atwell's *In the Middle* (1987), such as writing longer pieces, focusing on a single topic, using direct quotations to bring speakers to life, and experimenting with new and different kinds of writing.

Dear Mrs. Coombs,

My goal is to improve my typing skills and become better associated with the keyboard. I would also like to be where I was very confident that I was hitting the right keys without looking. I would also like to learn about a few new people and be able to help anybody who needs help.

In the way of projects I would like to work on some kind of a weekly magazine with a small group. I would also like to work on a short story.

SO FAR IT LOOKS LIKE A GREAT CLASS.

from Paul

Dear Mrs. Coombs

You asked me to write a letter to you explaining what I plan to work on in my time at the writeing lab. you asked for a goal that I would like to carry out and you asked me to think of a project that I would like to work on hear also.

I thought that a good goal for me would be to work on my spelling skills, my Mom always wants me to and to get good grades at this school it would be good for me to be a better than avrage speller.

I would also want to compleet a short story that I have been working on for way too long and that is a story that I have intitled simply, The Search which is a science fiction about manhaten island in the year 2020. I am looking foreward to finishing it.

Sincerely yours, Jeffrey

The next day, I summarized students' goals and writing projects from the letters; I wanted them to know what others in the class would be working on, and I also wanted them to feel free to add to their lists anything of interest that others had written down. I expected to see increased commitment to their work, since they were defining their own audience and topic. Still nervous about turning over all control, I told them that I also had some specific goals and assignments for them, including a poem and some informative and persuasive pieces. In addition, they could use the lab to work on assignments from other classes.

Then we began. Wayne, strongly concerned about environmental issues, wrote a poem about garbage, and Dylan worked on a medieval fantasy. Tom, the son of a clergyman, wrote an allegory about religion; Trevor, a product of public schools, wrote a letter to the school newspaper defending the school's interim learning program; and Burt wrote a personal narrative about his trip to London. Laurie wrote a slumber party horror story, Julie wrote about her little sister's trip to the emergency room, Annette, daughter of a poet, wrote poetry, and Eleanor wrote a fairy tale. Mindi wrote letters to everyone she could think of.

Some of the less traditional projects included Annette's questionnaire and results on "How Prepared Are You For Your Prom Night?" (Figure 5-3), Mindi's "Horoscope" (Figure 5-4), Suzanne's concrete poem, "The Eagle" (Figure 5-5), Robert and Peter's menu (Figure 5-6), and a soap opera from Winnie and Eleanor which traced three separate stories . Each scene represented a day's listening or viewing, and predictably, nothing significant happened in any single scene.(Figure 5-7).

After everyone had had several days to write, I announced that they would need to print a first draft by Thursday in order to begin response groups on Friday

When students walked into the writing lab on Friday, I handed them copies of George's character sketch, a first draft which had been written the previous term.

CHARACTER SKETCH

Ricky Torento is a thin and frail child. He doesn't have a lot of friends and the one's that he hangs out with are often a lot more nurdy than he is. He can be a very enjoyable person to be with. He sometimes gets talking about things that no one can understand. On the other hand he is really nice and friendly. He is about 15 years old and has brown hair that always leaves the house looking good, but after school it is a mess. He's about 5' 4" high and weighs 95 lbs. He tries to put in some slang words here and there, but the way he says them make them sound almost stupid. He is quiet in groups, but he answers questions very fully and well. He is a modest boy and in school does very well. He is a very honest person. His favorite hero is Flash. He would love to speed around at great speeds. If he ever had the chance to do things like Flash he would. He lives with his parents in a small house and he likes talking with them a lot. He could be greater than he realizes. I hope that he finds that out.

Figure 5-3
"How Prepared Are You For Your Prom Night?"

HOW PREPARED ARE YOU FOR YOUR PROM NIGHT?

1. You were very prepared for your prom. You ordered your dress to match the theme of the prom. Today you just found out that the theme has suddenly been changed. What do you do? You decide to:
   A) wear the dress anyway
   B) run and buy a new dress even though it will cost you plenty
   C) stay home and pout

2. Your date to the prom points out his hideous purple tuxedo with a top hat and tails that he is going to wear to the prom. It will clash horribly with your dress. What do you do? You decide to:
   A) refuse to go with him
   B) buy yourself a dress just as wild, such as a wild cherry dress
   C) reason with him

3. It's the night of the prom and your date brings you the ugliest corsage. What do you do? You decide to:
   A) start sneezing and pretend you're allergic to it
   B) accidentally drop it and step on it with your pointy heels
   C) wear it on your waist where it may be less noticeable

4. You go to the store and see the perfect shoes that totally match your dress. When you try them on you find that they are two sizes too small. What do you do? You decide to:
   A) resign yourself to suffering
   B) wear last year's pumps even though they don't match
   C) get them professionally stretched

5. You hear a rumor that the cutest boy in school wants to ask you to the prom. You then get a phone call from a good friend who is a boy asking you to the prom. What do you do? You decide to:
   A) say no and wait for the other guy to call
   B) say yes and decide to have a good time
   C) tell him to wait and you'll give him your answer later

6. You want to do something spectacular to your hair for the prom. What will you do? You decide to:
   A) get a new perm on prom's eve
   B) practice different hairstyles for a week
   C) dye it a funky new shade

7. After the prom, you and your date are invited to a party where there will be alcohol served. What do you do? You decide to:
   A) go to the party even though you may feel uncomfortable
   B) demand that your date take you home
   C) ask him to drop you off on the way to the party

PROM-ABILITY CHART

1. A) 3 points - Wear the dress anyway. You shouldn't be ashamed of your dress. B) 2 points. C) 1 point.
2. C) 3 points - Try to reason with him but do not be harsh. Explain your reasons. B) 2 points. A) 1 point.
3. C) 3 points - Wear it on your waist because you don't want to hurt him. After a short period, tell him you want to preserve it and take it off. A) 2 points. B) 1 point.
4. C) 3 points - Get them stretched because you want a prom perfect night. B) 2 points. A) 1 point.
5. B) 3 points - You go with your friend because, after all, the other guy may never call and, besides, your friend is a really great guy. C) 2 points. A) 1 point.
6. B) 3 points - Practice different hairstyles so your do will be the best. That way it will turn out the way you want. A) 2 points. C) 1 point.
7. C) 3 points - Have your date drop you off because you don't want to threaten him and you don't want to spoil the evening. B) 2 points. A) 1 point.

PROM PREPARED?

17-21 points: You are really prepared for your prom. You know what to do and the way you want to do it. Good luck!

12-16 points: You are almost there. You are starting to know how your prom will be. Start earlier next time and you'll be ready for sure.

7-11 points: Try harder. Know what you have to do before getting started.

Figure 5–4
Mindi's "Horoscope"

HOROSCOPE

ARIES
(March 21 to April 20)

Fun is your middle name in everything you do. Your money is going to change considerably in the next few weeks. Your birthday bash is going to be incredibly fun. Your lucky days are March 31 and April 19. Your lucky numbers are 19 and 31. You'll notice that magenta will catch your eye. Somebody strange but familiar will pass by, and your feelings for them will change soon!

CANCER
(June 21 to July 22)

Your main interest is in traveling. You seek new adventures in many parts of the world. You have not really been interested in friends lately but you have been taking time for school or your job. You have been wanting to spend more time with your relatives. You are not interested in what people think of you but of what you think of yourself. Your lucky numbers are 6 and 24 and your lucky days are June 24 and July 6. You will notice that a light shade of green will appeal to you.

LEO
(July 23 to August 22)

You have been happy lately. Your sweetheart has been finally noticing you. The mailbox will bring a new surprise to you. Your taste in clothes has changed considerably. Your friends have become closer to you and your friendship means a lot. Television has become quite boring and you do not spend much time watching it. Your lucky days are July 24 and August 1. Your new color is maroon.

Figure 5–5
Suzanne's Concrete Poem, "The Eagle"

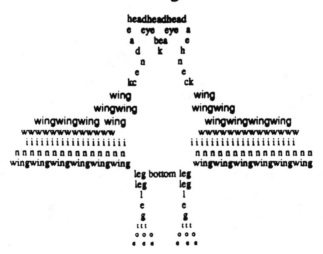

Figure 5-6
Robert and Peter's Menu

Parfaits

White Bunny Snow - $ 2.00
Ingredients-
Vanilla ice cream
Lots of whipped cream
Marshmallow sauce
And two cherries on top

Caramel, Marble -$ 1.90
Ingredients-
Any ice cream you want
Lots and lots of caramel
Nuts or peanuts
Whipped cream and a cherry on top
And a surprise--a bag of marbles

Chocolate Twister - $ 3.00
Ingredients-
Chocolate ice cream
Chocolate chip ice cream
Chocolate chocolate ice cream
Double fudge ice cream
Extra chocolate chips
More chocolate fudge
Blend all ingredients together
for 30 seconds.

I asked students to read through it silently; then we read it aloud. In the whole-group response, nearly every one of the eighteen students had something to say: "It's confusing the way he jumps around. He says something and then repeats it later on." "It sounds contradictory—'He doesn't have a lot of friends' and yet 'he is really nice and friendly.' What does he mean?" "Look at how so many sentences start with 'He.' That's monotonous." "He doesn't give any examples to show how he does well in school." "It sounds like his hair leaves the house by itself." "Why does he admire Flash?"

I categorized their responses on the marker board. I wanted to emphasize organization (their noticing that he jumps around and is contradictory and repetitive); development (asking for examples of how he does well in school and why he admires Flash); and sentence structure (seeing the many similar sentences and the misplaced modifier).

Then I handed out the transcript of the response group. Four members of the class volunteered to take the parts of the smaller response group and read their reactions and questions aloud.

Figure 5-7
Winnie and Eleanor's Soap Opera

As The World Crumbles

Story 1, Scene 1:
(Samantha hangs up the phone.) Julie, you'll have to keep yourself occupied tonight. I have a date.
Julie: Who with?
Samantha: Daniel.
Julie: The police officer!
Samantha: Of course.
Julie: Why him?
Samantha: Because he asked me. I'm going to get dressed, call me when he gets here.
Julie: Where are you guys going?
Samantha: I don't know, but I know it's really fancy.

Scene 2: (The doorbell rings.)
Julie: I'll get it. (She runs and opens the door.) Oh, it's you.
Daniel: Well, who'd you expect?
Julie: I was hoping it was someone besides you. Mom, your date's here. (She leaves Daniel waiting at the door.)
Samantha: (walking down the stairs) Why didn't you invite him in, Julie?
Julie: Because.
Samantha: Hi, Daniel.
Daniel: You look great!

Scene 3: (They both hop into Daniel's Mazda Miada and drive off.)
Samantha: So, Daniel, where are we going tonight?
Daniel: It's a surprise.
Samantha: I'm sorry about the way Julie treated you.
Daniel: It's all right. Can we just not talk about her tonight? I want to know more about you.

Story 2, Scene 1:
Nicole: Josh, I can't believe that they found Vikki. Start packing. We need to get to Utah.
Josh: How could she find her way there?
Nicole: I know. Utah's kind of far from California. It's a miracle she's still alive.

Scene 2: (at the airport)
Rental car clerk: What kind of car would you like?
Josh: Any car will do, just hurry! (The clerk hands him some papers to fill out. When he hands them back, the clerk hands him a key.)
Clerk: Lot 2. It's a white Jeep. Joe will take you there.

Scene 3: (on a street in Utah)
Josh: Where should we look?
Nicole: Why don't we ask someone if they've seen her. We have her description.
Josh: Have you seen this woman?
Man #1: No, I'm sorry.
Man #2: Why actually I think I have.
Nicole: What time? Where?
Man #2: I saw her coming out of that house over there about 15 minutes ago.
Josh: Did you see where she went?
Man #2: Yeah, she went back in the house.
Nicole: Josh, we have to get over there right now.
Josh: Thank you so much, sir.
Man #2: No problem.

Nicole: Josh, let's go.

Scene 4: (They ring the doorbell of the house.)
Cory, owner of the house, answers the door: Hello, may I help you?
Nicole: Yes, we were looking for a lady named Vikki.
Cory: Well yeah, she's here, but I don't think she'll remember you.
Josh: What do you mean?
Cory: Well, she's got a bad case of amnesia.
Nicole: Amnesia? Oh, no!

Story 3, Scene 1: (At the anniversary party for Brad and Veronica, Brad and a friend, Jasmine, have left the table for an important talk outside.)
Jeremiah: I wonder what is taking Brad so long.
Kendra: What could he be doing out there?
Veronica: I'm going to go outside and see what he is doing. (Veronica puts down her glass and goes outside)

Scene 2: (the next day, in the city)
Jasmine: Veronica, wait up.
Veronica: Who are you?
Jasmine: I'm Jasmine. (Veronica runs off in tears.) Veronica, wait, I want to talk to you.
Veronica: What about?
Jasmine: I'm so sorry for hurting you. I didn't want you to get hurt this badly.
Veronica: Can we talk about this some other time? I'm really not in the mood.
Jasmine: Okay, meet me in the park at 11:00 tomorrow.
Veronica: That's fine. I gotta go now. (Veronica turns away.)

TRANSCRIPT—Peer Response to Character Sketch

Randy: "No one can understand." Why don't you give examples of that because we can't really—

Eliza: Yeah, it's sort of jumpy. There are a lot of "He's" like—
"He is"
"He always leaves the house looking good."
"His parents."
You might want to say why or . . . If I was doing it, I might say he likes sports or add in something like that.

Jenny: It's pretty descriptive but I thought you could introduce a lit-tle more than you did. There was one question in here-

Eliza: I think one thing would make a little more is when he tried to put in slang words—I really like that line. I know people like that, can't say the words right. I sometimes give an example of what you say in a situation like that, that wouldn't fit.

Jenny: Yeah, that's what I was going to say. Maybe you could write a situation or think of a situation and find out how he would respond to it in that kind of situation.

Randy: And then you might want to do an example for "This modest boy" like what he would . . . if he's so modest, what would he do in this situation?

George: So, just more examples for everything that I state so you can understand.

Randy: Yeah.

Eliza: Yeah. Just put it into a situation so everyone can understand it. I like how you used Flash.

Jenny: Yeah.

Eliza: It was sort of entertaining. One thing, I was sort of confused. If you ever had the chance to do things like Flash would, what kind of things . . . I don't know. I guess I'm not exactly familiar with the hero Flash, so you might want to explore a little more.

George: All right. Explain him and what he would do in situations.

Jenny: Yeah. For instance, sometimes he would dash around the din-ing room table pretending to be Flash. [laughter and chuckling]

George: Yeah, this fifteen-year-old guy. [laughter]

Jenny: It's just an example.

Randy: You might want to know why. Like if he just wants to speed and get a speeding ticket or like maybe he wants to save people, like crime or something, you know.

Eliza: A fifteen-year-old guy. I guess that tells more about his personality. Ah, one thing—he doesn't have a lot of friends and the ones he thinks about were a lot more nerdy than he is. When you were writing this, did you think he might enjoy being around these people? Or were those the only friends he could get?

George: More like he tries to hang out. He hangs out with people and he tries to use slang words and the people that are supposedly better than he is, in their standards, think that the way he says them is stupid. The nerdy part is just the people start laughing when he'll say things and stuff.

Eliza: Do you consider him to be a nerd? I mean, what do you think of him?

George: Not really. He's in a way, how I pictured him was, he hangs out with a lot of different crowds. He's also a lot more in one crowd than the other. So he tends to . . . but he still hangs out evenly with both of them.

Eliza: Let's see, some more contradictory things. Does this person have enough confidence?

Jenny: I was thinking, would he be intimidated by a crowd of "popular" people?

Eliza: Is he shy?

Jenny: Yeah! I kind of get that impression.

George: Yeah.

Eliza: I guess I kind of get the opinion that he is a quiet and shy person. Like, you want him to be like a jock is shy? You know what I mean? Is that how you want him to be?

George: Well, it's kind of like he tries to be that in his character. He's trying to be that, almost. But he's trying to fit in with the higher crowd but when he's with the lower crowd, he's at the top. When in the higher crowd, he's at the bottom. So it's a strange balance, like almost because he hangs out with almost both of the groups at the same time. Also, there's something else I left out. If both groups are there at the same time, and he's with the high group, he sort of likes to put down the lower group. So he sort of tries to impress the higher group as much as he can and be better.

Eliza: I'd write that down.

George: Should I put that down?

Randy: It's like an example.

Eliza: You can't know that just from reading it.

Jenny: It seems like towards the end, you were saying that if he would gain, maybe, a little more self-confidence that he really could do a lot more than he thinks he is capable of as far as, you know, being around friends.

After reading the transcript, my students' first reaction was how imprecise and inaccurate written speech is—that thoughts were often broken off in mid-sentence. But they did see similarities in their responses: the need to explain the contradiction of whether Ricky is confident or shy; the lack of examples, including explaining why he is so modest and why Ricky admired the cartoon character Flash; and the repetition of "He" at the beginning of sentences and the hair walking out the door. Both the formal response group and my class were trying to help align George's idea of what he wanted his character to be with its depiction in writing. In addition, class members were putting themselves in the role of response partners to George's character sketch and feeling what it was like to help a writer.

Now it was time to set up our own class response groups. Rather than putting my three questions on the marker board and structuring their responses as I had done in the past, I asked students to get together in groups of three, asking those who had worked together on projects to place themselves in separate groups. I'd made some copies for them earlier that morning, since those who had worked with a partner had printed out only one copy. I asked that they take each piece of writing one at a time, reading it aloud and then responding to it before going on to the next. I hoped that their pride in their own work and interest in improving it would influence their leadership of the group when their own writing was being discussed.

The shuffle into groups was quick. The contrast with my earlier, more-structured response groups was dramatic. Before, students seemed to come into response groups worried about acceptance and nervous about sharing. This time, the author was in charge and didn't seem concerned about the effect of the writing at all. While I had always assumed that writers were not going to know what sorts of questions to ask and responders weren't going to know how to respond, everyone seemed eager to find out what others thought of their writing. When I glanced at the clock, it was 3:17. No one had noticed that it was time for school to end. Reluctantly, I said, "Oh, everybody, look at the time! It's time to leave."

"How did your response groups go yesterday?" I asked the class the next day. There was a long silence. No one spoke.

Finally Julie volunteered. "I couldn't figure out a title," she said, "and I finally put in something I didn't really care for, and then I asked somebody else to come up with something . . . and they thought of something I liked and so I used that."

"My group helped me with my spelling and punctuation," Phillip offered. I could see that the class was wondering what I wanted them to say; they were volunteering answers in a tentative way. I wanted to hear other responses, so I asked the question again. "Tell me about the ways the group helped or didn't help you," I said.

Trevor spoke next. "My group told me to put in more examples—to make it more appealing to the person who doesn't believe that interim should be going on," he said.

"Sometimes it's better to have a friend help you because you get a different perspective," Gloria said. "Your friends kind of know what you're talking about. If you talk about something you've done or something about school, they know how to change it."

"Also," Robert added, "sometimes you think in your mind something and as you write out the paper and then read it back to yourself, you can understand what is happening, but in some cases people are totally lost because one key part that you'd left out that seemed maybe obvious to you is not obvious to anyone else."

"Yeah," Burt summarized. "Your friends help you explain more of what you're trying to say."

"Did you use everything your group suggested?" I asked.

Julie responded. "There's always something that the writer's not going to agree with—so some you use and some you don't use."

I told my students that I was impressed with the intensity of the response from the day before: everyone was so engrossed that the groups hadn't noticed that the time for the end of school had arrived. In comparison to the response scenarios where I had structured the guidelines, this time I thought that students seemed more interested in asking for feedback when the writing was their own self-designed project.

But I noticed that a few students weren't on task. So before we began the next formal response group, I set up another role-playing situation. I chose a sample of student writing and passed it out to the class.

Third grade story draft, edited:

Saturday was my 9th birthday. It was a lot of fun. Jerry, Saul, Robbie, and Karl came. Karl screwed up my party! He made a fool of himself. Karl was the dunce of the party. We had pizza for dinner. Phillip was going to come but he didn't buy me a present. So he said "he had company" but he didn't have company. Tom didn't come either. I wish Tom and Phillip came. It would have been funner with Tom and Phillip. I like my watch the best. My watch has a stop watch. My party was pretty good. Even though it turned into a madhouse. We had cake a little while after dinner. The cake was very good. Jerry likes my brother's criss cross crash. Jerry gave me the Bumbling Boxing.

Using a sample of a much younger student's writing seemed to allow my students to see its problems more easily. While class members read the sample and wrote responses to it, I asked four students to accompany me into the hall where I passed out four cards that described the roles I wanted them to play:

Group member #1:

- Do not apologize for your writing.
- Read your piece aloud twice, so that others can concentrate on its message first and then listen for details.
- Take notes on others' comments, and underline the parts they liked.
- Do not defend your writing.
- Thank others for their comments.

Group member #2:

- Listen carefully.
- Be complimentary. Offer some of the following phrases:
    "It's good."
    "I like it."
    "It is really interesting."
    "It is descriptive."
    "I can just imagine it."
    "You write really well."

Group member #3:

- Listen carefully.
- Ask questions of clarification:
    "You say the party was 'a lot of fun' and 'pretty good'. How was it fun? What was good about it?"
    "What did Karl really do to screw up the party?"
- Ask questions about focus:
    "Why do you include Philip and Tom, since they weren't invited?"

Group member #4:

- Act bored. Yawn. Look around the room and compare the time on the clock to the time on your watch.

- Look carefully at your pencil. Roll it across the table. Try to balance it upright on its eraser.

- Roll your paper into a cone. Look through it. Fold it in different ways.

When we returned to the room, the four students sat at a table in the middle of the room, surrounded by the class. Group member #1 pretended that she or he had written the piece of writing I provided and read it aloud. The second group member offered complimentary but useless comments. The third member offered helpful suggestions, asking questions which allowed the writer to clarify the information and focus the piece. The fourth group member acted disinterested and impatient.

The exercise not only gives me the opportunity to mirror the behavior of those students who distract the group, but also the opportunity to distinguish between useful and useless responses. I remembered Alice's indignant response several years ago to a parent reader's praise. "We want suggestions on how to improve," she said, "not just praise." Students recognize that at first it is exciting to hear from others that "your story was good" and "I liked it," but they soon become very tired of hearing general comments and want more helpful responses to their writing. After the role-playing, the next set of response groups has fewer distractions and more useful and helpful responses.

Ten years ago, when I organized the first peer response groups in my public school classroom (eight groups of four students each), I structured the groups according to students' strengths. Included in each group, I told the students, was someone who was:

- a natural leader who would keep the group on task
- a creative person who had wild and crazy ideas
- a careful speller who would pay attention to detail
- an organizer who could help with the sequence and development of the writing and consider its effect on the audience

In some groups, one student fulfilled several of these roles. I also made sure that each group had a combination of strong and weak writers, so that students could learn from each other.

This term, I remembered some advice from Julie: "As we become closer, we become more sensitive responders," she said. "It's important to get to know the other people in your group. Then you can really tell how to help them in their writing." Now that students had had a chance to work in response groups with different groups of students and knew more about each other's writing strengths and weaknesses, I passed out slips of paper and asked them to jot down names of a few others in the class with whom they felt they could work comfortably in response groups—and asked if there was anyone in the class that they couldn't work with at all. Then I asked them to sit near those on their lists so that they could help each other. I am still not sure which method of grouping students is more effective. I want competent writers to have some influence on those who are less able, but I think the argument of closeness and comfort is a powerful one. And allowing students to state their preferences in yet another way gives them more autonomy over their writing.

Now that students were sitting near those who could help them, I noticed that even more of them were sharing their writing. The sharing was usually initiated by the author, not only at the end of an episode or when a particularly outrageous scene had been written and the writer wanted a reaction, but also for quick questions such as asking for a name for a character or what should happen next in a story. I noticed that less confident writers, who still saw the teacher as the controller, would ask me those same questions instead of asking their peers. One day, at the end of the class period, I asked who had received peer response from others, but no one indicated that they had. Winnie, who I knew had asked for suggestions about one of her characters, said emphatically, "I didn't get any peer response." Jeffrey was certain that he had not asked Peter for a logical name for his character. It was clear that students defined "peer response" as the response to a whole piece of writing which happened in formal groups organized by the teacher. The fact that peer response was a natural part of the everyday exchange between students escaped them.

I continually relayed to students what I was observing, encouraging them to share their writing in progress with those around them and reminding them that "peer response" meant also the offering of and asking for suggestions as they were composing. Because of the arrangement of the computers in the writing lab, most of the students' writing became a community project, and the informal talk, a natural outcome of the layout of the lab, further encouraged their writing development. At times, the whole writing lab represented a giant response group. A comment by one student could cause a rush of movement in the room, with everybody within earshot wanting to read the draft. Wayne's constant discussions with himself about the wording of his poem on the environment were occasionally punctuated by suggestions, corrections, and jokes from Robert and Dylan, and the giggles over the lines of the soap opera being developed at the next table frequently drew attention from others who made suggestions about the turn of the story line. The widening circles of interest made students even more aware of writing for a wider audience. It was difficult for me to document the response in the lab because the composing and responding were inseparable. I praised students for the purposeful talk I was hearing and learned to live with the noise.

Still, I needed a system to manage the class and avoid chaos. A notebook paper-sized chart adapted from Nancie Atwell's *In the Middle (1987)* worked for me. Using a new chart every two weeks (Figure 5-8), I fill in daily data on student work; I can see easily who is and isn't progressing and can plan my time accordingly.

At the beginning of each class, I walk around and jot down notes on each student's plans for the day. Conferring with every student not only provides direction for those who do not begin projects immediately but also gives me an opportunity to talk with everyone, even if just for a moment. Then I can circle back to work with individuals who have questions or who need an idea for a new project.

And the role of the computers? They contribute to more than a little chaos: the writing lab is a less predictable environment than a regular classroom. Computers contribute to varying stages of progression in writing—some students can type faster than others—and that, coupled with the variety of individual projects, means that everyone is at a different stage in writing. The resulting confusion was uncomfortable for me until I understood it. When I listened to the purposeful talk going on and realized that students were in charge of their own writing, I became more comfortable and the routine in the writing lab—in a different way—also became predictable.

Computers contribute as a catalyst for an interactive classroom, just as any project or writing event in a classroom can provide a similar context for social interaction. It has been interesting to observe that after the informal in-class response was in place, students made the decisions on when to sit down with each other to go over whole drafts. The "formal" response groups were only formal in that a number of students (2–5) agreed to work together on their drafts. I no longer set the guidelines or time and place of the formal response groups. Students' autonomy over their writing and their continual informal response to each other in the classroom seems to be the most important factor in influencing the success of the group response when drafts are completed. Along with the socializing and fun, Wayne and Robert and Dylan were serious and committed to their writing. In several ways, students showed pride in their work in the writing lab. In his graduation speech, Trevor said that "in writing lab, the most important projects are the ones we create ourselves." And, on the last day of school when I asked students to give me feedback on peer response, Robert summed up what I like to think was the feeling of every student: "I like peer response. You get to read other people's work and you get to comment on it and feel maybe that an idea

Figure 5-8
Two-week Progress Chart

8th Grade Weeks of ___February 1 – 12___

Student's Name	Mon.	Tues.	Wed.	Thurs.	Fri.	Mon.	Tues.	Wed.	Thurs.	Fri.
Laurie	advice column	advice column	response: Annette, Suz.	diets	response with A + B (absent)	slumber party story →	→	→	beauty guide	beauty guide
Trevor	hospital poem	poem	poem	revisions	(absent)	wine label	cat story	cat story	interviews	interviews
Annette	poem	(advice) prom	response: Laurie, Suz.	prom	response: Log	poem	poem	response with Suzanne + Eleanor	revisions	shopping list
Jeffrey	(absent) → [Chicken pox]			→	→	alien story	alien story	→	→	revision
Suzanne	story art collage →	→	response: Laurie, Annette	concrete poem	concrete poem	prom – the eagle	revision the eagle	response with Annette + Eleanor	response with Burt tale	tale
Burt	(absent)	London writing narrative →	→	→	response with Paul + Tom	revisions	movie review	look review	response/rev with Jeff	typing puzzle
Paul	choose your own adventure	→	→	→	response with Burt + Tom	look review	movie review	want ads	rsp/rev: Tom	typing practice
Wayne	garbage poem →	→	locker sign	response with Paul + Dylan	goxy poem	lost in the refrigerator	→	→	The fly	want ads
Phillip	choose your own adventure	→	→	Hypercard: map	fairy tale	choose your own adventure →	→	→	locker sign	fairy tale
Eleanor	soap opera	SOAP	soap	rsp + response: Winnie + Julia	fairy tale	→	→	response with Annette + Suzanne (absent)	ice cream menu	→
Robert	bean story	→	→	response with Wayne + Dylan	bean story	bean story	typing practice	→	rsp/revision with Paul	typing puzzle
Tom	list of new projects	alien story	→	→	response with Burt + Paul	bt. review	movie review	book review	rsp/revision with Paul	response with Winnie + Julia
Mindi	letter (friend wrote)	horoscope	horoscope	letter	(absent)	(absent)	response with Winnie + Julia	horoscope	horoscope	response with Winnie + Julia
Gloria	poem "rul'"	→	concrete poem	→	response: Laurie + Annette	fantasy	fantasy	tongue guide	tongue guide	zoo guide
Winnie	soap opera	soap	soap	running snap? J + Eleanor	locker sign	typing practice	response with Mindi + Julia	soap	soap	response with Winnie + Julia
Dylan	Dragon Killer story	→	→	response with Wayne + Robert	Dragon Killer	→	want ads	want ads	sky diving poem	str. to acting
Julia	soap opera	soap	soap	revision + response: ant	emergency poem story	→	response with Mindi + Winnie	soap	soap	response with Mindi + Winnie

you had went into something—an expanded idea—that they came up with. That makes you feel proud."

Works Cited

Atwell, Nancie. (1987). *In the Middle: Writing, Reading, and Learning with Adolescents*. Portsmouth, NH: Boynton/Cook.

Frank, Marge. (1979). *If You're Trying to Teach Kids How to Write, You've Gotta Have This Book*. Nashville, TN: Incentive Publications.

Part III

Decentering the Classroom

6

Revising Responding

Kristi Kraemer

"Once I was very naive about the environment"; Hannah wrote, in the cover sheet summary of her paper, "now I am very aware." She continued:

> What I like best about this piece, are the statistics and specific information I included. That was the most difficult part of writing it, though, because I had lots of trouble organizing it. Between the first and final drafts, I changed the incident I was using to show the reader what I was talking about and make it more obvious. I added the statistics, too. I'm still not entirely comfortable with the overall flow of the paper . . . I think that if I'd had more time, I could have rewritten it to be even better than it is. As you read and respond to this paper, I'd like some feedback on how you think it flows, and whether or not that additional information takes away from the basic idea, okay?

Hannah had been working on this piece for three weeks, and it was one she was passionately interested in. The original assignment, which I had taken from Ponsot and Deen's *Beat Not the Poor Desk*, (1982) had been to complete the sentence, "Once I was _____ ; now I am _____ ." After listing changes like "Once I was a bicycle rider; now I am a driver," "Once I was in junior high; now I'm in high school," and "Once I quit school; now I am a student again," she decided that the most important change she had made recently was that of realizing her responsibility for the environment.

She was excited about the assignment because formerly she had had difficulties with school, and now she was proud of her recent political involvement. She wanted to share her new awareness with her classmates, most of whom seemed far more interested in social life than in social issues.

Sitting across the room from Hannah was Sarah, another senior, a cheerleader whose tenth-grade brother was making life difficult. When the prompt was given, Sarah had no question about what she wanted to write about. She had recently been dreaming of a brotherless life, and as she filled in the blanks in the sentence, she began to resent the fact that this dream had come true before she was old enough to appreciate it, back when she was just a toddler.

Back then, she didn't have to worry about driving him around, putting up with his puerile sense of humor, or negotiating with him over bathroom and telephone privacy. Now, he bothered her constantly, and she realized that her chance at nirvana had long since passed her by. She would use this assignment to get revenge.

Unlike Hannah, Sarah chose to write about immediate experience, about everyday life, and once she decided on her focus, the paper, she noted later in her writing log, almost wrote itself. Where Hannah's initial draft was 436 words of struggling over two and one-half pages to try to explain her former ignorance and current insight, Sarah's was only 299 words, 299 that Sarah, generally, liked. Where Hannah's purpose was to persuade a resistant audience by sharing both personal experience, facts, and figures, Sarah was writing purely for entertainment, taking enjoyment in playing the martyr in a well-told tale.

Two very different writers with two very different pieces. Two very different purposes, problems, potentials. One prompt. One class. One teacher.

There was a time in my teaching career when this "heterogeneity" would have been daunting, and I would have been plagued by how I could possibly teach, given such a range. In those days, I must admit that I tried to thwart such situations by giving highly structured assignments and demanding that all of the students follow the same sequence of prewriting activities. After they wrote their first drafts, I gave them focused response sheets so they could see whether or not they'd met my criteria for success. I was also careful to choose their response groups carefully so that they'd stay "on task" and get the best responses, and I regularly presented whole-group grammar lessons to ensure that everyone accumulated the requisite skills for clear communication.

That was, after all, my job. Though I was a process teacher, committed to teaching my students to have both competence and confidence in their writing, I also believed that sequencing and accountability were important. My classes, five each day, ranged in size from 32–36. Though I realized that each of these 165 students was an individual, I believed that my job was to teach for the common good by presenting, in sequence, the rules of clear communication.

Like most teachers, I also realized that my students were largely apathetic about my quest to find their voices, and nowhere was this apathy more evident than at the response/revision stage of the writing process.

When I put my students into response groups, no matter how carefully I balanced writing abilities, no matter how far apart I seated friends, no matter how clearly I wrote the response sheets or how many points were attached to their completion, my students seemed to harbor the belief that discussing the weekend was more important than discussing a paper. They also seemed to believe that being nice was more important than being helpful.

Because of my ever-present determination and Teacher Looks, they did, I'll admit, complete the response sheets and they occasionally proffered good advice, even though they rarely talked about the papers they had read. Students came alive when they stapled the completed response sheets to the rough drafts (a process that took more energy than their reading had). Despite my best efforts, recopying papers in ink (perhaps with some spelling or punctuation improvements) continued to be synonymous with revising them. Since, in my view, real revision rarely occurred, response groups were the most frustrating and fruitless component of my process of teaching, and I often considered abandoning them entirely.

Study after study, though, has shown that it is at the point of response that young writers learn the most about how to write and how to effectively translate their ideas and information for their audience. Looking back, I'm not sure that my students were even aware that they had an audience; they cared only about meeting the stated requirements for each assignment. They were not interested in communication; they were interested in grades, and their own criteria for effective writing began and ended with their sense of grammatical correctness. When they read each other's papers, they did not see themselves as an interested audience, but as editors who felt imposed upon. Understandably, the writers were less than enthusiastic about the process and rarely used any but the most concrete suggestions that I was able to wrench out of their classmates.

They took suggestions from me, though. They would make substantive changes whenever I took part in response groups or gave mini-lessons or wrote notes in the margins of their rough drafts. If I suggested a change, it appeared, regardless of whether or not they understood the reason behind it or even understood the suggestion itself. Occasionally, I would find that my suggestions were used, verbatim, in places other than those where I had hoped they would appear, and when I asked the writers about these, they always indicated that they "liked the paper better" when my suggestions were used.

So, for a long time, I stripped response groups from my teaching repertoire altogether, and read and responded directly to all of my students' rough drafts, taking care to place the suggestions clearly next to the text I was changing. If, during this period of my teaching, I had read Sarah and Hannah's papers, I am sure that I could have helped them make "effective" revisions.

Had I read Sarah's draft at this point, I suspect that I would have lauded her style and her voice, and I would have noted that the way she juxtaposed images often made me laugh. I would have suggested a few changes in syntax and word choice, and recommended that she look at the rhythm and meaning of a few of her phrases. I would also have made some suggestions about writing her conclusion. When she received her rough draft and my response, it would have taken her just a few minutes to revise it.

By the same token, if Hannah had been in my class back then, I would have noticed a number of serious flaws in her first draft: early on, for example, her piece focused on her new environmental awareness. Later, however, it veered toward comparing her old friends with her new ones. Neither topic seemed developed adequately. I would have probably urged her to choose a direction for the piece early on, and either focus on the change in her awareness or the change in her friends.

I am sure that I would also have told her to "be more specific" in some sections, and to think about the third paragraph, where she states that the generation of the 1960s and that of the 1990s differ in that *my* generation tried to force change, while *hers* wants only to share knowledge. Depending on the amount of time and energy I had, I might have written a brief epistle about the two eras or else I might have simply suggested that she delete such erroneous thinking from her text.

I would also have directed her attention to the logic contained in the final paragraph, but, being a good teacher (and a child of the sixties), I would certainly have applauded her maturity and awareness. I am sure that I would have echoed her hope that "little step(s) . . . start an entire movement." Despite my encouragement, Hannah's revisions would have taken a great deal of time and energy.

Since she was interested in the paper and committed to succeeding in school, however, I'm sure that she would have done all that I suggested. She probably would have asked for some time outside of class so that I could help her with the "specific details" she needed to "clarify" her points. I would have been more than willing to make suggestions and add what information and resources I knew, and I have no doubt that the resultant piece would have been complete, cohesive, and perhaps even compelling. I suspect that we both would have been satisfied with the product.

But whose paper would it have been?

Though both writers might have produced better papers than those they submitted the following week, the structure, focus, and much of the new content and phrasing would have been mine, not theirs. I would have identified all of the flaws, and I would have suggested possible solutions. I'm good at that, and besides, I'm the teacher. Dutiful students that they are, they would have done what I told them to do. The papers, no doubt, would have been better.

But would the writers be better? Neither would have learned how to find these problems on her own, and neither would have had the opportunity to sort out her own thoughts or compare them with the words on the page. In a sense, their content—their ideas, their information, their responses, and their insights—would have been dictated by their audience, a powerful audience who holds the authority of both experience and the gradebook. Their growth as writers would have been stunted.

Years ago, I'd often wondered why student writers weren't more "committed" to their work, but it's obvious that if what they say is subject to being rewritten by their audience, no real communication is going on, and there is little to be committed to. Under this system, the role of the writer and the reader is completely reversed . . . somehow, instead of the writer informing the reader, the reader informs the writer about how to tell the reader what the reader wants the writer to say.

Interesting.

Confusing.

No wonder students loathe writing so much.

When I think of all of the hours and all of the energy I've devoted to rewriting my students' texts, I could kick myself. I think, too, of all of the time I've spent not only reading and fixing students' rough drafts, but later flipping between the final drafts, the rough drafts, and my comments to be sure that my suggestions had, indeed, been followed.

Then there are all of the hours I wasted in having students fill out the response sheets, which I hoped would act as surrogate teachers and provide the same witty advise I would give. These were followed by those hours I spent, again flipping between the final drafts, the rough drafts, and the comments the "peer responders" made on the response sheets to see whether their insights were as insightful as my own and whether the writers were insightful enough to put them to use.

No wonder response groups didn't "work" in my classroom! They weren't response groups. They didn't respond; they parroted. They answered questions. Students avoided and encouraged and edited and sought my help, but they didn't respond.

Clearly, neither the hints I provided nor the hints I forced their friends to provide were seen as clues to communication; they were clues to success. The writers had no questions about their writing; they questioned how I wanted them to write. Despite my good intentions, communication wasn't the driving force in my writing classes; grades were.

And real revision, the kind real writers do, comes from a completely different origin: real revision comes from the feeling that something isn't right, that the words on the page, somehow, don't match the ideas in the brain or might not be clear to a reader. Real revision is triggered by comparing text with intent, and my powerful suggestions had served to completely preclude this process for my students.

After I read Karen Spear's book, *Sharing Writing* (1988), I realized what was going wrong, and I began to switch my efforts from fixing my students' writing to fixing my own teaching. My first task was that of convincing my students that they could work independently to produce clear, coherent text, and that it would be worth their while to do so.

This clearly was not going to be easy. Many of my students caredc only about getting good grades, and believed that it was my job to tell them how to do so. Because I had always been able to translate their thoughts into correct and occasionally stylish prose, they believed that I always knew what they meant, regardless of what they had written. All of this reinforced their belief that English teachers were simply picky people who had rules for everything and got paid to impose these rules on each and every piece of paper a student handed to them.

When I set them into response groups, therefore, they mimicked my efforts, beginning with giving the impression that they truly understood each writer's message and proceeding to fix the errors they knew they could handle, mostly those in spelling and punctuation. Once those errors were taken care of, the writers believed that their writing was perfectly clear, and even if it wasn't, changing it was too hard, with no one willing to help and no assurance that the grade would be any better.

I knew, as most teachers do, that my students needed to see their writing more objectively, to switch back and forth between being readers and writers in order to improve their texts. This sounded simple enough, but in reality, it was a tremendously demanding cognitive task, and my job became that of breaking this switch into manageable and meaningful steps.

Step 1: The Readaround

In Hannah and Sarah's class, I began this process of decentering by modifying Jenee Gossard's "Readaround" (1987), a sequence wherein students read a vast number of their classmates' papers in a relatively short amount of time.

The desks were arranged in a huge circle, and students were asked to pass papers from person to person rapidly, allowing each reader only a few moments to skim each paper. Students were instructed to keep in mind that these were rough drafts and, as such, weren't polished or perfect. Ignoring errors, then, they were to read each paper quickly and to use a highlighting pen to indicated the words, phrases, sentences, ideas, and sections they found most effective and/or interesting. That was all.

When students finished reading and "coloring" a paper, they passed it to the next student, whose job it was to do the exact same thing. If, when they received a paper, they liked something that had already been colored by a previous reader, they were asked to simply "lay down some more color" to let the writer know that at least two people were impressed by that section. If, on the other hand, the previous readers had not highlighted something they liked, they could go ahead and add color to the page.

In the readaround, each paper was read by at least five readers, and when they got their colored rough drafts back, both Hannah and Sarah found that the main points of their papers, along with vivid details and clever phrasing, were highlighted. Both agreed with what other students identified as strengths, and felt good about their efforts.

More importantly, though, they read lots of other rough drafts themselves. At first, they later noted in their logs, they were both drawn to highlight interesting words, surprising facts, dialogue, and other specific, vivid details in the papers they read—the same things they later found colored on their own papers. After three or four papers, though, they said that they started to "read" not only the papers, but the highlighting on them as well. In some cases, they said, they found that they agreed with the pattern of color on a paper; in other cases, though, they wondered about the criteria other readers might be using in deciding what to color. Occasionally, both reported that "stupid stuff" was colored, and other times, "things that were really good" were missed. They both found themselves wanting to talk with the writers. Interestingly, too, both Hannah and Sarah reported that they "sort of forgot" about their own papers because they were busy passing papers around, reading, and highlighting.

This is a very different sort of reading than most of my students have done before. Both private and evaluative, the process of reading, highlighting, and passing encourages students to consider not only the overall effectiveness of the papers, but the parts as well. Because some sections are highlighted while others are left white, the implication is that the various sections offer different possibilities to the writer: some may be kept as is, some may be changed a bit, others may be eliminated entirely. This is quite different from the more holistic judgments my students had always made about writing.

Students enjoy this activity, even those who are "reluctant writers." As readers, their only responsibility is to read and celebrate good writing. It's fun and they get a lot of good ideas without having to justify their highlighting in any way.

Step 2: The Writers' Response Sheet

The next step in the process of helping the students become more "objective" about their writing is one that I modified, over the years, from Charles Cooper's work on "Writers' Response Sheets" (1983).

After the papers had been passed five or six times, I interrupted the students in Hannah and Sarah's class by asking them to stop reading and to tell me what they thought was necessary for an effective response to this assignment. Immediately Carol said that, obviously, there had to be "stuff about some sort of change," and the writer had to tell what they'd "been like" both before and after the change.

Other students seemed to agree. Francisco added that he thought that there had to be at least two parts, the "once" and the "now" parts. He said that some of the papers he'd read were missing the "now." Everyone agreed that those papers needed additional work.

Since we had now agreed on three criteria for these papers, I listed them on the board:

Change

"Once" section

"Now" section

While I was writing, someone suggested that, really, there should be three parts, that the best papers he'd read included not only the "once" and the "now" sections, but some sort of transition as well. Gerardo took exception to this observation, pointing out that his piece was simply a comparison between his life in Guadalajara and in Davis, and he didn't want to write about why he moved or about the long drive—he just wanted to write about how different his life was in the two places.

Some discussion ensued about whether transition sections should be required, since some, like Gerardo's, explored the contrasts between the two stages of life rather than the reasons for the change from one to the other. I let the discussion go, and finally, the general consensus was that I shouldn't add "Transition" to the list of criteria on the board.

After this, there were discussions about whether or not writers had to include how they felt about the changes, whether or not they should have to include specific incidents, and whether they had to include the original prompt in the first paragraph. For each point, various members of the class took sides, often citing either their own paper or the papers they read to support their viewpoint. The talk continued until the end of class.

My sense is that this sort of discussion is incredibly important for young writers. By talking about what might and might not be necessary to write a good paper, points are raised, evaluations are made, suggestions are given, and thinking is stimulated in a way quite different from the old days, when I simply told everyone what they had to do to get a good grade. This sort of discussion is grounded in both writers' purposes and readers' responses, and the issue of grading seems to recede into the background.

As the students in Hannah and Sarah's class talked, I rarely spoke. Mostly, I waited with my chalk in my hand until they finished talking, and then I called for a vote on those points for which there seemed to be no consensus. Majority vote won.

Ultimately, the list on the board read:

Change

"Once" section

"Now" section

Story/Incident

Reflections/Feelings

Detail/Description

Lead

Next, I asked the students to make their own response sheets by copying what I wrote on the board:

Writer's Response Sheet

1. I have presented information about how I once was and how I now am.   yes   no

2. I related a story or incident in one or both sections of this paper.
   yes   no

3. I included a sense of how I feel, what I learned; a sense of reflection.   yes   no

4. I described scenes clearly enough that the reader can "see" them.   yes   no

5. My lead was highlighted, showing it to be interesting to my readers.   yes   no

When they were finished, I asked the students to return the drafts they were holding to their writers. After a brief period of chaos and chatter, everyone—EVERYONE—became completely silent. They were reading their papers.

Step 3: Time to Think

Back in the days when I took all of the responsibility for checking the drafts, setting up the response groups, asking the questions and, more often than not, providing the answers to the questions I had raised about their papers, this simply never happened. No one ever read their own paper unless forced to, the prevailing wisdom being that there'd be no point in reading something that they'd just finished writing.

And they probably would have been right; however, after going through this process of reading, highlighting, discussing, and questioning, they were able to read their work with a very different set of eyes . . . and all of them read.

When we talked later in the day, both Hannah and Sarah told me that they knew, of course, how well their papers matched the criteria we'd listed, but they both found themselves reading their papers carefully before they responded to the statements on the Writer's Response Sheet.

Both, of course, received only positive feedback from the readaround, but both said that they privately focused on the "white" areas of their papers to think about how to make them better. Both girls thought that the feedback from the highlighting alone was both safe enough and specific enough that they could have improved their papers with that alone.

Hannah said that she was absolutely stunned to see so much color on her rough draft when she first got it back (Figure 6-1). Evidently, she thought, it was better than she'd thought. She immediately circled "yes" to statement #1.

As she read it through, she first looked to see what had been colored, but later, she said, she began wondering why some sections had been

Figure 6-1
Hannah's Rough Draft (boldface = highlighted parts)

When I look back and remember how I used to be, how **little respect for the environment** I had, I feel sad and stupid. I don't believe it was my fault: I didn't **have the awareness** around me to know any better. I look back to my sophmore year of high school . . . **driving everywhere, parties every weekend, friends & fun were everything to me. Who cared about the environment; this wasn't the 60's. It was my time to have fun.**

Towards the end of my sophmore year & beginning of my junior year, **I lost touch with most of my old friends & began to hang out with a whole new crowd. Our afternoons & weekends consisted of hot and heavy environmental discussions and information trade-offs.** Although I lost a lot of the social "scene." I **made closer friends than I had had before.** These people I found stimulating & always something new to add to the conversation. **We'd talk especially about the things each of us gave up for our beliefs.** (i.e., not eating meat, animal products, non-use of the car, product boycotts, etc.) We were all open to new information & growth & lots of new friends we met from one incident or protest to another.

Today I find myself a lot more confident. I don't **feel naive.** I tend to know a lot more about saving the environment than most. I almost agree this is the 60's again, but I don't really think we (my generation) are trying to achieve the same things as the generation. I feel, rather **than trying to convince the world, I want to share my knowledge and let everyone come to their own realization of what they themselves feel is necessary.** No real incident made the change except being open to information **and awareness.**

I personally feel, although no one person can do it all, **every small thing I helps.** I know there are things I do that hurt the environment, but equally there are things I do that help. The fact that **public opinion can change government** and company policies, believe more & more that by standing aside & not attempting to do anything you *are* letting government & company owners know what they are doing is alright with you. I can only **encourage more people to begin to be aware** and try to make that little difference. It does help, it is every citizens right to speak out & to believe in what they want. **We are all open to change** & it just takes that first little step to start an entire movement.

highlighted. She felt good about most of it, but she began to realize that some things simply weren't right. She was bothered, for example, by the fact that a number of readers had highlighted her memory of being a party girl, and she wondered if that image was more appealing to them than the one she really wanted to convey, that of being a serious and thoughtful citizen.

She wondered if focusing more on the activities she'd shared with her two sets of friends might be useful. Originally, she had written that her old friends cruised the party scene and that her new ones spent "afternoons and weekends [in] hot and heavy environmental discussions and informational trade-offs," and, though both of these sections of her paper had been highlighted, she realized that the party section sounded like a lot more fun.

She jotted a note in the margin next to the "environmental discussions" sentence to "Show, not Tell" on the next draft.

She then crossed out her "yes" after statement #1 on the Writer's Response Sheet and circled "no," adding a note that said "not really."

When she read statement #2, she circled "no," and realized that the only specific incident she could think of was one that would go into her "now" section, a time when three guys were so drunk during a protest at the state capital that they fell down the steps. Since this wasn't exactly the kind of image she hoped to promote, she wrote herself a note to "Call Kathy for an incident."

She thought that she'd "pretty much" met criteria #3 and had not done #4 "at all." Her lead, she judged, was "okay," and she decided to "add in lots of statistics and stuff to let people really know what was going on." She decided to do this later, since the class session was almost at an end.

Sarah, meanwhile, followed an entirely different process in her reading of the paper about her brother. She told me later that she mostly read to see whether people got her jokes and enjoyed her phrasing. The pattern of highlighting told her that they did (Figure 6–2).

She noticed, though, that there was more color at the very beginning and end of her piece, and that the center, where she reflected on her early days, had absolutely no highlighting whatsoever. She thought that was important, so she quickly changed some of the phrasing, deleted some words, and changed her punctuation to see if she could make it read more smoothly. When she finished, she had Letitia listen to her read it aloud. Letitia thought it was "great," and urged her not to change anything.

In response to the criteria on the Writer's Response Sheet, Sarah answered "yes" to all but #3. She expected to put her reflections in the conclusion, and she planned to write the conclusion later that evening.

Figure 6-2
Sarah's Rough Draft (boldface = highlighted parts)

Once I was an only child, now I am suffering . . .

I missed out on two of the best years of my life. For my first two years in this world, I was an only child. Years I have always dreamed of, **years without my brother, have actually existed. Unfortunately, I have no recollection of this blissful period.**

I've sifted through stacks of pictures **of myself as a baby, and of my mother pregnant, but my** memory has never been jarred. **It isn't so much that I want to remember life without my brother, but I want to know** how I reacted when he was born, and how my life has changed. **I've stared at pictures of myself with my** tiny hands placed on my mothers inflated tummy, **straining to remember this time, but it never works.** The first two solitary years of my life will forever be locked in the depths of my mind.

Unfortunately, my early memories of life with my brother are not erased. Somewhere around age 3 or 4 my memories pick up. Let me tell you, these memories are not all good and happy . .

I feel like he is always around. When we my brother and I were small, we were inseparable. Not by my choice, of course. This situation was definately not my choice; he followed me everywhere.

He is always around. **Wherever I go, my brother follows.** Ever since we have been **very small, we have been inseparable, not by choice, of course, but inseparable nonetheless.** Whether I'm going to the park, to **the bathroom,** or into high school, I know my brother isn't far behind.

My brother and I **usually get along,** but **when we fight, we really fight.** When we were young **we would have no mercy. Karate chops to the head and punches to the gut would continue flying recklessly until I would take a cheap shot.** In looking back, **I realize that most of our fights were completely pointless, but I think they were just part of our job.**

By the next day, most of the students had finished reading, writing notes, and responding to the five statements we'd developed. At the beginning of the hour, therefore, I asked them to add some information to their response sheets by completing some open-ended sentences. On the board, I wrote:

6. The part of this piece I like the best is:

and asked them to finish the sentence. Some, like Sarah, immediately knew how to answer (she liked the section where she fought with her brother). Others, like Hannah, took some time to re-read their papers in order to decide what they liked. Some students found that they agreed with their classmates, and cited the section which had been most heavily colored; others didn't especially like anything at all, so simply went with majority opinion. A few, like Hannah (who planned to write her conclusion about how much she'd grown up), decided that what they liked best was something they'd not yet written, so they simply wrote themselves a note on their drafts to be sure to include the new information.

The next open-ended sentence was:

7. To make this paper even better, I think I might:

Most of the students glanced over the criteria, wrote a little bit, and then began re-reading their papers. I waited a few moments, then quietly suggested that they place stars in the margins of their drafts next to any section where they thought they might add information later. I also suggested that they could write themselves brief notes to remind them of what the stars referred to so that rewriting would be easier.

Once again, everyone was quiet, and the re-reading took quite awhile. Addition is the most common form of revision, and many of the students had gotten ideas from reading others' papers, from the previous day's discussion, from the re-reading, and from thinking about the papers overnight.

They seemed willing to spend time on this step, too, perhaps because it was so easy. They didn't have to actually write anything more than the stars and the notes. The writing would come later.

Stars appeared everywhere, and I put a star on the board and wrote "add" next to it to serve as a reminder. Then I made another quiet suggestion, that they just cross out the things that they didn't think were worth recopying later, things that seemed unnecessary or awkward. Most were already doing this, so I put a line under the star on the board and wrote "delete" next to it.

By this time, some of the students had already moved on to the third method of revision, substitution, by writing their corrections above the sections they'd crossed out. I quietly added that strategy to my blackboard list of ways to revise.

The last method of revision, rearrangement, was one that I mentioned near the end of their reading time. I began by commenting that, often, writers write for awhile before they find the "center" of their piece and end up embedding an excellent lead in the middle of a half-page or so of initial rambling. I suggested that they "look at the color" on their drafts again to see if that pattern seemed to be highlighted on their first page. If it was, I suggested that they draw an arrow to show where their paper actually started, and to think about whether or not any of their early ramblings ought to be included, somehow, later in the paper. I pointed out that they could use arrows and notes to remind them of how to reorganize their paper when they recopied it later.

This, again, took some time, since most of the students read their papers yet again (their third or fourth reading) to see how they might reorganize them. To make things easier, I pointed out that they could write an informal outline of their papers on the last page if they wanted.

Some did so; most did not.

Though they had received some initial response from the highlighting on their papers, the writers in Hannah and Sarah's class had worked alone on their papers until this point in the process, and we had devoted one and one-half class periods or so to revision. Most students' papers were now covered with marks—highlightings, stars, notes, deletion lines, arrows, and question marks—and they were ready to begin rewriting. Many now had questions about the possibilities they'd considered, and wanted help in rewriting, so I posed one last statement for them to complete:

8. When I read this to my group, I'd like them to help me with:

When they'd completed that statement, they were finally ready, in my estimation, to make good use of meeting in response groups.

Step 4: Response Groups

They met in groups of three and took turns reading their drafts aloud, telling each other how they'd completed statements # 6 and #7, and asking for help with whatever they had noted in statement #8. While they did so, I simply wandered from group to group, enjoying the conversations, the reading, the interactions.

In Sarah's group, her partners, David and Amy, laughed as she read her paper (Figure 6-3). They both enjoyed her description of her plight because both have younger brothers. They, too, liked the idea of using writing as revenge. When Sarah mentioned that she was particularly proud of the sentence where she said that her brother followed her " . . . to the park, to the bathroom, [and] into high school," they both laughed and said it was an incredibly accurate account of their own lives.

Sarah also liked the description of the fights she'd had with her brother. When she mentioned this, they both launched into telling stories about the fights they'd had with their brothers and went on to talk about other ways of dealing with "sibling stress," as David called it. When he used the word "sibling," Sarah immediately realized that it was the word she needed in her topic sentence and, that problem solved, she asked them for some help with writing the conclusion. She said that she actually liked her brother now and wanted to say so, but she didn't want to sound "stupid." David and Amy both had some ideas, and ten minutes later, Sarah was finished. They moved on to Amy's paper.

In Hannah's group, meanwhile, the discussion of her paper and its issues was still going on when the bell rang twenty minutes later. Hannah had lots of questions about the writing, but she got to explaining how vegetarianism conserved water and food while it decreased the amount of agricultural chemicals released into the atmosphere. Her group was very

Figure 6–3
Sarah's Final Draft

Once I was an only child: now I am a suffering sibling.

I missed out on two of the best years of my life. For my first two years in this world, I was an only child. Years I have always dreamed of, years without my brother, have actually existed. Unfortunately, I have no recollection of this blissful period.

I've sifted through stacks of pictures of myself as a baby, and of my mother pregnant, but my memory has never been jarred. It isn't so much that I want to remember life without Lucas, but I want to know how I reacted when he was born, and how my life was changed. I've stared at pictures of myself with my tiny hands placed on my mommy's inflated tummy, straining to remember this time, but it has never worked. The first two solitary years of my life will forever be locked in the depths of my mind.

Unfortunately, all of my early memories of life with my brother are not erased. Somewhere around age three or four, my memories pick up . . . and let me tell you: these memories are not all good and happy!

Ever since we have been very small, we have been inseparable, not by choice, of course, but inseparable nonetheless. Wherever I go, my brother follows. Whether I'm going to the park, to the bathroom, or into high school, I always know my brother isn't far behind.

My brother and I usually get along, but when we fight we *really* fight. When we were young, we would have no mercy. Karate chops to the head and punches to the gut would continue flying recklessly until someone (usually me) would take a cheap shot. In looking back, I realize that most of our fights were completely pointless, but I think they were just part of our jobs.

Today, now that my brother and I are much older and much more mature, we fight much less. He still can be one of the most annoying people on earth, but we've learned to deal with each other in a more peaceful manner. I ignore him, he ignores me, and everything is fine. Actually, the truth of the matter is, I love my brother (don't tell him that), and if he wants to follow me around forever, that's fine.

---

interested in what she had to say, and they asked her lots of questions. This led Hannah to add facts and figures and information until she had so many notes in the margins that the draft was almost impossible to read, and the focus of the paper was completely lost. She was aware of this, and was never able to solve the problem. Whenever she re-read the paper, it seemed confusing. Whenever she talked about the paper, her partners asked more questions and she added even more information.

As she stated on the cover sheet, she wasn't sure how it " . . . flowed, whether or not the additional information takes away from the basic idea." I had to respond that, while I wasn't sure that leaving the information out would have been the right choice, I did find it difficult to follow her thesis as it developed through the paper.

Hannah's final paper was not, in fact, an excellent piece (Figure 6–4); in fact, if I had not seen the trail of her thinking from rough draft through response sheet and notes to final draft, I might have questioned her effort, her commitment, her skill, my teaching ... any of a number of things. Because I had her drafts, her notes, her response sheet, and had been able to listen to some of her group's conversations, however, I could clearly see the issues, the problems, and the solutions she had worked with as she wrote the piece. Clearly, it was the due date rather than her "motivation" or "skill" that left the final draft so flawed. If she were in my class now, I would simply encourage her to continue her work and include all of her drafts in her portfolio.

When I discovered the power of highlighting and the effectiveness of helping my classes develop their own criteria and take responsibility for revising their own papers, my teaching took a quantum leap. Response groups have become one of the most fruitful and favored components of my teaching. Because my students have time to think about their papers before sharing them publicly, they seem to have plenty to say and have no problem staying on task. They seem comfortable, too: in their groups they share their papers, their thinking, and their problems. They ask for help and they offer suggestions, and, increasingly, they do so without my bidding.

There is more of a community of writers in my classroom these days. Responders find that they no longer have to deal with poor penmanship and spelling or searching for nice ways to criticize their friends' efforts. Writers seem less on guard than they used to be.

My purpose in all of this is to help my students read their writing more objectively and remain interested in revising it to make it more clear. I want my students to own their writing.

For Hannah and Sarah, the sequence worked. They both acted, first, as their own audience, and later invited the feedback of others. Both young women used their friends' comments in developing their final drafts.

The longer I tinker with this sequence, the more committed I am to helping my students learn how to take responsibility for their entire writing process. No longer am I writing their papers, suggesting improvements (unless directly asked for ideas), rewriting leads, correcting usage, or asking questions that no one cares about answering. Now I leave my students alone to look at their papers and tinker with them. This approach results occasionally in poorer papers, but more confident, competent writers, and seems to generate more learning and commitment than the old one.

At the end of this sequence, Sarah liked her piece well enough to present it as an anniversary gift for her parents. Hannah, meanwhile, continued to work on hers even after the due date in the hopes that it would be included in a local environmental newsletter.

Figure 6–4
Hannah's Final Draft

When I look back and remember how I used to be, how little respect for the environment I had, I feel sad and stupid. I don't believe it was my fault: I didn't have the awareness around me to know any better. Now, I look back to my sophmore year of high school . . . driving everywhere, parties every weekend: friends and fun were everything to me. Who cared about the environment? This wasn't the 60's; I was young; it was my time to have fun.

Towards the end of my sophmore year and beginning of my junior year, I lost touch with most of my old friends and began to hang out with a whole new crowd. Our afternoons and weekends consisted of hot and heavy environmental discussions and informational trade-offs. Although I lost a lot of the "social scene." I made closer friends than I had had before.

These people I found stimulating, and always had something new to add to the conversation. We'd discuss issues such as being or not being a vegetarian. Most everyone could add facts or opinions to this discussion, such as how much water is used to produce grain to feed the cattle, and how much is really "wasted" in this (1 pound of wheat uses 25 gallons of water: 1 pound of beef uses 2,500 gallons of water. If this water were not government subsidized, a hamburger could cost $35 . . and a pound of steak about $89.)

We all would express our opinions about this, and then someone might bring up starvation that exists because of the waste in raising livestock (including all of the water, land deforestation and its effects on the environment, but even the problems of starvation within our own country.)

One of us might make a point of how, if everyone in the U.S. were to cut their meat consumption by 10%, we could feed 60 million people with the saved grain (This is *only* the meat eaten in the U.S. — there are 243 million people in the U.S., eating ten times the amount of meat necessary to feed all of the starving people in the world)

Many other points could also be brought into this discussion, all of us realizing how little we really know, but how may different ways we know to help in a positive way.

We all respected the things each of us gave up for our beliefs. (i.e., not eating meat, boycotting animal products, less use of the car or specific product or company boycotts.) We were all open to new information and growth, and met lots of new people from one incident or project to the next.

Today, I find myself a lot more confident, or, at least not as naive. I tend to know a lot more than most people about saving the environment, but still I feel that I know very little I don't agree that this is the 60's again: history may repeat, but I don't really think we (my generation) are trying to achieve the same things as the 60's generation was. I feel that, rather than trying to convince the world, I want to share my knowledge and let everyone come to their own realization of what they themselves feel is necessary. No specific incident made the change except being open to information and awareness.

I personally feel, although no one person can do it all, every small thing I do helps. I know there are things I still do that hurt the environment, but there are also things I do that helps. The fact that public opinion can change government and company policies makes me believe more and more that by standing aside & not attempting to do anything, I am letting government and company owners know that what they are doing is alright with me. I can only encourage more people to begin to be aware and try to make that little difference.

Action will help. It is every citizen's right to speak out and to believe in what is right. If we are all open to change and to new information, our awareness may cause us to take positive action.

This is the kind of effect I want my teaching to have, and I'm convinced that the more I teach my students how to take responsibility, the more independent they will become. At the end of the semester, Hannah wrote a final entry in her writing log:

> I know that I did not do amazingly perfect work, but I did put much time and effort into [it] . . . I think I still have a huge hump to still climb over in dealing with organization, facts, statistics, etc. in long essays, [but] I feel that my greatest improvement has been in my *realization* of what I need to do. This class has given me some new techniques to use and new things to think about . . . I feel much more prepared for college. I know now what I need to do and I think I can handle whatever comes up.

What more could a teacher of writers hope for?

Works Cited

Gossard, Jenee. 1987. "Readaround." In *Practical Ideas for Teaching Writing As A Process*. California: California State Department of Education.

Cooper, Charles. 1983. "The Cooper Guides."

Ponsot, Marie, and Rosemary Deen. 1982. *Beat Not the Poor Desk*. Portsmouth, NH: Boynton/Cook Publishers.

Spear, Karen. 1988. *Sharing Writing*. Portsmouth, NH: Boynton/Cook Publishers.

7

Letting Go
Rebecca Laney

Getting Ready

I have heard it said that parenting is the process of holding on to a child with one hand while pushing away with the other. Parents guide and protect their children while allowing them to gradually move into an ever-expanding world of experience. The ultimate goal, of course, is to develop a confident, responsible adult. This model can also be applied to a teacher wishing to implement the writing/response process in her classroom. Our goal as teachers of writing is to guide students in finding their writing voices. Over the years I have sought to develop a classroom where students were given the freedom and trust to learn. It was quite a shock to me when reviewing a videotape of my own students in a response group, that even though my goal was to develop independent writers and responders, I was actually better at guiding and directing than at letting them go.

My interest and involvement with peer response began in the summer of 1986 as a participant in the Utah Writing project. This was a turning point in my career as an English teacher. One of the most profound experiences of the four-week institute was my participation in a peer response group. Prior to that time I had the notion that writing was supposed to be a solitary, tortured endeavor. When I found out that I was to share something I had written with a group of other teachers, I nearly panicked. However, what I feared would be a humiliating exercise ended up providing a forum from which to share my writing and receive ideas for improvement. This group ended up being a supportive, helpful group of *writers* committed to improving their own writing through assisting others in writing.

Another experience of the UWP summer institute that forever changed my approach to writing instruction was observing a group of upper elementary students participating in a peer response group. I was

151

amazed at the ease and sophistication with which they discussed their writing. It was evident that they took their writing and the writing of others quite seriously—that they saw themselves as writers with something worth saying. Their teacher had given them the opportunities necessary to become committed writers. I was determined to make my classroom a similiar place, one in which students receive the kind of encouragement and support necessary to find their writing voices.

So, in the fall of 1986, I entered my classroom fresh and enthusiastic about the writing process and the potential of peer response groups. I had something close to a missionary's zeal when it came to peer response. I jumped right in and established peer response groups and was more than a little disappointed when my students' performance didn't match that of the students who had visited the institute. Not defeated, I stepped back and evaluated what had happened. This process of placing students into groups and then evaluating what happened continued over the next four years. During this time, I also read, studied, observed, and thought about the nature of peer response and how students could be prepared to participate meaningfully in such groups. During that time of study, I decided to document what was happening in my classroom through the use of videotape, with the hope that some of that footage might be useful in peer response group training. I began showing the videotapes to my students so they could comment on what they saw happening. These review sessions became a powerful response group training tool. After viewing several taped segments, it became clear to me and the students that the balance between teacher control and student decision making was a delicate one which required careful attention.

False Start

In the following transcript, three boys from one of my sophomore classes were in a response group to share essays they'd written in response to their reading of *I Heard the Owl Call My Name* (Craven, 1973). These essays were the result of my "guiding" the students toward a more "academic" piece of writing. Upon reflection, it's more than a little ironic that in an attempt to implement natural response, I encouraged artificial writing. I may have been intellectually prepared to create a writing workshop in the classroom, but I was not psychologically ready to trust these students to write something real. The results are as follows:

Three boys sit in front of a video camera obviously a little nervous and embarassed. Matt begins reading tentatively from a paper he has written. As he begins to read, Steve averts his eyes from the camera and begins to doodle on his notebook. Ryan, the third member of the group, isn't on screen as Matt reads, but his presence is acknowledged by Steve's occasional sidelong glances and sly smiles.

Matt reads his paper without much enthusiasm or vocal variety, and Steve alternately taps on his microphone and his notebook with his pen. When Matt finishes reading, the response session begins.

Ryan: I liked your—your story because it had a lot of imaginative examples like the—the school children when they're at school, they come home and they're different than they used to be. And specific examples like how the owl called—calls your name—if you're gonna die and about how the potlatch—the white man took away the giving so it changed the meaning. And it [the paper] was long which is fruitful for a story like this.

[At this point Ryan signals Steve that it is his turn to respond by looking at him and nodding. Steve squirms uncomfortably in his chair and begins]

Steve: I liked what you had to say. You—uh—you said something about Mark—Mark experienced the death—deaths within the village— in the villages and that what—you know—the owl—the owl did call his name and people knew he was going to die and so there really wasn't a surprise when died. [He then begins taping his notebook again]

[Matt looks at the camera (me). I direct him to look at the chalkboard where response steps have been listed]

Matt: Uh—What—what can I do to improve?

Steve: [Exhales in frustration and whispers and shakes his head] I don't know. [Begins tapping again and shakes his head again]

[Matt reaches over and grabs some notes that Ryan had been taking]

Matt: Go, Ryan.

This response session was extremely uncomfortable, and had the feel of a staged production. Most teachers and students alike would probably not find this a useful experience. These boys were clearly not motivated to respond and were simply doing what they had been instructed to do. After such an experience teachers might be tempted to quit trying to implement response groups and students would probably prefer to have their papers responded to by the teacher rather than their peers. What could be done to make peer response more relevant to both teachers and students? How could students become more enthusiastic over writing, responding to writing, and revising pieces of writing?

Those critical questions are not easily answered, and they keep popping up year after year. I have not yet answered them completely or to my own satisfaction. In the meantime, I have found one variable that seems to make a difference in student commitment to writing—choice. Whenever possible in the writing process choice must be built in. Students are usually compliant with teacher mandates, but compliance does not equate with involvement and commitment. If we expect students to be engaged with their writing and that of their peers, we must involve them in decisions concerning what they write, what their audience and purpose for the piece is, and with whom they will share that piece of writing. Furthermore, they should set the ground rules for the response group's procedures. This does not mean that the teacher will abdicate all responsibility for the writing and response process. It means that the teacher will become a facilitator rather than a director. Accountability can be built in without usurping student ownership of the process.

Matt, Steve, and Ryan had few choices in the writing process documented earlier. The writing assignment was teacher mandated. As they read *I Heard the Owl Call My Name*, they wrote three in-class essays on topics outlined by their teacher (me), then they got to choose one to take to their response group.

As Matt read his paper, it became clear that this piece of writing was really not very important to him. He had completed the writing assignment meeting the basic requirements of the prompt. But there was no emotion or feeling or voice; in short there was nothing of Matt in the writing. He had done what all good students do: he had completed the assignment. It's not hard to guess what Matt did with this piece of writing once he got his grade. In effect, this paper was not his; it was his teacher's.

The teacher's control is evident in the group itself. While students got to choose their own groups, the procedures for response were dictated by a list of steps written on the chalkboard. The woodenness of Steve and Ryan's responses is really not surprising. While there was no written script for the boys to read, the unwritten script outlined by the teacher was clear. Note in Ryan's response the use of teacher language: "I liked your story because it had a lot of good, imaginative examples." On the face of it, this might sound like a pertinent response, but what did Ryan mean? We're not sure because Matt either didn't feel free to ask or it didn't occur to him to ask because the directions on the board didn't include asking follow-up questions. The "script" was followed carefully by the boys but there was little, if any, honest response in this session.

At one moment though, there was an honest exchange. Steve, the most visibly uncomfortable of the group was nervously tapping something through most of the session. His faltering speech pattern might indicate that he was grasping at something to say. He didn't feel free to respond honestly except at the end of the session when in great frustration he exhaled, shook his head and admitted he didn't know what to suggest to

Matt. In a way it was refreshing to hear him express his genuine frustration after suffering through the five-minute session with these boys.

Tune-Up/Alignment

This transcription supports what much of the literature has to say about the effects of teacher control and control structures on peer response. In a traditional classroom the teacher makes most of the educational decisions and therefore holds the power. When peer response groups are implemented, teachers must be prepared for a change in roles. Indeed, they may need to assess their attitudes about power sharing or abdicating power altogether. This is not just an intellectual exercise, as my experience shows; it is necessary to be ready psychologically and emotionally to share power and trust students.

DiPardo and Freedman (1988) discuss the strength of peer influence on learning and cite a number of studies. They conclude that peer interaction can support or complement instructional goals of a school. However, because of powerful peer influence, teachers can feel threatened by the potentially undermining effects such influence may have on organizational norms. Many teachers may question whether student-centered learning groups will enable them to maintain classroom management and discipline. Additionally, once the power is shared as in peer response groups, it may be difficult to switch back to a teacher-centered classroom. Even though teachers may be willing to share power, they cannot share the ultimate responsibility for what goes on in the classroom.

As a result, some teachers search for a middle ground. They seek to establish peer response groups while retaining control over the groups. For example, Lamberg (1980) attempted to channel response through the use of editing sheets. Similarly, Lynch (1982) used a number of methods that allowed her to monitor student writing throughout the entire process. She developed a number of analytic and self-evaluation scales for students to use in responding to their own and others' writing. Matt, Steve and Ryan's group illustrated my attempt to find a middle ground. Out of insecurity over what I saw as "off-task" behavior, I sought to make sure students were responding, not socializing, by establishing a series of steps they were to take in the response process. I established what I felt were logical steps in response and wrote them on the board.

Freedman (1987), in her study of groups in two ninth-grade classrooms, found that interaction between students depended upon the task they had been assigned. If a written evaluation sheet was given to the students to complete, student response to writing was minimal, and they would avoid evaluation. Rather, students would work collaboratively to complete the sheet in a way that would preserve their relationships with peers and at the same time satisfy the teacher. The patterns of feedback and response to feedback were determined largely by the design of the sheets. The students did appear to remain on task when the task was filling out a sheet; however, they avoided evaluation of one another, and any talk about writing was usually initiated by the writer, not the peer listeners. While I did not give Matt's group a sheet, the steps on the chalkboard had the same effect. The boys did exactly as I had instructed—no more, no less. Their primary goal was to satisfy the stated teacher requirements, not to respond honestly to writing.

The guidelines I had written on the board communicated that the highest priority was to meet the teacher's expectations. DiPardo and Freedman (1988) believe that when peer groups are denied the opportunity to interact as peers, constrained in their feedback by the guidelines of a teacher, the teacher may retain power, but deny divergent feedback. Further, Freedman (1987) found that use of such lists resulted in reduced student-to-student talk. When this happens, the groups tend to assign tasks traditionally completed by an instructor. Consequently, the students are more concerned with addressing teacher-mandated concerns than providing a thoughtful, personal response to a peer's writing. This was certainly the case in Matt's group. The artificiality found in the transcript stems from a failure on my part to recognize the importance of letting students struggle toward honest peer response. By keeping students rigidly on task, I had taken the "peer" out of peer response and created teacher-mandated response.

Brannon and Knoblauch (1984) indicate that this form of teacher control "appropriates the writers' texts." They assert that when teachers determine the subject of the writing, the form it will take, and the criteria that will determine its success, students have to try to accommodate both their own personal intentions and the teacher-reader's expectations (p. 158). They also believe that once students perceive the teacher's agenda, their motives for writing change. Students no longer write for their own purposes; rather, their task is to match their writing to the expectations of the teacher-reader. Often the consequence is that students lose commitment to communicate ideas they value; eventually they may even lose incentive to write.

In attempting to pick and choose from the writing/response process to accommodate my comfort level, I had unintentionally subverted the entire process. Honest peer response to genuine student writing requires careful, intentional planning by the instructor. The teacher contemplating implementing the writing/response process must first establish a clear, defensible concept of the value of student centered-writing and response. In doing so, he or she will need to assess personal feelings about sharing power and delegating responsibility. The transcript of Matt's group illustrates what happens when a teacher isn't prepared to share power. It is critical to remember as well that students need to be moved gradually from teacher-centered activities to student-centered groups. I am not suggesting that putting students in groups and walking away will produce the desired effect either. The teacher's influence is still important, but he or she will want to become a more subtle presence, doing less controlling and more facilitating. Ideally the teacher becomes a knowledgeable coach who presents options instead of prescribing solutions and who, through listening and asking questions, guides students to workable solutions. This is exceedingly difficult for most teachers. For one thing other teachers and administrators may not be supportive of student-centered classrooms. Often these classroom don't look "academic" enough because the teacher isn't standing in front directing. In addition, many students resist the notion that they can and should be responsible for their own learning.

Redirecting Response

On the same tape there is another response session that contrasts with Matt's session rather significantly and demonstrates what an exciting place the student-centered classroom is. The following transcription will show some startling differences in interest and commitment to response and writing. These students were from an honors sophomore class and were initially more fluent writers. The students had written several short memory pieces taken from "Road of Life," an exercise found in Kirby and Liner's book *Inside Out* (1981). The students drew maps of their lives from birth to the present with all the hills and valleys. Then the only instruction I gave them was to choose an experience from their "Road of Life" map to write about. This piece of writing was closer to their own experiences and they were allowed to write about something they chose. Adam is reading a piece that previously had been responded to by the members of his group, Melissa and Taralee.

Adam: I liked our last group better without any rules.

Taralee: Okay.

Melissa: Yeah.

This exchange refers to the last response session where, after a class discussion, it was decided that the groups could determine what procedures would be used in the response session. Adam then begins reading his paper. It was apparently decided off camera who would begin. As Adam is reading aloud, Melissa and Taralee are reading silently. At one point Melissa turns the paper as if reading a margin note:

Melissa: Did you forget that part? [Points to a note in the margin]

Adam: I didn't want that, it was part of my revision.

After reading his narrative, Adam begins the discussion by revealing what he plans to do with his paper.

Adam: I think I'm gonna go back and put in more about the checks— ya know—ah—as they built up and what I did to get them and stuff like that.

His commitment to his writing is evident in this comment. It's obvious that he wants to work further with this piece and has given thought to what he wants to do.

Taralee: Yeah.

Melissa: It sounds good to me.

Adam: [Sounding just a bit ironic] What feelings impressed you about this paper?

Taralee: It's just funny. It's—it's—it's you. No, I see you doing that— 'cause of your personality.

Melissa: It's like you're speaking it. [Recognition of writer's voice]

Adam: What—what do you think I should change or do different or how can I make my paper better?

Melissa: Just—ah—just talk more about the checks and uh—

Taralee: Maybe mention like if there was anybody else being disruptive— uh - when they changed to assertive discipline or if it worked—if everyone else knew what was going on.

Adam: Everybody else knew what was going on so they quit—I remember Blair and I used to—uh—be covered with lipstick by the end of the day but—

The writer here is now engaged in the memory and thinking more deeply about its relation with his writing.

Melissa: So put that in there like. . . .

Adam: I don't know—maybe she just liked me. [The group laughs at this]

There are a few moments of silence at this point as the three seem to be thinking what else could be done. Melissa then attempts to make a suggestion.

Melissa: You could say how everyone else in the class—that they were like really good—uh—'cause the discipline changed and how you were the only one and—that's how and like that's how you could tell—you'd—uh—I don't know—[She looks at Taralee uncertainly]

Adam: Is that kind of clear anyway or—but is it not clear?

Taralee: But maybe just explain that—ya know—that the—ya know—that the lipstick didn't work so they switched to assertive discipline—

Melissa: I pictured you were the only one—

Adam: Yeah, that's what I have, "After a while I got so used to the lipstick that it ceased to bother me."

Taralee: Yeah—but see everyone else followed the assertive discipline.

At this point they digress a bit when Taralee asks if the teacher kissed even the girls. Still not ready to close off discussion Melissa suggests they read the paper again. As they are reading silently Adam points to an area he has a question about.

Adam: I have a question you guys might help me with. Okay the second page, paragraph—uh—oh I guess it's not written in paragraphs [He and Melissa chuckle] uh—okay down by where all the scribble—see where—

Melissa: Yeah.

Adam: Okay—"I came to school the next day being my usual disruptive self." What's a better way I can say that?

Taralee: I like it that way.

Adam: It just sounds kind of—unprofessional to me or something—ya know—cause I did have my "usually disruptive self" but I don't know if it's usual or usually or—

Melissa: Usual sounds better than usually or—

Adam: That sounds all right?

Melissa: Uh—huh—yeah, I think it sounds right.

Adam: Okay.

This discussion lasted approximately fifteen minutes—three times as long as the previous group. There were no signs of boredom or nervousness. In fact, the members were engaged and interested in the piece of writing being discussed. While the students seemed aware of the camera initially, as they became involved with the response session, they seemed to forget it was on. They worked without the presence of written procedures or a teacher.

What would account for the different results in these two groups? There were three critical differences in my approach with the second group: expectation of success, solicitation of students' involvement, and trust in student decision-making abilities. While ability levels did differ between the two groups, I don't believe that variable was nearly as critical as the way I approached the two groups.

Letting Go

After carefully analyzing the experiences of the two groups, it became painfully clear that I expected the students in Matt's class not to be very skilled in writing. So, I made all the decisions—what they would read, what form their written response would take, who their audience would be, and what steps they would take to respond to the writing. On the other hand, from the first day I met the students in the second class, I expected them to be able to draw from personal experience and create interesting pieces of writing. Both groups fulfilled my expectations. Adam's interest and commitment to his writing showed when he planned changes, asked questions and received feedback. Melissa and Taralee were obviously interested in Adam's story. As Taralee said earlier, the paper was Adam—it was a true picture of his personality. The girls enjoyed the narrative and had a stake in helping Adam revise. Matt's group didn't display as much skill as Adam's group displayed. Of course, had Matt's group been given the same opportunity to write within their own experience, they too may have created more interesting, lively pieces.

Because I saw early and immediate enthusiasm in the second group of students, I found it easier and more fun to solicit their ideas. I spent much more time sharing student models of writing and listening to them talk about that writing. They were especially interested in viewing the tapes of other response groups and then discussing what they saw happening within those groups. These discussions were lively and student-directed. They usually began by a simple set of observations, then the group would begin to speculate about the reasons for different group behaviors. A great deal of divergent thinking took place in these sessions. The students would piggy-back on one another's ideas and often end up with very insightful conclusions. Also, after each of their own response sessions, we would have a debriefing session where students would talk about their own experiences in response groups.

These discussions led to the final and I think most critical factor in this group's success—I trusted them to make good decisions about the writing process. Often a suggestion concerning a writing prompt or a change in group procedure would come from a debriefing session. Because I found their discussions so intelligent, I often implemented their suggestions. My trust in them encouraged them to trust one another and a genuine feeling of respect and friendship began to emerge. The chance to make decisions together with minimal teacher interference had made this group a cohesive unit. When viewing the tape of Adam's group, it was clear these kids liked each other, they could move from serious response to lighthearted joking. This happened, in part, because they had more freedom to function.

Implementing peer response in my classroom has been at times difficult and frustrating, but at the end of five years of using the groups, I'm still enthusiastic about the results. A process-oriented classroom has an organic feel to it—it's alive and developing. I contrast this with my classroom prior to 1986—it was an orderly, task-oriented place and deadly boring to both the students and me. More importantly, students were totally dependent upon me to guide them in their learning. Now students struggle to find meaning and gradually develop confidence in their abilities. I have to add too, that I continue to struggle along with my students. I struggle to maintain that organic atmosphere when I am tempted to retreat back to the teacher-directed classroom. I struggle to keep my goals focused on student-centered writing and response. I struggle to remain patient when the process bogs us down and I feel pressure to "mother hen" my students—and, in the process, seize ownership of writing and response. After five years I can say the struggle is worth it.

Works Cited

Brannon, L. & C. H. Knoblauch. (1984). *Rhetorical Traditions and the Teaching of Writing*. Portsmouth, NH: Boynton/Cook Publishers.

Craven, Margaret. (1973). *I Heard The Owl Call My Name*. New York. New York: Dell Publishing.

DiPardo, A. & S. W. Freedman. (1988). Peer Response Groups in the Writing Classroom: Theoretical Foundations and New Directions. *Review of Educational Research*, 58 (2): 119–149.

Freedman, S.W. (1987). Peer Response Groups in Two Ninth-Grade Classrooms. (Oeri/Ed Technical Report No. 12).

Kirby, D. & T. Liner. (1981). *Inside Out*. Portsmouth, NH: Boynton/Cook Publishers.

Lynch, D. (1982). Easing the Process: A Strategy for Evaluating Compositions. *College Composition*. 33 (3): 310–314.

8

The Writing Workshop
Student Writers in the Classroom

Cheryl Ause

"I have always been on my own when I had to write a paper."
Heather C.

Our experience as students and training as teachers often teach us two things about student writing: students write it and teachers read it—both, usually, in isolation. Writing seems to be full of silent suffering on everybody's part: for the student who sweats it out and for the teacher who disappears behind a never diminishing stack of papers. Furthermore, in the end, writing almost always leads to that shared angst, the inevitable "letter grade," the final blow given and received in silence. Occasionally teachers read papers out loud to the class. (Usually only the "best," but also, on occasion, the "worst." What some students wouldn't have given for an invisible shield—or ray—on those Monday mornings!)

I say "student" and "teacher," but I include myself in both categories. Who better knows the anxieties, fears, and, yes, even successes silently suffered by student writers than the teacher who writes. In an attempt to break the silence and end the isolation, each year I turn my classroom into a writers' workshop, if only for a short time. Every new year brings some change or other to my approach, but the basic structure remains the same. In terms of content, focus, and pace, the writing workshop offers an endless variety of possibilities. When applied to a discipline that has the tendency to fragment language arts skills into separate "units" or content areas, the student writing workshop format is unique in that it smoothly integrates four critical communication skills: reading, writing, thinking, and discussion.

Flexibility is perhaps the workshop's greatest advantage. Over the years, I have adapted it to accommodate every genre, including poetry, fiction, playwriting, creative nonfiction narratives, and even the more conventional forms of expository and persuasive essays. In conjunction with the writing, I have used a wide range of readings to introduce and explore every genre with my students. In addition, the workshop approach provides a framework into which all steps of the writing process fall naturally. Writing review sessions may be scheduled daily, weekly, or as needed. Pre-writing and editing work may be included as appropriate.

The writing workshop, along with its associated reading strand, may vary in length from a few weeks to a full term or longer. All phases involve some form of peer review. It is also important to note that the writing workshop is not an activity that should be reserved for honors or gifted students. I have conducted workshops with students of all ability levels, and I encourage other teachers to do the same. While unit objectives require that students participate to the best of their abilities in each of the curriculum areas, no minimum achievement ability level exists. The workshop process breaks down into three main segments, each applying writing and peer review in different ways.

Phase One—Pre-Writing: Reading, Journal Writing, and Discussion

Students read a variety of selections within a particular genre and keep reading journals, focusing on the content and style of each. Graded discussions about the readings replace traditional quizzes, although on occasion I have been known to give a pop reading quiz just to keep my students "honest." Taking my cue from the elements the students find most interesting about the readings, I guide them through a discussion about the ideas the writer conveys and the style he or she uses to convey them. Students also produce in-class "freewrites" on topics related to their readings. Part of each class period is set aside for students to share these very informal writings with each other in a casual, nonjudgmental manner. Both the reader's journals and the freewrites later become a resource pool for each student's writing projects.

Phase Two: The Writing Process

After completing the literary study, which may vary in length from one day to a couple of weeks, students refer to their journals to find "kernel" ideas they can develop into longer writing projects. Peer review, in a variety of forms, plays a major role in the development of each student's work. Some class days are devoted to read-around groups which help the writers clarify the main ideas of their work and focus on what works best in the writing. On other days students prepare written evaluations ("round-robin reviews") of each other's work, reading closely for technical aspects such as organization, style, and language.

Throughout the various phases of writing, students assist each other in focusing their ideas and refining the final product. They learn to trust each other and to see themselves as active participants—even as experts—rather than simply as passive learners. By the end of the second phase, each student will have created a "workshop draft." Students submit this piece of writing, which is as close to a final draft as possible, to a workshop group for in-depth review.

Phase Three: The Workshop Evaluation

This final stage of the workshop also uses peer response, but differs significantly from earlier situations. Prior to this time, I have remained more or less in the background, supervising writing and peer response activities from afar, but making a point never to read or comment on any of the students' early drafts. I never read any draft earlier than the workshop draft. This frustrates those students who want to know if they have done it "right" or those who are reluctant to trust peer reviewers.

The reason I do not read their early attempts is because I hope students will discover two things. First, they need to trust in their own sense of what works. Students must learn to recognize the sound of their own voices in writing, rather than relying on what I tell them they should sound like. Second, they must learn to trust one another as valid respondants. The authority of the peer reviewer, while providing positive benefits in terms of feedback, is far less imposing than that of the teacher and allows the writer more room to make his or her own choices when revising. The longer I forestall my involvement, the more committed my students are to their own voices and to the power they have over their writing.

Another difference between this phase and that which preceded it is that each member of the workshop group, including me, has copies of manuscripts for each writer in the group. Homework consists of reading each work closely and then writing a thorough critique of it. I meet with each of these small groups, in the same room but separate from the rest of the class, and we discuss each writer's work in detail.

Peer Review as an Essential Element

Although process writing does not always require peer review, it is a crucial element within the workshop format. Student writers experience numerous benefits by interacting with other writers. Besides the act of writing itself, peer review is the most important element of the workshop experience. It provides students with feedback throughout all steps of the writing process; at the same time, it frees me from having to respond to multiple drafts of dozens, if not hundreds of students. Students welcome peer review in all its forms. One student, Elaine, commented on the various steps of the peer review process this way:

> In the read-around groups, I liked listening to other people's stories. Some of their comments I stuck into my story when I rewrote it. The round-robin evaluations gave me a better idea about spelling, ideas, etc. that I didn't think of. The workshop evaluations were the best, I thought. I found a lot of super ideas that I had never thought of.

Elaine is not alone when she says the last phase, the workshop groups, was the "best." Students rate it by far the most popular of all the peer response formats. Many simply enjoy the verbal, face-to-face aspect of this part of the process; others like it because the teacher takes an active part. Students need to connect with the teacher at some point in the process in order to give it validity, if only in their minds; however, it is essential that students also stand on their own so they can discover their own strengths if they ever are to become independent learners. If students are reluctant to trust each other's opinions in the different phases of the writing process, it may be because they have become too dependent on teachers within the "traditional" classroom setting. Unfortunately, students too often learn implicitly if not explicitly that when the teacher is not in charge, the activity is meaningless.

The workshop format, by emphasizing peer interaction, thrusts students into positions of responsibility to themselves and others. It frees students to take charge of their learning, reluctant as some may be about the experience. Giving students control over their own learning can be a threatening experience for many of them—and for many teachers as well. However, any teacher who hopes to prepare students for a future in which problem-solving and cooperation will play key roles must in some way transfer the responsibility for learning how to learn to students. The writing workshop does just that.

A Look at a Workshop in Action

To clarify what happens in a writing workshop, I want to show a class in action. In deciding which class to use as the basis for a case study, I selected an average English writing class to show that even "regular" students are capable of the complex activities associated with the workshop format. Effective Writing is a semester-long writing class, mainly comprised of juniors. These students generally fill the other semester of their junior English requirement with an American literature or novels class. As seniors, most will enroll in a college preparatory class which focuses on advanced grammar and composition. Students in Effective Writing classes, in addition to continuing their review of grammar and usage fundamentals and expanding their vocabulary, learn to write more effective sentences, paragraphs, and essays.

I begin with a brief grammar and usage review during the early weeks of the first term, and then shift the focus to paragraph development for the remaining weeks. By the time second term is under way, students are ready to tackle longer writing projects. The students also participate in a number of group process and peer response activities throughout the first term to prepare them for working together in a workshop format.

The students spotlighted here were in my class from September, 1990, through January, 1991. Prior to teaching them, I had taught only one other effective writing class, in the spring of 1990. Although I was still developing my curriculum for the course, I was well on my way to the class as I described it above. These students wrote a number of short compositions: reviews, resumes, business letters, and two brief, rather loosely-structured expository essays.

I had set aside six weeks starting at the beginning of second term for the workshop so that we could finish before we dismissed for the holidays in late December. Six weeks may seem like a long time, but not when it is spread out over the "block," the class scheduling system used at the high school level in our district. On the block system, instead of meeting with our students each day for forty- or forty-five-minute class periods, we meet every other day for roughly eighty-five minutes per block. Taking the Thanksgiving break into consideration, I knew we would have only about a dozen class sessions in which the class of thirty-two students would have to discuss readings, do in-class writings and peer reviews, spend at least part of a day reviewing an essay I had written, and meet with the workshop groups. Group meetings alone would take five days. I also wanted to reserve the last day of class in December for a debriefing meeting about the workshop process itself. It was definitely time to get things moving.

Phase One: Pre-Writing Reading, Journal Writing, and Discussion

Activities during the pre-writing phase of the workshop prepare students to write their own pieces within a specific genre. Students read an average of three to five selections, sometimes as homework at the rate of one or two a night and sometimes singly in class. From time to time, I bring in readings which are more current, but mostly I try to use texts that are readily available at school. When choosing narrative essays, I include material that reflects a variety of topics and approaches to writing. I also look for things that mesh with students' lives, if only in a small way. I hope the readings show students how writers make the ordinary aspects of life unique.

In the interest of time, I assigned this Effective Writing class only three readings: E. B. White's "Once More to the Lake" (1982), Langston Hughes's "Salvation" (1979), and a passage from Jean Paul Sartre's autobiography, *The Words* (1964). All are memory pieces recalling some defining moment or experience in the life of each writer. The serious tone in each essay apparently influenced the students, for their essays touched on moments of their own lives with greater seriousness than they might otherwise have done.

So I could guarantee full participation in our discussion of the pieces, students read all three narratives in class on three different days. Following each reading, they wrote short journal entries, focusing on the issues and ideas they found most interesting. A brief, graded discussion followed the reading and journal writing. As a class we talked about each of the elements that made each story work for the students. The readings and discussions led students to review the events of their own lives as sources for writing ideas.

This is not to say students agreed on the question of how useful these readings were as writing models, but overall most students responded favorably to them. Those who objected said the material did not reflect their own way of writing; others complained that some selections were too challenging. Most of the negative views came from weaker readers, while their more reading-adept classmates tended to express more positive views about the models.

Through the reading, I hoped students would acquire a broader view of the narrative essay, and find at their disposal some clear structures they could use in developing their own essays. Students like Amy liked having the readings available:

> It was helpful to read the essays in order to get an idea of how a personal essay could be written. They were related to what we were working on. Besides, they were interesting to read. I did not write like them; however, when I wasn't sure of where my paper was headed, I referred back to them.

After we discussed each selection, the students freewrote on topics related to the readings. For example, after reading the Sartre passage, one in which he recalls the Paris apartment where he lived as a child, my students wrote about a place from their childhood which was significant to them in some way. Students need and appreciate this kind of writing direction. In an effort to get students to care about their subjects, teachers often tell them to write about whatever they feel like. This type of unstructured writing assignment sounds like a good idea, but it is usually far too open-ended for the developing writer. It is not that we should choose topics for our students; rather, we need to teach them how to gain access to topics derived from their own experience.

At our debriefing session at the end of the workshop unit, Krista wrote: "I thought out of all the things we did to prepare for writing, the free-writing activities helped the most by helping to learn how to get ideas to flow, give ideas for other papers, or give an idea that would start another idea." Joel recognized that the final pieces of writing the students did had their roots in these earlier forms: "Free-writing helped me a lot with my paper. The topic I wrote on was one I had done in a free write." This was the case for a number of students. Janna said she found freewriting enabled her to spend less time "figuring out what subject to write about. I had really good ideas on what subject there was a lot to write on and which subjects had limited information."

As mentioned earlier, I reserve some time in each class period for students to share these informal writings with each other, usually immediately after they have written them. Because no one expects anybody's writing to be "good" at this point, students feel free to exchange their ideas. This is an important first step in bringing their ideas into the open. Making students accountable for their writing beginning with the first step of the process makes it easier for them to accept responsibility for later, more complex compositions. I find that anonymity in the writing classroom is counterproductive because more often than not it separates writers from their writing and from one another. Although private writing has its place in our lives, the writing class is probably not an appropriate forum for it.

As my Effective Writing students began the first phase of the workshop, I hoped that over the course of the weeks to come I would find at least one student who would choose to sustain the same piece throughout the entire sequence of writing activities. Aron turned out to be that student. Aron, a junior, was college-bound and highly motivated to do well in school. He was and is the kind of student most teachers love to have in their classes. Although Aron did well in all of his classes, his true talents and interests lay in art. In fact, I thought of Aron as an artist first rather than a writer, which is one of the reasons that his writing file was of such interest to me. A number of students produced final manuscripts which had evolved through two or three different phases, but Aron's file was the only one in which I could trace the evolution of his final essay from a brief freewrite he had done almost a month earlier (Figure 8–1) in conjunction with our reading of E. B. White.

Phase Two: The Writing Process— Drafting, Sharing, and Revising

The second phase of the workshop process, including drafting, revising, and editing—more or less getting something substantial down on paper—

Figure 8–1
Aron's Freewrite

The Train Inceoent:

late one night

We were driving around when we suddenely saw lighted up, one of the mines on the west mountains. Phsycically together we had a great idea to drive down and see how close we could get. There were private roads, which were rated, but no pobulc roads leading to the mine. Laying east of the mine was a long field about two miles. We parked the car and started walking through the field towards the mine.

(Not Finished)

---

is usually the toughest for student writers. By the end of this stage, the students must produce a "workshop draft" which they then submit to their workshop group for detailed review. Students must write at least three separate drafts prior to the workshop draft: the rough, the first, and the second drafts. I build into the second phase as many days of in-class writing activities as students need, usually about three. Each day's schedule includes both writing and reviewing time.

Sharing Rough Drafts

Allowing students to write rough drafts in class often works better than assigning it for homework. They respond well to the extra support inherent in the structure of the classroom atmosphere, the result being a high level of participation at this important formative stage. My students had already done a number of freewrites in connection with their readings, so they needed only to select one to develop as a rough draft during class.

The rules for rough drafting are simple. Students read the freewrite they have selected for revision. Then they close their eyes and focus their memories on the original experience or place. After getting the picture clearly in view, they rewrite the experience as if it were happening to them right at that moment, trying to capture as much immediate concrete detail as they could summon. Reading the freewrite first acts as a catalyst for memory. It provides the basic structure which students embellish in the rough draft.

After the timed writing period—about fifteen minutes—students read their writing aloud to one or two others sitting nearby. The procedure is familiar because it is similar to the freewrite sharing they had done on previous days. The simple act of reading aloud helps writers hear problems, including the basic fact of whether one word fits after another. Because the listeners are not bound to comment in any particular way on the readings, they are in the most rudimentary sense sounding boards for each other.

More often then not, however, these sharing sessions initiate some very lively discussions about story events and meanings. When students comment to one another, they respond positively to the parts that interest them and offer helpful tips on problems. I encourage writers to talk about the things they feel aren't working, too, and to ask for suggestions. In this way the fragile beginnings of writing are brought out into the open in a constructive and positive way. Hearing another student's writing also has an impact on the listener. While listening to others, students get new and better ideas about how to approach their own topics.

During one class session, Aron and his classmates repeated this process three times with three different freewrites. By the end of class the students had three good rough drafts from which they could choose to write the next draft, called the "first" because it is the first formal attempt to give the writing a definite shape. During the last fifteen or twenty minutes of class, I reviewed the basic elements of the narrative essay, directing the students to keep those concepts in mind as they constructed their first drafts at home.

Aron's rough draft (Figure 8–2) was a continuation of an incident he had first written about almost three weeks earlier. Obviously, he had a story inside that needed to be told. Through the freewrite/rewrite process, Aron was learning to uncover the key stories of his life.

Read-Around Groups (RAGs)

In addition to having a more well-defined structure, the revised first draft should be roughly four to six hundred words in length, neatly written in ink or typed, and double-spaced. On the day the first draft was due, the class followed a more structured evaluation procedure within an assigned read-around group. The students would continue to work with these assigned groups for the remainder of the workshop, so I wanted them to get used to working with each other early in the process. Students were supposed to bring their completed drafts to class with them; of course, not all students came prepared. Nevertheless, I like to emphasize the

Figure 8-2
Continuation (three weeks later) of Aron's Freewrite, Figure 8-1

-THE RISK-

My FRIEND AND I WERE ON THE EDGE OF A TEN FT. DROP-OFF WHICH WAS LIKE A PIT WITH TRAIN TRACKS LEADING DOWN IT. WE WERE SPYING ON ONE OF THE MINES DOWN AT KENICOT, WHICH WAS BEYOND THE TRACKS. IT WAS 11:00 PM AND WE FIGURED THERE WOULD BE NO TRAINS, SO I DECIDED TO CLIMB DOWN FIRST. WHEN I REACHED THE BOTTOM I WENT OVER TO THE TRACKS AND THEN MOTIONED MY FRIEND TO CLIMB ON IN. AT THAT MOMENT I HEARD A FAINT NOISE, LIKE A HORN. SUDDENELY, A PIERCING BRIGHT LIGHT CAME CHARGING AROUND THE CORNER, IT WAS A TRAIN! I LOOKED AT MY FRIEND AND SAW THAT HE HAD RETREATED BACK. I THEN RAN TO THE OTHER SIDE AND CLIMBED FRANTICALLY IN THE LOOSE DIRT OF THE HILLSIDE

importance of group commitment, so I required even those who were unprepared to participate in the groups, even if only on the most minimal level. Students soon discover it is more difficult to hide among four or five people than it is to disappear into a class of thirty-five.

I always decide ahead of time which students will be in each group of six. I try to create an interesting mixture of ability levels and personality types. Often students say they want to do their own grouping. They say they work best with friends, but I disagree. Friends have a difficult time sorting out the writer from the writing. Friends working with friends creates a situation which often results in vacuous commentary and weak writing development. My choosing the groups also eliminates the painful problem of "leftovers," the students nobody wants in their group.

The first read-around sessions always have an air of tension, so I try to keep things as low key as possible. In spite of the fact that I have imposed the groups on them, students still need to feel comfortable within them. I constantly remind the class that our purpose is to evaluate the writing, not the writer. With the great proliferation of sharing that goes on in this atmosphere, most students soon learn to see their writing as product, separate and apart from them as people. They learn that criticism of the writing is something very different from criticism of them as people.

In Aron's class, it was the first time the groups had worked together, so the instructions were simple. Students had to take turns reading their work aloud to their group (see Figure 8–3 for Aron's first draft). After listening carefully to each piece, the other writers in the group would comment briefly on its strengths and weaknesses while the author took notes on their comments. Listeners easily recalled vivid details and specific examples while trying to pinpoint unclear or undeveloped ideas. During the activity, I moved throughout the room, listening in on student discussions and encouraging any groups that needed assistance.

At this point students discovered a number of critical problems: lack of preparation on the part of some group members, disinterest in the other members' writing, the failure of some students to work with the other members of the group or in group settings at all, and unwillingness to share writing with other group members. In isolated writing situations, one student's lack of preparation or involvement affects no one else. In a workshop format, that changes. Students did not tolerate indolence from anyone in their groups. They made those who were not prepared talk about what they intended to do for the next time, subtly pressuring them to get in step. As a result, the number of prepared students increased with each round of revisions.

Group dynamics is the key to success, the variable in the equation which is often outside my control. Contrary to my own belief, the groups who saw themselves as most successful were those in which a feeling of friendliness prevailed. On the other hand, the groups which I felt were the most successful in terms of finished writing product did not have an especially strong sense of camaraderie. What they did show was a willingness to maintain writing as the central focus of their discussions. For them the issue was never personality; it was the writing. Aron's group, although cordial to each other, kept the idea of writing and the experiences that inform it, at its core.

Following the thirty-minute read-around sessions, we discussed what they had accomplished in their groups and any problems they encountered. They then spent the remaining time either working on revisions for their next draft or making more detailed notes on the group discussions.

Round-Robins

As homework, students had to write a second draft, focusing on changes in content and organization. The second draft would be evaluated at the next class session in a round-robin peer review. In this activity, students

sit in a formal class seating arrangement and systematically pass manuscripts around the room. Since students are not in their assigned groups,
this review admits "outside" views on the students' writing and offers an
interesting contrast to the insular opinions which begin developing
almost immediately in the RAGs.

Any evaluation rubric that suits the needs of the assignment may be
used. After reading a second draft, preferably twice, the peer reviewer
writes a detailed evaluation based on the rubric. For each category, the
critic assigns a numerical score followed by an explanatory comment. On
the draft itself, the evaluator underlines particularly effective words,
phrases, or sentences; brackets problematic items; and marks or corrects
as many mechanical errors as possible. Each evaluation round is supposed to last approximately ten minutes, at which time students pass the
manuscripts and reviews to the next evaluator.

After the first round, Aron's class asked for more time. I extended
the review periods to fifteen minutes, but no doubt could have easily
given them twenty. I wanted to balance the time needed by those students
who were capable of writing more complete reviews with that needed by
those who could not or would not write more complex responses. During
class, each student evaluator completed three reviews. A fourth reviewer
only had time to write a general response. Near the end of the class
period, the final peer reviewers returned the drafts and comments to the
authors. Students spent the last few minutes of class reviewing the written
comments and consulting with peer critics when necessary.

Many students liked the element of privacy inherent in this activity.
Debby wrote: "I liked these a lot because you could tell your honest feelings. If there is something that needs improvement, you can be honest
because you don't have to say it to someone's face." The most frequent
complaint cited was insufficient time. Students felt that fifteen minutes
was not long enough to address all the areas of the evaluation form thoroughly. Actually, I received this complaint happily because I knew then
that the writing process had begun to engage their attention.

They had another complaint as well. They understood that not all
evaluators approached the writing with the same skills or equal interest in
the topic. What upset them were those critics who either through lack of
self-assurance or just plain laziness read the comments of a previous
reviewer and then copied the same comments into their review. It was a
valid complaint. In response to it, I have since altered my procedure. I
now have the reviewers paperclip completed reviews to the back of the
manuscript, out of sight from the next critic. Most, if not all students,
welcome this "no-peek" approach. It has, in fact, led to a greater diversity of opinion (see Figure 8–4 for Aron's second draft).

Following the round-robin reviews, I passed out copies of my "Basic
Rules and Guidelines" (see Appendix 8A) for phase three, the workshop
groups, along with a schedule of their group meetings (see Appendix 8B).

Figure 8-3
Aron's First Draft

ARON
PERIOD 6

500-1000
WORDS

DRIVING WITHOUT
A PURPOSE

- FIRST DRAFT -

It was late Friday night, around 11:00 PM. My friend Matt and I were spying on one of the mines down near Kennecott. The only way to get close to the mine was through a long field east of the mine. While walking through the field, Matt and I came upon train tracks that were dug into the field, like a gulley, ten feet deep. After surveying the area, I decided to climb down first. It was very steep, but I managed to jump down safely. I went over to the tracks and then motioned Matt to climb down. At that moment I heard a faint noise, like a horn, and it was getting louder. When I looked at Matt he was still on the top of the hillside and starring off in the distance where the noise came from. Suddenely, a piercing bright light came charging around the corner, rattleing the tracks and roaring with noise; it was a train! When I looked back at Matt I saw that he had retreted into the field. Quickly, I ran to the other side and began to climb the steep hillside as fast as I could, but it was no use. As I clawed vigorously, the loose dirt of the cliff would collapse out from under me. I wasent going anywhere! Realizing that it was no use, I suddenely had a thought. What if

continued

Figure 8-3
continued

THE DRIVER OF THE TRAIN CAN SEE ME? AT THAT MOMENT I PRESSED MY BODY FLAT AGAINST THE HILL, HOPING I WAS FAR ENOUGH AWAY AND NOT BE SCRAPED OFF BY THIS SPEEDING LOCOMOTIVE. WHEN I FINALLY FELT THE BURST OF WIND, I TURNED AROUND TO NOTICE THE LIGHT WAS GONE. I THEN WATCHED AS THE REST OF THE TRAIN FLEW BY WITH GREAT SPEED, RELIEVED THAT IT WAS OVER. I THEN NOTICED MATT STANDING ON THE EDGE OF THE CLIFF LOOKING AT ME AND LAUGHING. HE FINALLY BLURTED OUT, IGNORANTLY, "DID YOU SEE THAT!"

I went over the workshop group procedures in detail, explaining that once we began meeting in workshop groups, we would all continue to work in the same room, but I would be in direct contact only with the workshop group of the day, while the rest of the class worked at their desks on other class assignments or on reviewing manuscripts for their upcoming sessions.

Following the round-robin reviews, students prepare their workshop drafts. This is a "first final" draft in the sense that it should be as near to perfect as possible, but that it would not be the last draft of the piece they would do. Although I prefer they type this draft because it is used to make multiple photocopies, I allowed them to do it in ink if their penmanship was neat, legible, and did not take up an extraordinary amount of space. Although the small group meeting dates vary, the due date for the workshop drafts is the same for everyone in the class.

On the day the workshop drafts were due, I had the students critique one of my own narrative essays. They used the same form to critique my writing as they used to critique each other. To make it a little easier on them, I put them into their RAGs to do an initial review. Each small group then selected a representative who became part of a demonstration group that evaluated my paper in front of the class as a whole. I did this for a number of reasons.

While the students responded to my writing—airing their likes and dislikes or asking questions about it—I had the chance to model appropriate author responses to criticism. I was also able to alleviate problems

Figure 8–4
Aron's Second Draft

_read
around
round
robin_

- SECOND DRAFT -

IT WAS LATE FRIDAY NIGHT, AROUND 11:00 PM. MY FRIEND MATT AND I WERE DRIVING WITHOUT A PURPOSE, WASTING PRECIOUS GAS ON BOREDOM. ~~WE WERE SCANNING THE AREA FOR SOMETHING TO DO WHEN~~ MATT NOTICED A PECULIAR ~~FORMATION OF LIGHTS ON THE~~ WEST MOUNTAINS. WE DECIDED TO GO CHECK IT OUT. AS WE CAME CLOSER, WE COULD SEE THAT IT WAS A LARGE MINE NEAR KENNECOTT. WE DROVE THE CAR ON A PRIVATE ROAD WHICH SEEMED TO BE LEADING TOWARD THE MINE. AS WE CAME OVER A HILL THE MINE WAS ABOUT <u>A QUARTER OF A MILE AWAY,</u> AND YET THE <u>LIGHTS FROM IT NEARLY BLINDED US.</u> ALSO LIGHTED UP, WAS A LARGE ROAD BLOCK, WHICH FORBID US TO GO ANY FURTHER. WE WERE BOTH READY TO TAKE THE CHALLENGE OF SEEING HOW CLOSE WE COULD GET TO THE MINE, BUT THE LIGHTS WERE SO BRIGHT THAT WE WOULD SURELY BE SEEN. WE THEN NOTICED A FIELD JUST EAST OF THE MINE THAT WAS A WALKABLE DISTANCE WITHOUT BEING SEEN. WE GOT BACK IN THE CAR AND BACKTRACKED TO A HIGHWAY WHICH LED US TO THE FIELD. [IT] LOOKED LIKE EASY ACCESS TO THE MINE SO WE PULLED THE CAR AS FAR OFF THE SIDE OF THE ROAD AS WE COULD AND PROCEEDED TO WALK THROUGH THE FIELD. WHILE WALKING THROUGH THE FIELD.

continued

Figure 8–4
continued

MATT AND I CAME UPON TRAIN TRACKS THAT WERE DUG
INTO THE FIELD, LIKE A GULLEY, TEN FEET DEEP. AFTER
SURVEYING THE AREA, I DECIDED TO CLIMB DOWN
FIRST. IT WAS VERY STEEP, BUT I MANAGED TO JUMP
DOWN SAFELY. I WENT OVER TO THE TRACKS AND THEN
MOTIONED MATT TO CLIMB DOWN. AT THAT MOMENT
I HEARD A FAINT NOISE, LIKE A HORN, AND IT WAS
GETTING LOUDER. WHEN I LOOKED AT MATT HE WAS
STILL ON THE TOP OF THE HILLSIDE AND STARRING OFF
IN THE DISTANCE WHERE THE NOISE CAME FROM.
SUDDENLY, A PIERCING, BRIGHT LIGHT CAME CHARGING
AROUND THE CORNER, RATTLING THE TRACKS AND
ROARING WITH NOISE; IT WAS A TRAIN! WHEN I
LOOKED AT MATT I SAW THAT HE HAD RETRIETED
INTO THE FIELD. QUICKLY, I RAN TO THE OTHER
SIDE AND BEGAN TO CLIMB THE STEEP HILLSIDE AS
FAST AS I COULD, BUT IT WAS NO USE. AS
I CLAWED VIGOROUSLY, THE LOOSE DIRT OF THE
CLIFF WOULD COLLAPSE OUT FROM UNDER ME. I
WASENT GOING ANYWHERE! REALIZING THAT IT WAS
NO USE, I SUDDENLY HAD A THOUGHT. WHAT IF
THE DRIVER OF THE TRAIN [CAN] could SEE ME?. AT THAT
MOMENT I PRESSED MY BODY FLAT AGAINST THE
HILL, HOPING I WAS FAR ENOUGH AWAY AND NOT TO
BE SCRAPED OFF BY THIS SPEEDING LOCOMOTIVE.
WHEN I FINALLY FELT THE BURST OF WIND, I
TURNED AROUND TO NOTICE THE LIGHT WAS GONE.
I THEN WATCHED AS THE REST OF THE TRAIN FLEW
BY WITH GREAT SPEED, RELIEVED THAT IT WAS
OVER. I THEN NOTICED MATT STANDING ON THE
EDGE OF THE CLIFF LOOKING AT ME AND LAUGHING.
HE FINALLY BLURTED OUT, IGNORANTLY, "DID YOU
SEE THAT?!"

they were having with the evaluation form. If nothing else, this exercise set the tone and created a rapport between the students and me. The act of teachers and students writing and sharing writing together lends a spirit of creative egalitarianism to the class, an important aspect of any successful writers' workshop. Timing is important in this tone-setting exercise, though. Had I introduced my writing at an earlier date, it might have had a daunting effect on their writing.

Phase Three: The Writers' Workshop Group Evaluation Meetings

Unlike the teacher, who is a member of every group, student writers deal only with manuscripts written by members of their writing cluster. Each group member receives copies of the manuscripts to be reviewed at least two days in advance of their group meeting. Students need enough time to consider each piece of writing carefully and to complete thorough evaluations. Comments are less visceral, and the commentators are less easily swayed by the opinions of others in their group. That is not to say opinions do not change during the course of the session. In fact, their careful preparation inevitably results in substantive discussions, both pro and con, about the ideas and elements in the writing.

With the exception of their own pieces, student evaluators prepare a written critique of every manuscript in their section of the workshop. These critiques follow the same format established in the round-robin review, although the critics do tend to be more detailed and explicit when reviewing the writers in their cluster. Following the group session, these critiques become the property of the writer whose work has been evaluated. In most cases the evaluators also return their copies of the writers' manuscripts, which they have marked for mechanical errors.

Putting the comments in writing makes the critique more concrete in both the evaluator's and the writer's mind and provides writers with hard copies of issues that arose in group. It also reveals how much time the student critics have taken in considering their classmates' writing. Most make a serious effort to communicate their feelings and thoughts in detail.

How a Workshop Group Functions

All workshop groups follow the same procedure. After checking to see that everyone has written a critique for the first writer, I tell the student reviewer to the right or the left of the writer to begin. Each group member contributes in turn to the discussion. Student critics usually begin and end with things they like about the piece. They do this naturally, it seems, revealing a surprisingly well-developed awareness of sensitivity to each other. Still, they speak freely about problems they see in the work or raise questions it created in their minds. Meanwhile, the author must adhere to a strict ground rule: he or she is not allowed to speak or respond to questions until all the student evaluators have had a chance to comment. I found early in my experience that a writer's defensiveness can put an end to productive discussion faster than anything else. Once everyone has had an opportunity to speak, the discussion becomes more freeform, enabling the writer to address particular issues or questions and giving student critics a chance to agree or disagree with each other.

My role is different than might be expected. I listen carefully to their comments, making notes on what they say, without speaking. I purposefully keep my comments to a minimum so as not to stifle their efforts. Rather than playing the all-knowing mentor, I act as a clearinghouse for the ideas that emerge in the discussion, answering questions about more complex issues of structure and style or helping student critics clarify what they are trying to say by raising questions about their responses. After the student reviewers have had their say, I try to draw together the two or three most common threads that run through the discussion, formulating them into a unified, cogent response to the piece that I hope will be helpful to the group as a whole and to the writer when he or she revises.

Although I have read each writer's work before our workshop session, I reserve my own judgment about the piece until I have heard what the other writers in the group have to say about it, keeping my mind open to their sometimes more acute perceptions. I also prepare a written commentary for the writer, but not until after the workshop session. That way I can include ideas that arose during discussion and either augment or defuse them. I also mark the manuscript for mechanical errors, referring the writer to sections in the grammar text if I see the same type of error being repeated frequently.

A Closer Look at Aron's Group

Aron's essay was the second of five manuscripts we reviewed on that day (Figure 8–5). His group had a lively discussion of all the manuscripts they reviewed that day. They gave him high marks on topic and language choice, but they all found areas that needed improvement. Jason pointed out problems with point-of-view and tense shifts. The group as a whole offered solutions for the trouble spots. Two groups members, Janna and Krista, wanted to know more about Aron's state of mind at the moment of crisis. They said he did an effective job of setting the scene, but the lack of emotional content made the main incident difficult to comprehend. As Krista said, "I could picture the place and everything else about it, but I was confused about your feelings at the time."

Figure 8–5
Aron's Workshop Draft

GROUP GROUP C   G   ARON
   9   G   PERIOD 6
   GROUP   GROUP C

GR

·FRIDAY NIGHT·

IT WAS LATE FRIDAY NIGHT, AROUND 11:00 PM. MY FRIEND MATT AND I WERE DRIVING WITHOUT A PURPOSE, WASTING PRECIOUS GAS ON BOREDOM. WE WERE SCANNING THE AREA FOR SOMETHING TO DO WHEN MATT NOTICED A PECULIAR FORMATION OF LIGHTS ON THE WEST MOUNTAINS. WE DECIDED TO GO CHECK IT OUT. AS WE CAME CLOSER, WE COULD SEE THAT IT WAS A LARGE MINE NEAR KENNECOTT. WE DROVE THE CAR ON A PRIVATE ROAD WHICH SEEMED TO BE LEADING TOWARD THE MINE. AS WE CAME OVER A HILL THE MINE WAS ABOUT A QUARTER OF A MILE AWAY, AND YET THE LIGHTS FROM IT NEARLY BLINDED US. ALSO LIGHTED UP, WAS A LARGE ROAD BLOCK, WHICH WAS FORBIDDING US TO GO ANY FURTHER. WE WERE BOTH READY TO TAKE THE CHALLENGE OF SEEING HOW CLOSE WE COULD GET TO THE MINE, BUT THE LIGHTS WERE SO BRIGHT THAT WE WOULD SURELY BE SEEN. WE THEN NOTICED A FIELD JUST EAST OF THE MINE THAT WAS

continued

Figure 8–5
continued

We got back in the car and backtracked to a highway which led us to the field. It looked like easy access to the mine so we pulled the car as far off the side of the road as we could and proceeded to walk through the field. While walking through the field, Matt and I came upon train tracks that were dug into the field, like a gulley, ten feet deep. After surveying the area, I decided to climb down first. It was very steep, but I managed to jump down safely. I went over to the tracks and then motioned Matt to climb down. At that moment I heard a faint noise, like a horn, and it was getting louder. When I looked at Matt he was still on the top of the hillside and starring off in the distance where the noise came from. Suddenely, a piercing, bright light came charging around the corner, rattling the tracks and roaring with noise; it was a train! When I looked at Matt I saw that he had retrieted into the field. Quickly, I ran to the other side and began to

continued

Figure 8–5
continued

CLIMB THE STEEP HILLSIDE AS FAST AS I
COULD, BUT IT WAS NO USE. AS I CLAWED
VIGOROUSLY, THE LOOSE DIRT OF THE CLIFF
WOULD COLLAPSE OUT FROM UNDER ME. I
WASENT GOING ANYWHERE! REALIZING THAT
IT WAS NO USE, I SUDDENELY HAD A
THOUGHT. WHAT IF THE DRIVER OF THE
TRAIN CAN SEE ME? AT THAT MOMENT
I PRESSED MY BODY FLAT AGAINST THE HILL,
HOPING I WAS FAR ENOUGH AWAY AND NOT TO
BE SCRAPED OFF BY THIS SPEEDING LOCOMOTIVE.
WHEN I FINALLY FELT THE BURST OF WIND,
I TURNED AROUND TO NOTICE THE LIGHT WAS
GONE. I THEN WATCHED AS THE REST OF THE
TRAIN FLEW BY WITH GREAT SPEED, RELIEVED
THAT IT WAS OVER. I THEN NOTICED MATT
STANDING ON THE EDGE OF THE CLIFF
LOOKING AT ME AND LAUGHING. HE FINALLY
BLURTED OUT, IGNORANTLY, "DID YOU SEE
THAT?!"

Amy and Krista wanted a more detailed description of Matt, feeling more explanation of his personality might lead to a more complete appreciation of the story as a whole. Jason also suggested that Aron remove the first reference to the railroad tracks, saying it would add an "air of mystery."

At this point in the conversation, Amy brought up the question of *purpose*, saying she was uncertain about how it was supposed to function in any of the essays they'd written. By referring to their writing and discussing what each of them was trying to do through it, I was able to clarify what had been a problem for at least two members of the group. The lively, conversational nature of these small groups allows for immediate discussion of issues that are on the students' minds. The workshop provides opportunities to approach problems directly, spontaneously, and actively.

Following up on the group's comments about Aron's piece, I agreed that Aron should delete the first reference to the tracks. This led to a brief discussion on the idea of withholding critical information as a key element in any well-told story. I also agreed Aron should do more with the moment of the train's passing, suggesting that when he sat down to rewrite he should imagine himself back in that gully and write about it as if it were happening to him at that instant, trying to see the moment in the detailed, slow-motion way we see things when we come face-to-face with a potentially fatal situation. After some brief questions about Matt, intended to help Aron decide whether he wanted to reveal more of Matt's personality, we ended our roughly fifteen-minute discussion of Aron's work and moved on to the next writer.

The group review session is by far the most popular of all the peer review formats. Most students like the fact that the teacher takes part, but even those students who may have once viewed the teacher as the central figure in the classroom, now see me as one among many more-or-less equal critics. By closely critiquing the work of other student writers, in both oral and written forms, students learn to construct effective comments for real writing problems while being sensitive to another's feelings about his or her work. Perhaps the students speak best for themselves about this process:

> I really enjoyed the group review. You get a lot of feedback, plus I like getting the teacher's viewpoint on papers. — Marni

> I finally found out what was wrong with my paper and a way to fix it. Nobody was afraid of telling me what they thought. — Chrys

> I liked this because you could speak to the people who were evaluating your paper. — Jeff

By the time we reach the close of the workshop, each writer has received an impressive amount of feedback on his or her writing, beginning with the verbal responses between pairs and in read-around groups, continuing with the rubric-based round-robin written reviews, and finishing in the workshop groups which couple discussion with written evaluations. The various peer review experiences provide each writer with far more information about the writing than I could possibly muster.

In my written critique, I offer my expertise through very specific technical suggestions based on the group's discussion. My review combined with the writer's memory of the group meeting enhances the effects of both. The written comments assign permanence to many ideas which might otherwise be lost to memory. Likewise, each student's memory of the group experience adds depth to the otherwise flat expression of the written critiques. In retrospect the reviews make a great deal more sense and are more useful to the writer than the usual isolated comments found on papers graded by more traditional means.

Grading is, of course, a concern, but the workshop approach puts the grade issue in proper perspective. Chris mentioned this idea in his unit evaluation: "We got more out of the workshop. It was done with the teacher so she could basically help us individually, not like in other classes where the teacher only cares about giving grades." As a teacher, I must care about grades, too. But if my students feel better about this process, then so much the better.

Following the workshop meetings, the students use the group's suggestions in revising their last drafts, which they turn in to me for final evaluation (Figure 8–6). Because I am familiar with the papers already, they are easy to review. Quickly scanning the manuscripts, I keep an eye out for changes made between the workshop and the final drafts. Obviously, revisions may be more or less extensive, depending on the quality of the workshop manuscript. Mechanical errors are minimal if not nonexistent.

I admit I grade the process as much as anything else. If a student sticks it out from beginning to end, I reward his or her perseverance. My justification comes in the form of comments like Charlotte's: "I have never done anything like this workshop in another class before. It was definitely worth the time. I liked the outcome. I wrote a paper and I never thought I could before." If grading the process rather than the writing makes nonwriters into writers, I'll grade the process every time. I realize some of my students' work lacks sophistication, but at least they are writing to a coherent finished product.

The Workshop as Community

The most significant effect of the workshop is the sense of community it engenders among the students in the groups and the classroom as a whole. Students learn quickly that they can rely on one another for help and feedback. Krista wrote the following about the workshop experience: "I learned more, and the workshop helped me with my writing more than any other class. All the different personalities in my group made it so I got a variety of suggestions. They had comments for everything."

Figure 8-6
"Friday Night": Aron's Final Draft

FRIDAY NIGHT

It was late Friday night, around 11:00 PM. My friend Matt and I were driving without a purpose, wasting precious gas on boredom. We were scanning the area for something to do when Matt noticed a peculiar formation of lights on the west mountains. We decided to go check it out.

As we came closer, we could see that it was a large mine near Kennecott. We drove the car on a private road which seemed to be leading toward the mine. As we came over a hill the mine was about a quarter of a mile away, and yet the lights from it nearly blinded us. Also lighted up was a large road block, which was forbidding us to go any further. We were both ready to take the challenge of seeing how close we could get to the mine, but the lights were so bright that we would surely be seen.

We then noticed a field just east of the mine that was a walkable distance without being seen. We then got back in the car and backtracked to a highway which led us to the field. It looked like easy access to the mine so we pulled the car as far off the side of the road as we could and proceeded to walk through the field. While walking, Matt and I came upon a gulley dug into the field about ten feet deep. It looked to me like a dried up canal. After surveying the area I decided to climb down into it first.

It was very steep, but I managed to jump down safely. I backed away from the cliff and motioned Matt to climb down. At that moment I heard a faint noise, like a horn, and it was getting louder. When I looked at Matt, he was still on the top of the hillside and staring off in the distance where the noise came from. I began walking backwards down the gulley when I almost tripped. I looked down to see what it was and noticed that this was no dried up gulley. Train tracks were at the bottom of this pit. Suddenly, a piercing bright light came charging around the corner, rattling the tracks and roaring with noise; it was a train!

When I looked for Matt I saw that he had retreated into the field. Quickly, I ran to the other side and began to climb the steep hillside as fast as I could, but it was no use. As I clawed vigorously, the loose dirt of the cliff would collapse out from under me. I wasn't going anywhere! Realizing that it was no use, I suddenly had a different thought: "What if the driver of the train can see me?" At that moment I pressed my body flat against the hill, hoping I was far enough away so as not to be scraped off by this speeding locomotive.

From head to toe my body stood trembling with fear as I clenched my fists and tightened my eyes shut. I stood most impatiently ready for impact, when I felt a great burst of wind. I turned around and noticed the light was gone. I then watched as the rest of the train flew by with great speed, relieved that it was over. I then noticed my friend standing on the edge of the cliff looking at me and laughing. Matt blurted out, ignorantly, "Did you see that?"

Students also come to understand in a very short time how beneficial this type of interdependence is for all involved. The workshop also eliminates the "everybody's-a-better-writer-than-I-am" attitude among students. Janna wrote: "The workshop was very helpful. I like having every-one's paper and seeing how I'm doing compared to everyone else. I think this is one of the most effective things I have ever done in school."

Of all the comments I received from students on their written evalu-ations of the workshop unit, Heather's response, which stands just under the title of this chapter, struck me most deeply. Hers is a simple state-ment, but it reflects on the most essential writing problem that peer-review-based writing workshops attempt to overcome. Heather wrote: "This is the first time I have ever done a writing workshop. It helped me a lot. Before this, I've always been on my own when I had to write a paper." It is that sense of aloneness that I hope the workshop eliminates, or at least diminishes. More than that, I hope my students learn a more effective way to proceed when writing.

Works Cited

Hughes, Langston. (1979). "Salvation." *A Writer's Reader*. Eds. Donald Hall/D. L. Emblem. Boston: Little, Brown and Company. 198–200.

Sartre, Jean-Paul. (1964). *The Words*. New York: George Braziller. 59–60.

White, E. B. (1982). "Once More to the Lake." *One Man's Meat*. New York: Harper & Row, Publishers. 198–203.

Appendix 8A
Basic Rules and Guidelines

1. Each writer must prepare one workshop manuscript of a narrative essay, 400–600 words in length. The workshop submission must be in standard manuscript form and must follow the guidelines established for narrative essay.

2. Each writer must prepare a written critique of each manuscript that comes through his/her section of the workshop. Evaluations are due at the beginning of each workshop session and become the property of the writer being critiqued.

3. Organization: One group per day will meet with me on a rotating basis. We will critique manuscripts of all group members on the day we meet as a group and only on the day we meet, so *attendance is crucial.*

4. In-Class Assignments: While in class but not in group, you must work independently and silently at your desks. Use this time wisely to work on reading, critiques of other writer's works, writing, or the daily assignment due. I will distribute a list of the daily assignments. They are *due* on the days listed. *Separate yourself from others who may negatively affect your behavior. You can ruin your grade by being a pain in the neck.*

5. Grading: The workshop represents one-half of second term's grade. You will earn three-fourths of that grade in workshop-related activities. You will earn the remainder by doing in-class assignments and acting appropriately.

   Grades will be based on the following:
   A. In workshop
      1. Workshop manuscript (25%)
      2. Final post-workshop revision (15%)
      3. Written critiques of others in your group (15%)
      4. Contribution to workshop group discussion (10%)
      5. Writing folder (10%)
   B. In-class work
      1. Completion of daily assignments (15%)
      2. Behavior (10%)

6. Final post-workshop revisions are due on the next class day following your workshop session. You will lose credit for any work you turn in late.

Appendix 8B
Workshop Schedule

*ALL WORKSHOPS DRAFTS ARE DUE MONDAY, DECEMBER 3.

Group A meets Wednesday, December 5:
Glenn, Steve, Adrienne, Debby, Elaine, Melanie
[Pick up workshop packets from me Tuesday, December 4.]

Group B meets Friday, December 7:
Tandea, Dennis, Jeff, Chrys, Neda, Charlotte
[Pick up workshop packets in class Wednesday.]

Group C meets Tuesday, December 11:
Aron, Jason, Krista, Wendy, Amy, Janna
[Pick up workshop packets in class Friday.]

Group D meets Thursday, December 13:
Sean Paul, Heather, Jodi, Marni, Amy
[Pick up workshop packets in class Tuesday.]

Group E meets Monday, December 17:
Joel, Chris, Missy, Melanie, Juliann, Charlynn
[Pick up workshop packets in class Thursday.]

3	4	5	6	7
ALL WORKSHOP DRAFTS DUE		WORKSHOP GROUP A		WORKSHOP GROUP B
10	**11**	**12**	**13**	**14**
	WORKSHOP GROUP C		WORKSHOP GROUP D	
17	**18**	**19**	**20**	**21**
WORKSHOP GROUP E				

Final revisions due *on* or *before* the following dates:
　　Group A: Tuesday, December 11
　　Group B: Thursday, December 13
　　Group C: Monday, December 17
　　Group D: Wednesday, December 19
　　Group E: Friday, December 21

9

Discovery
An Essential Outcome of Response Groups

Beth Johnson

By the end of my first ten years of teaching, I was becoming the teacher I didn't want to be. I was so concerned with marking every error and correcting every problem in my students' writing that I never heard their voices or thought about their ideas. I spent hours writing comments and suggestions that my students only ignored. I kept trying to get them to improve the *next* paper before they knew how to write *this* paper. My teaching felt hollow and frustrating, yet I stuck with it out of some bizarre sense of duty, some uncritical devotion to tradition.

It wasn't until I began to redefine teaching as learning and thought about myself more as a seeker than a dispenser of knowledge that things began to change. I began searching the literature for a better understanding of how students learn, the way they think, and the ways they use language, and the importance of language to their social and intellectual development. I rediscovered Piaget, who taught me that the key to intellectual development, as it pertains to teaching and learning, is the activity of the student. The significance of language in the development of thought is central (Bybee and Sund 1982, 70). More reading in Vygotsky, Luria, Piaget, Moffett, Spear, and a host of others reinforced that message. Because I found that response groups actively involve students in their own learning, I became committed to creating a curriculum in which response groups would be central.

Although my first attempts were disastrous, I was determined to experiment and to learn, just as I was beginning to encourage my students to do. As my students became adjusted to working in repsonse groups, I noticed that they became more like the active learners I wanted to teach.

They responded to what interested them in their peers' writing, to what confused them, to what mirrored the problems they were having in their own writing. They began to integrate and assimilate information from their own experience. But most important, their writing began to improve as a result of their own discoveries—from comparing, formulating hypotheses, making inferences, and drawing conclusions, in other words, from discovering the essentials of reasoning.

I turned to James Moffett's *Active Voice (1981)* for guidance. Moffett shows how meaning begins within the person: we do not know in any but a trivial way when we receive knowledge simply as fact to be memorized, and, more significantly, we do not develop an ability to internalize abstractions to help us determine the importance of any discrete piece of data in the first place (Petersen 1982, 17).

Building a New Environment

In this chapter, I want to focus on the methods I use to create a writing community, an environment that stimulates and nurtures growth. There are three essential ingredients. The first is getting a sense of what students' attitudes are toward writing. The second is implementing a sequential writing program. And the third is establishing for myself a role as a participant while students are in different stages of writing.

Students' attitudes and reactions to writing are critical to how they will participate in response groups. Experience always frames perception. As Combs states in *Perceptual Psychology*, children can only see themselves in terms of their experience and the treatment they receive from those responsible for their development (1947, 113). Before writing is assigned, I find it helpful to ask students to write to me about how they feel about writing. This task reveals a personal history. These histories often have an influence on how I initially group my students. Figures 9–1 and 9–2 illustrate very different views about writing. Both students were seniors in my college prep English class.

Kip's statements about loving writing (Figure 9–1) refer to his relationship with words and the connections they create with his world. He gives singular insight into the private and rewarding place he creates with writing: "I've never been able to express such feelings to others but in writing its my own world which has me starring in it." Kip is not simply egocentric here. Rather, he enjoys what he writes and can make connections to the "eternal aspects of things." For Kip, words carry what Luria called "fundamental units of consciousness reflecting the external world" (1983, 99). His remarks highlight the confidence that he has with writing. Although it is impossible to ascertain whether this example illustrates a totally positive writing past, it offers enough to suggest that he will be easy to work with and will enjoy writing.

Figure 9-1
"How I feel about writing": Kip

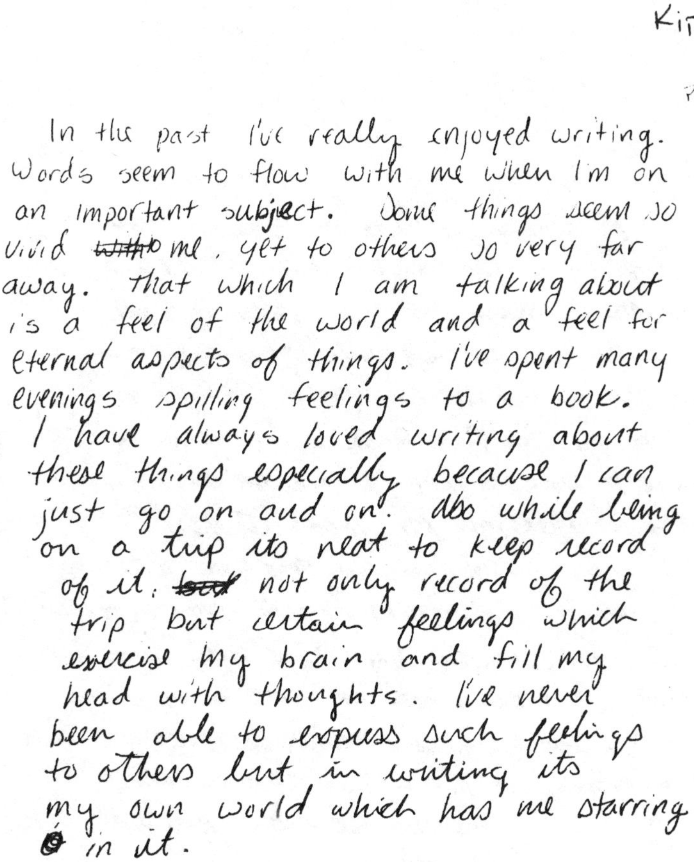

Kip

Per. 3

In the past I've really enjoyed writing. Words seem to flow with me when I'm on an important subject. Some things seem so vivid ~~with~~ me, yet to others so very far away. That which I am talking about is a feel of the world and a feel for eternal aspects of things. I've spent many evenings spilling feelings to a book. I have always loved writing about these things especially because I can just go on and on. Also while being on a trip its neat to keep record of it. ~~but~~ not only record of the trip but certain feelings which exercise my brain and fill my head with thoughts. I've never been able to express such feelings to others but in writing its my own world which has me starring in it.

In contrast to Kip, Eric's perception of writing brings to light what many students feel but rarely express (Figure 9-2). This example reflects the impact a past experience can have on writing and on oneself.

Eric's example illustrates the powerful influence a teacher has on a student's writing and how important it is to understand what happens when teachers respond to students' writing. Writing is intricately connected to the writer's emotions and self concept. What these two examples have to do with success or failure in response groups is important. Students vary widely in their attitudes toward writing. Developing insight into who these students are and how they react to writing allows me to

Figure 9–2
"How I feel about writing": Eric

Eric

My Sophomore year was the time I Decided I didn't like to write. I doot even know if I'm Good or bad at it. All I know is that my Honors English Teacher would put every writing assignment of mine down even when I felt good about it. She would tell me that my work didn't symbolize anything and w/out symbols my work was trash. I took her advice, but she never understood my symbols. I used to say to myself "why does everything have to mean what she wants, cant anything mean something different to." I haven't written any type of story, since then in fear of it being rejected, but someday I would love it if something I had done was published (not that I want to be a writer). And if it was I would be sure to find   and show her what I had done. And say I must not be that bad

---

better understand the way groups will function. For me, these early writings clarify how certain students may relate with one another and thus how the groups will function. For example, placing Eric in a response group with others who share his feelings about writing would not be wise. The students would simply reinforce each other's dislike of writing. In contrast, placing Kip in a response group with others who share his attitude would probably produce an ideal response group.

Although such a group would be delightful, the idea is to get the whole class into successful writing experiences so that their success can influence their writing development. Using student writing histories provides me with the initial guidance I need in forming workable response groups.

Changing Student Roles

To get students ready for response groups, I use James Moffett's *Active Voice* during the first quarter. I take students through several assignments which include Spontaneous Sensory Monologue, Spontaneous Memory Monologue, and Composed Memory. These three assignments in particular lead to writing a final narrative. These sequential assignments allow students to gain momentum in reaching the final draft stage. From these three assignments, students choose which one they want to work on for a final narrative. Response sheets are used to make students feel they must accomplish a task, and discuss one another's paper in the group. Through the discussions, students select, manipulate, and organize information in their narratives, and apply this information in their revisions. Response sheets also direct students to participate in dialogue which engages them without the teacher. While students are in small groups discussing, I move from group to group and listen rather than direct how they should respond or suggest what they should say. However, I do pause and question or probe occasionally to keep students going. The emphasis is more on the students talking rather than on my commenting. I feel that my limited involvement at this point empowers students.

However, there are specific guidelines for response group behavior. Everyone in the group must contribute to the discussion and everyone must stay on task. There can be no sideline discussions which would derail the group. In order to insure these guidelines, I appoint a group leader who tells me if everyone has been involved. I put no more than three students in a response group and, early in the term, I don't have the groups spend more than ten to fifteen minutes in discussion. I have found that a time limit pushes students to stay on task and accomplish more. Later phases of the class require more time and more guidance.

Redefining the Teacher's Role

As students progress through their drafts, response groups change. I try to vary their purpose and function. For instance, I set in motion several procedures and activities while students are drafting and participating in response groups. First, in order to engage myself as a co-respondent, I ask them to write to me explaining how they feel about their writing while they are in the process of composing—what frustrates them, what pleases them. This writing is important because it engages me as a respondent to their writing while they are in the process of composing and it also opens up written communication between me and the student. Since little conference time is possible, I find this method helpful in understanding what attitudes students are forming in their writing. My role shifts from teacher/grader to teacher/listener and teacher/responder. The purpose of my becoming a co-respondent is to establish a rapport that takes on a different shape from my role as the one who gives a grade. In this co-respondent position, I want to build trust. I don't want to be one who merely slashes through students' work and determines a grade. I would rather be one who shares, at least to some extent, in their struggles. I have found that when I know the trials students have been through, I have a more sincere regard for their work. It also establishes a foundation in understanding the point at which students begin in writing and how far they develop.

Second, while students are writing to me about how the process is going for them, they are also revising their drafts. These dual experiences allow me and my students to see how they explore ideas and feelings and how they formulate changes from response group participation. I am trying to help them open a window into their thinking. Figures 9–3A and 9–3B, examples by two twelfth-grade students and my responses, illustrate the rapport I want to establish and the engagement of students thinking about their writing. These examples were written after students were in the first response group and were now trying to figure out in what direction they wanted to move.

To me, these examples reflect the influence from response group participation in that students have become aware of certain facets of their writing that they probably would not have glimpsed without the response group. Kendra picked up on the problem of dealing with two different subjects and her need to focus on one (Figures 9–3A and 9–3B). She questions and thus puts into play the thinking process of differentiating. She states, "I also am having a hard time figuring out my main point (subject). I guess I'm kind of talking about trying to go into detail about to [two] different things and can't figure out how to leave one of them behind." By examining and distinguishing her subjects, Kendra is analyzing what she needs to do to put material together to form a new whole.

Kristi noticed that each draft became more focused. When she states,"My first draft was exactly that, just alot of ideas thrown together. A type of brainstorm" (Figure 9–4), she relates her understanding of moving from recalling to reshaping and describing. She recognizes her draft as more focused because she has moved beyond the brainstorming stage into translating what she wants to do with "one of the basic ideas." The response groups gave Kendra and Kristi the opportunity to think critically about their papers while they were in the early stages of drafting and could benefit most from peer discussion. By having them write to me, I helped them to become more aware of their own thinking.

Figure 9–3A
Students Think About Their Writing: Kendra

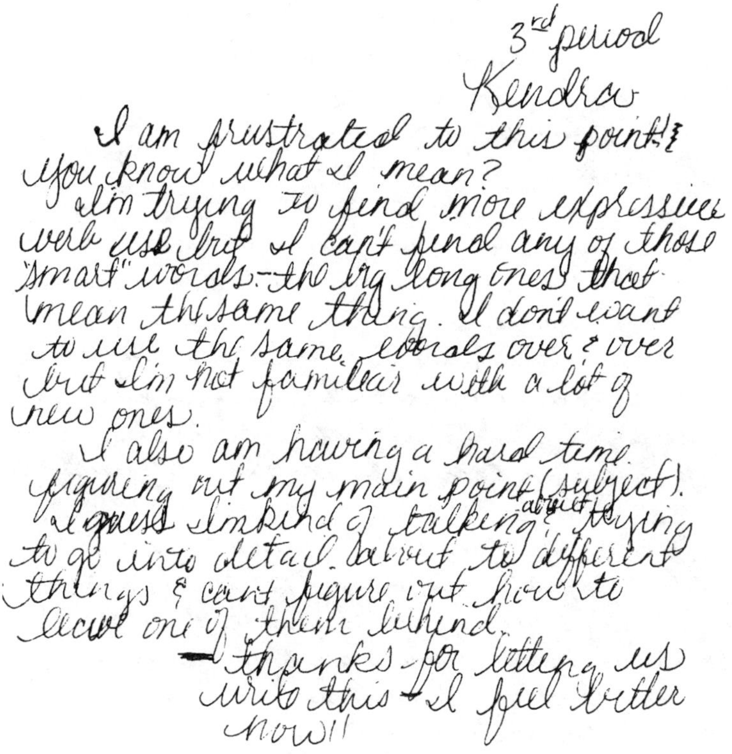

3rd period
Kendra

I am frustrated to this point!! you know what I mean? I'm trying to find more expressive verb use but I can't find any of those "smart" words—the big long ones that mean the same thing. I don't want to use the same words over & over but I'm not familiar with a lot of new ones.

I also am having a hard time figuring out my main point (subject). I guess I'm kind of talking about trying to go into detail about to different things & can't figure out how to leave one of them behind.

thanks for letting us write this—I feel better now!!

Because I become more supportive as a participant in their compos-ing, students feel comfortable about voicing their thoughts. A collabora-tive relationship emerges between me and my students in uderstanding and elaborating writers' intentions. Response groups can incorporate teachers, too, as responders at different levels and in different stages. The premise here is to develop a positive attitude toward writing as a process and not necessarily as an end product. Students writing to me while they are in the process of composing, coupled with participation in peer response groups, teaches them to talk with one another about writing. My main objective in using such practice is to lessen the threat of talking about writing to others and to build a vocabulary for discussing writing.

Figure 9–3B
My Response to Kendra

Kendra,
  I do know what you mean about being frustrated. I often feel this way, too when I'm writing. Don't despair — it's normal.
  Don't worry about "smart" words. Use words you're comfortable with. Vocabulary will increase this year — promise.
  Your comment about having a hard time figuring out your main point interests me. I think you're on the right track about trying to go into detail about two different things.
  I've been in this muddle, too. You're capable enough to gain your focus. Your work is always a delight. Your comment about writing making you feel better made me smile. I'm glad you feel this way.

Igniting Change

The next two examples show the effects of response group interaction. One example illustrates diversity in development from the original composed memory assignment to the final draft. The other draft remains generally constant in its focus but changes developmentally through extension of detail. The improvements that students make are often recursive and are made in smaller increments and in different ways contingent upon where they are in their own development. The expectation is that all students move in some direction that elicits improvement. Response groups will not make all students equally good writers. They should never be established for this intent. Instead, response groups should recognize

Figure 9–4
Students Think About Their Writing: Kristi

Kristi

period 1

Talk to Me!

Mrs. Johnson—

My first draft was exactly that, just alot of ideas thrown together. A type of brainstorm. The second draft was more focused on one of the basic ideas. Each time I focus more on the subject. forcing more detail and description. I feel my paper has advanced more since the first draft

Kristi, your "talk to me!" feels urgent. Stop by for a paper conference. I'm here after school, just let me know. Many times first drafts are "a type of brainstorm" — nice observation. Interestingly, you've noticed that each draft takes on a new shape and form. Did the response group help you make changes? I'd like to discuss this. I would guess that your paper has advanced more. Keep going!

students' individual capabilities and afford them the opportunity to make their own improvements.

Ty's first example is rather typical of a student who just aims to "get this assignment done" (Figure 9–5). Even though class discussion targeted purpose and audience, Ty's example shows what he has been taught a writing assignment should be: perfunctory and pointless. At this point, he would defend his example as meeting the criterion of writing an essay based on a personal memory. However, once his essay was read aloud in class and then went into response group, it changed dramatically. In fact, Ty abandoned his first topic, waking up early, and chose an entirely new subject. When interviewed about why he made such changes, he admitted, "I recognized that there was something wrong about mine. It was the one read in class so there were a lot of people talking about it."

Specifically, in Ty's revised example he has "re-visioned" and refocused the entire piece. He actually resaw the paper as something he wanted to convey rather than just finishing a writing assignment. In his revised piece, "A Time to Dance" (Figure 9–6), he's writing more deliberately to an audience. Because he has become more aware of someone else reading or listening to his paper, Ty realized that something had to be done with the original example.

Interaction with another person is the only factor that can tell writers they made sense or if the reader "got some kind of feeling from it." This factor is critical for all writers. It is the human capacity to listen and respond with sensitivity and emotion to a piece of writing. It is the exchange and interaction over a piece of writing that guides its form and intent. Development is strengthened when students are nudged, if not forced, to rethink and evaluate. Conversation is the vehicle for this to happen.

Something specific occurred within the response group to facilitate Ty's readjusting his topic and focus. His post-writing interview did not reveal any one statement which would indicate exactly what was said in the response group to direct his shift. However, the overall impression he gained was that this audience was not particularly engaged. This was enough for him to make changes. An excerpt from this interview with me (B. J.) follows:

B.J.: Your composed memory paper has changed a great deal. What made you make these changes?

Ty: I felt that I wasn't going anywhere with this [Saturday Morning paper]. It wasn't very clear.

B.J.: Was there something specifically said in response group which made you change your example?

Ty: I don't know just that there wasn't a clear purpose in mind, I guess.

Figure 9-5
Composed Memory Assignment, First Draft: Ty

---

1. Purpose   Narrative based on memory
2. Who are you writing to

EXAMPLE #5

Composed Memory

One Saturday morning I had to do the most dreaded thing. Wake up early! It was terrible. ~~The I was~~ ~~alarm~~ rudely awoken ~~me up~~ by the alarm so I almost threw it off the dresser, but realizing that the alarm clock was just doing its job, I gently turned it off. ~~The~~ since the silent sound was so refreshing, ~~that~~ I almost fell right back to sleep, but I caught myself. Knowing ~~that~~ I had to be ready in about an hour. I grudgingly crawled out of bed and felt my way out of the room almost running into the bed and ~~the~~ wall. It was almost like an obstacle course ~~since~~ with my eyes ~~weren't~~ not functioning ~~totally right~~ correctly. After making it out of ~~the~~ my room I still had the (menacing) stairway up ahead. Knowing I had to go up the (towering) steps I began the long trek.

continued

Figure 9–5
continued

I ~~finally~~ made it up the stairs just in time because my legs were beginning to feel a little weary. By this time, a shower sounded like the ^most wonderful ~~best~~ thing in the world. I got into the bathroom and rested for awhile looking forward to the refreshing shower I was about to take. After a short rest I mustered up enough strength to turn the knobs and as I turned the hot water on the steam began rising ^like a helium filled balloon. I knew then that it was going to be a ^great ~~good~~ shower as well as an ^excellent ~~good~~ day.

B.J.: What do you mean by clear purpose?

Ty: I don't know. I'm independent and can tell. I recognized that there was something wrong about mine. It was one that was read in class, so there were a lot of people talking about it.

B.J.: So from this discussion, what do you remember being the force that made you feel it wasn't right?

Ty: They weren't able to tell what I was trying to say. They were bored. I could tell. And I wasn't reaching them. My audience I mean. I did the Saturday morning paper and thought it was okay. Everyone hates to get up on Saturday morning so I thought I'd better change. I don't like this writing anyway. I'm better at writing analytical papers. I know what I'm supposed to do there.

B.J.: In what way are analytical papers easier?

Figure 9-6
"A Time to Dance": Ty

A TIME TO DANCE

Have you ever felt the exhileration of dancing the jitterbug? Well, this stimulating experience came my way when I was in the third grade.

The excitement began on a gloomy winter evening when my brother and I attended a dance festival. As we approached the building, the excitement electrified our somber spirits. The invigoration heightened immensely as the two of us scurried into the building. We anxiously sat in our seats like vultures anticipating their prey, hoping the show would begin shortly. The performance finally began and it lived up to our expectations. Each dance aroused our enjoyment, but one particular dance, the jitterbug, overpowered us. In this dance the teenagers gracefully glided around the dance floor while swinging each other around like dolls. After many more dances the show ended and the crowd sadly proceeded to exit like a herd of cows out into the cold. We all wished the performances would go on like a never ending circle. As we left and began cruising down the street, I could not cease thinking about the jitterbug dance and suddenly, a brillant idea popped into my mind — to learn a jitterbug.

My brother and I felt overwhelmed with joy since we were going to create our own excitement. But the hard part still lay ahead. We had to find girls to be our partners and become as graceful as the teenagers at the show. The task of locating girls to help us thrill an audience turned out to be a simple as riding a bike since two lovely, hardworking girls in our neighborhood willingly accepted our invitation.

We spent many long afternoons that cold winter becoming skillful dancers and many times it seemed as if all hope had disappeared like a setting sun, but we all struggled through and conquered all our adversity in the end. We all grew during these trying times proving to ourselves that if we worked hard and never gave up, things would always turn out great. After finally conquering the difficult dance, we scheduled a time for us to perform in front of our school.

The moment of truth had come! We anxiously waited for our opportunity in our slick fifties outfits, acting like newly wed husbands waiting for their first child to be born. While we positioned ourselves in the correct spots behind the curtains we knew our time of reckoning had finally come. As the curtains slowly parted and I stood there staring at my peers, the butterflies tripled in size, but they quickly vanished when the music began.

We dazzled the audience as we glided effortlessly around the floor with our artistic moves. After finishing, the audience roared with approval. The joy we felt from completing the dance and hearing the applause of our peers clearly showed in our wide grins as we exited the stage. The praise and approbation rang in my ears for days. I vowed then that I would take advantage of many more choice opportunities to come like this in which to grow and create excitement for others.

Ty: I don't know they just are. For me anyway.

B.J.: They're easier because they follow a specific format, perhaps?

Ty: Yeah.

B.J.: What made you change the Saturday morning paper to the dance one?

Ty: When I was younger I danced a few times and I remembered what went on so I decided to write about this experience because I figured I could do more with it. It was so vivid. I thought I could show it more clearly. I thought others would be more interested in it.

B.J.: Is writing something interesting important?

Ty: Yeah. No one likes a boring paper.

B.J. : Do you think you would have changed the Saturday morning paper if you had not been in a response group?

Ty : Not that much.

In the Saturday morning paper, Ty had begun to make small changes in substituting one word for another, circling active verbs, and minimally changing syntax in a few sentences. In "A Time to Dance," there is more attention made to adjusting sentence structure, substituting one word for another, adding more transitions, and extending the essay length. The differences between these two examples show Ty's thinking processes at work in comprehending what was identified in the Saturday morning paper, and in applying this informaiton in another draft. There is more effort made selecting words and in manipulating sentence structure in the first draft of "A Time to Dance" than there was in the draft of the Saturday morning paper. More importantly, however, Ty's discovery of an authentic audience elicited the changes he made. His interview underscores his awareness of someone other than a teacher listening to his paper. In reference to the "A Time to Dance" paper, he says, "I thought I could show it more clearly. I thought others would be more interested in it." In reference to the Saturday morning paper he says, "They weren't able to tell what I was trying to say. They were bored. I could tell. And I wasn't reaching them." In essence, Ty realized that he was actually communicating with a live audience and this discovery triggered his desire to reach them.

The next example (Figure 9–7) does not illustrate the broad changes that Ty's example does. Instead, Mike's example shows how his response groups helped him to become more descriptive and to focus the paper more on the chase. Suggestions from the response group directed Mike to give more detail and description.

Figure 9–7
Mike's Early Draft

Writing
Composed Memory

It was a (cold) Thanksgiving night in 1987. That night my dad was working the afternoon shift as the records sergeant. His shift was coming to an end, so we decided to leave and go out and drive around. The cop car needed gas so we first stopped at the traffic sub-station and filled up before we started to head for home.

The car was filled up and we proceeded to drive up 4500 south when we both noticed a car behind us with its (high) beams and (driving) at a high rate of speed. The car got even closer and decided to pass us in a no-passing zone, which was against the law. My dad (flipped) on his grill lights, because his car was unmarked, and tried to pull the suspect over. Instead of (pulling) over the car (sped) up and the chase was on. The suspect was driving

continued

Figure 9–7
continued

What's a burnout

east on 4500 south when he ran a red light and was trying to ditch us. He turned down 600 east off of 4500 south driving south when he came upon an L.D.S. church and tried to do a (burn out) to turn around but his car failed and we had him (trapped) The only problem was that he (jumped) out of the car and ran west towards State Street. (Word of a Jump, maybe ease in) It move

A traffic sergeant (spotted) the suspect at a pay phone on 4500 south and State and he (apprehended) the suspect. The suspect was taken to the county jail for evading, warrant numerous traffic violations, and O.U.I. This incident was fun to watch. something for me to studying on for the future.

The development of the paper gets significantly better as Mike adds detail to the sequence of the event. He also begins to manipulate sentence structure. His thinking reflects his comprehension of what needs to be improved and how. In some ways Mike makes these gains recursively by reworking his original material (Figure 9–8). At first glance, Mike's piece does not indicate significant changes. Yet he does respond to the evaluative feedback and makes improvements in differentiation and formulation of new ideas. He analyzes the suggestions made and applies this new information to his paper. Each student will work from his or her own writing performance level. Understanding this aspect is exceedingly important. Although Mike can evaluate feedback and make improvements in differentiation and formulation of new ideas, the wonderful feature of Mike's piece is that it illustrates the trust he has in his response group. This trust builds Mike's confidence to write a better paper.

In contrast to Ty, Mike credits the response group for helping him write better. He highlights the benefits of information from the response group and addresses its abililty to help "even those people who don't write that well" (Figure 9-9). Although Mike has centered on the response group's telling him "right out" where his problems were in needing more description, he has demonstrated some degree of confidence in expanding his paper. He may have seen development in terms of length primarily, but as he expanded his ideas, the fluency helped create a more detailed paper. The major effect here is the positive attitude Mike has in participating in response groups. He views them as helpful. This is the result that response groups should have in order for them to work successfully. Essentially, both Ty and Mike made changes in their drafts from their individual discoveries and self-realization in assimilating information into new cognitive structures.

The element of discovery is an essential outcome from the use of response groups. What students discover is twofold: first, that revising is a process of discovery, and second, that response groups help them in this process. Jerome Bruner believes discovery learning increases intellectual potency because it forces the individual to use cognitive abilities in generating meaning. Realizing how his or her mind is capable of functioning, the student receives the self-satisfaction of intrinsic rewards. Bruner believes that in order for individuals to want to use their minds and to continue to explore and become knowledgeable, they must have had success in doing this many times. He argues that what is really needed (in school) is to have students become aware of using their minds. The only way a person learns to discover is to be involved in discovering. It is, therefore, essential for students to have multiple opportunities to make discoveries so that they develop their cognitive abilities. If orchestrated effectively, the use of response groups will provide the atmosphere conducive to engage cognitive growth.

Works Cited

Bybee, R. W., and Sund, R. B. (1982). *Piaget for Educators*. 2nd ed. OH: Charles E. Merill.

Bruner, J. (1966). "The Course of Cognitive Development." *American Psychologist* 19: 1–16.

Figure 9–8
Mike's Revised Draft After Response Group

The Turkey Chase

It was a cold Thanksgiving night in 1987. That night my dad was working his regular day shift, which started at 3:00 p.m. and ended at 11:00 p.m. My dad asked me if I wanted to go with him and I said that I would. Since it was Thanksgiving, my dad let the records clerks on his shift go home for a couple hours and eat their Thanksgiving dinner. While they were gone we did some of their work and maintained the office just to make the shift go by quicker.

There were 45 minutes left in the shift and with the shift coming to an end we decided to go home. On the way home we had to stop at the traffic office, which is where the Traffic Division is stationed, and fill the car up with gas because it was on empty. We left the traffic office with a full tank of gas and proceeded to head home. We were driving east on 4500 south when we noticed a car with its high beams on and it was driving at a high rate of speed. The car about ran into us but at the last moment it swerved and passed us in a no-passing zone. My dad's car didn't have a light bar but it did have sheriff stars on the doors and red and blue grill lights mounted behind the grill.

My dad bent over to flip the switch to the lights, but he couldn't find the switch. The switch was screwed in by my left knee, and when I saw that he couldn't find it I reached down and flipped the switch on myself. The lights came on, the car sped up, and the chase was on. My dad picked up his radio transmitter and radioed in that we in pursuit of a later model blue mustang and he also gave the license plate number to the dispatcher. This was a high priority call, so the dispatcher sent out the emergency beeps to get cars in the area to give my dad some assistance.

The suspect car was dodging in and out of others in an attempt to try and ditch us but it didn't work. At this point we were up to speeds near or above 60 MPH. We were driving east on 4500 south when a traffic signal turned red at 500 east and the suspect proceeded to go through it. We were still on the suspect when he suddenly made a sharp turn at 600 east and proceeded to drive southbound. In a desperate attempt to get away for good the suspect drove onto the grass of a L.D.S. church and tried to make a 180° turn which failed and he slid to a complete stop. My dad trapped his car with the cop car as he was getting out the suspect opened his door and ran westbound towards State Street. I had a chance to stop the suspect by slamming my door into his mid-section but I was so excited that I didn't even think about it.

My dad radioed in his location again and also gave a bodily description of the suspect and which way he ran. We took the keys out of the mustang and got in our car so that we could go and look through the neighborhood that we saw the suspect run into. We couldn't find anything so we went back to the scene to process the situation. Different patrol cars were searching the area for the suspect but they couldn't find anything.

Thirty minutes had passed since we stopped the car when suddenly a traffic sergeant came over the air and told dispatch that he has the suspect in custody. We drove to the location of the arrest, which was 4500 south State at a gas station and we made sure it was the right guy and it was. The traffic sergeant said the suspect did resist arrest and the suspect was taught a major lesson, if you know what I mean. From there the suspect was taken to jail and being charged with evading, warrants, and numerous traffic violations and D.U.I.

Apparently the suspect ran through the neighborhood, came upon a muddy canal and ran through it to get to a payphone at the gas station. The suspect was muddy from knee to toe and he also made a trail of mud tracks all the way across state street and to the payphone. The suspect was a used car salesman and was wanted for odometer tampering, which is turning back the mileage on the cars that he was selling. This car chase was a fun experience because I was in the middle of it and it's funner being there than watching it on T.V.

Figure 9–9

Mike Highlights the Benefits of Response Group

> The response groups really helped me out a whole lot. The group told me that I needed more description in my story and that is what I worked with. I turned a two-paged paper into a seven in a half paged paper in a matter of minutes, it was easy. The group was informative and told me right out where my problems were and what I needed to do to make it better.
>
> The response groups was a great idea because it helped me to write better and to me my writing has improved. The response groups would work out, even for those people who don't write that well. I think that it is better to talk about a paper because it helps those who don't write well improve on their mistakes. Talking about a paper before turning it in also helps to fix mistakes and add more description which makes the paper more superb and better to read.

Mike

Combs, A. W., Richards, A. C., and Richards, F. (1949). *Perceptual Psychology A Humanistic Approach to the Study of Persons*. New York: Harper and Row.

Luria, A. R. (1983). *The Development of Thought*. New York: Houghton Mifflin.

Moffett, J. (1981). *Active Voice A Writing Program Across the Curriculum*. Portsmouth, NH: Boynton/Cook.

————. (1983). *Teaching the Universe of Discourse*. New York: Houghton Mifflin.

Petersen, B. (1982). "In Search of Meaning: Readers and and Expressive Language". In T. Fulwiler and A. Young (Eds.), *Language Connections: Writing and Reading Across the Curriculum*. IL: National Council of Teachers of English.

10

To Look Again
Reevaluating the High School Research Paper

Nolyn Starbuck Hardy

The research paper is an essential part of any good English class. Unfortunately.

Actually, writing the paper itself isn't bad, it's the other stuff. When you first start, some underpaid librarian will probably drift into your English class to tell you how exciting research is. I mean, he'll *really* get excited about it. And he'll invite you to come down to his library any-time, including Saturdays and late week-nights when you don't have anything better to do. You'll probably be persuaded to write notes from your research on tiny note cards, with the illusion that this will actually make things easier, until you lose half of them in a freak windstorm.

After wearing down the carpet in the library entrance and after you have accumulated a few thousand note cards, you will be instructed to attempt writing a rough draft, to form a rational, flowing, concise train-of-thought (if you have any rational, flowing, concise thoughts left by this time).

Length is a very important aspect of the research paper. Your teacher will probably require some unheard-of length. But it's usually not necessary to pay any attention to this. And you can just ramble on about anything; it can be totally different from your subject, as long as you make it sound good.

Footnotes are exciting. (If everyone who committed plagiarism was caught, our public school system would not exist today.) It is important to footnote all intelligent-sounding parts of your paper, because no teacher is going to believe that *you* were smart enough to make such a statement. And teachers never really look at footnotes let alone check your sources, so any book will serve as a reference.

In conclusion, the conclusion is the most important part of any research paper. This is where you remind the reader exactly what it was you were writing about, because he has most likely become thoroughly confused by this time. . . .

The student who wrote this was being facetious, of course, but (*unfortunately*) if you examine his essay, he has identified many of the ideas students, and often teachers, too, have about a research paper:

1. It's an assignment which is "essential to any good English class." In other words, a type of writing unique to schools and not something people do in real life.

2. Looking things up in the library is something you only do when compelled. (OK—so compelled by what?)

3. Length is an external criterion not related to the subject matter or the audience and is subject to the teacher's whim.

4. It isn't necessary to become involved in what you write, you can just "ramble on about anything."

5. Footnote style is the most important skill to know in writing a research paper.

6. You don't have to worry about reliable, accurate information; any old book will do because teachers don't have time to check your sources.

7. Plagiarism is really what it's all about, you just don't call it that.

8. You don't have to think or write anything original because the teacher wouldn't believe you are capable of it, anyway.

9. You don't have to be involved with your subject or even like it; in fact, you don't even have to understand it.

10. It isn't *meaningful*; it's not something you do for your own enrichment, or anyone else's; its just another makework assignment.

It was autumn quarter of my second year of teaching high school. I had been less than impressed with the research papers my first class of seniors had written the previous spring. Out of curiosity, I asked my current sixth-period seniors class to write an essay explaining what a research paper was. When I read their essays, most of them said the predictable, bland things that sounded like what they thought a teacher would want to hear. But the student who wrote the paper quoted above—Chris, who was always truthful behind his sarcasm—struck a nerve. I had to admit that, if I were honest with myself, I would have to agree with what he said.

It made me think about what it was I really expected in a research paper. What should my students understand about research papers when we were finished? What should they be able to do? And why? The previous year I hadn't been ready to do anything more than follow the formula the other teachers in the department used, which consisted of consulting *Warriner's Complete Grammar*, trudging down to the library for a few days, doing endless note-card checks and making sure they got the footnotes right. I still have a copy of the handout I gave them at the beginning of that assignment. It includes things like: "A research paper is an indepth composition that follows a specific format, giving information gleaned from readings from a number of sources. . . . It will include a title page, text that is double spaced, and it must have footnotes and a bibliography. . . . Its purpose is to discover the facts about a subject. Personal opinions and prejudices are out of place. Do not use the pronoun I. . . . Your paper should be completely impersonal. . . . " I did manage to suggest that "your paper will work best for you if you choose a subject to investigate that you have some real interest in." The papers they wrote certainly were impersonal. And uninspiring and boring and trite, for the most part, consisting mainly of plagiarized excerpts pasted together with hastily composed sentences that didn't necessarily relate to the excerpts in any meaningful way. They were the efforts of high school students trying to sound like middle-aged scientists who supposedly hadn't used the personal pronoun 'I' in years.

But what had I expected? I had gotten back the papers I should have gotten, considering the instructions the students had been given. Some of them had certainly been competent, as well-done as any of the other senior classes' papers. No one questioned that we had 'done the senior research paper' as we were expected to do it. No one, it seemed, but me.

I wasn't looking forward to dragging my students through it again. Even more, I dreaded having to read their papers. They weren't meaningful to the authors and they were certainly not meaningful to me.

I thought about some of the papers I had written in college. Most of them I had forgotten the minute I handed them in, just as my students probably did. The few I remembered were, of course, the ones I *liked*. They were the ones I had really invested in, in terms of time, effort, involvement, understanding, and, most of all, *self-interest*. They were assignments that had an element of the unknown, of discovery, and they had been satisfying to me because they had helped me to learn something I had *wanted* to learn, not to impress the teacher, but to benefit myself. I got an emotional payoff from doing them that had nothing to do with handing them in for a grade.

What I needed was a way to get my high school seniors to invest themselves in their papers. What I wanted them to feel was that same kind of emotional payoff, that same kind of quenching of a thirst for knowledge, that I had experienced.

I enrolled that fall in a composition theory class at the university and through some of the readings in the texts required for the class, I began to find some possible methodologies I could implement.

It was nearly Christmas before I decided to bring up the issue of research papers at a lunchtime gathering of the department faculty. Being the newcomer in the English department, I procrastinated through several opportune lulls in the conversation before I interjected with "Well, it's time to think about doing research papers."

A chorus of moans and groans went up. Every teacher had a war story and each one was worse than the last. They laughed over the blatant examples of plagiarism and the ubiquitous papers that kept turning up, hastily modified, year after year. One honors teacher confessed she had her students' papers come due the last day of school so she didn't have to read them. She just gave a grade on the paper based on what they had already done that year. "You don't want to give them back their papers anyway," she said, "or they will just give them to a sibling or a friend to use some other year." I had to admit she was probably right.

Why, then, I persisted, deciding to be the devil's advocate, were seniors expected to do a research paper? Why didn't we just forget the whole thing?

One teacher, eyebrows raised, asked why I was asking. "Seniors have *always* done a research paper," he said, folding his arms across his chest and eyeing me with the look teachers reserve for a student who just might turn out to be the class non-conformist.

Fortunately, before he could say anything more, someone added, in all seriousness, that the purpose was so students could learn to use footnotes. We argued about notation styles for a few minutes. (About half the teachers favored the traditional footnote to the newer *MLA*.) There was a lag while we caught our breath, and then another teacher suggested the purpose of the research paper was so we could be sure that students had paid at least one visit to the library before they graduated, and another declared that it was because students would need to know how to write a research paper when they got to college. As they talked, I realized that, despite the kidding and the laughter, they dreaded bullying their students through the project and reading the resulting papers just as much as I did, and they had no surer justification for it than I had been able to come up with—the best reason any of us could give was that it was, like castor oil, *good for you,* but no one was sure exactly why.

Most of all, I hated resorting, as so many high school teachers do, to that old excuse about how useful something is going to be when a student gets to college. I knew that when they got to college most of them wouldn't remember their high school research papers, and their professors would discount what they had learned in high school, anyway. I was coming to believe more and more that if a writing assignment didn't have inherent value, it wasn't worth doing. And if what I needed to do was to teach them how to use footnotes, perhaps the best thing I could give them was a copy of Turabian. I certainly can't write a college research paper without referring to it. Neither, I suspect, can anyone else.

Just as the end-of-lunch bell rang, a veteran of many years teaching declared that the purpose of the research paper was to demonstrate that a student could write an evaluative paper without expressing any opinions of his own—that the student could be "objective." Warning lights came on in my mind but there was no time to pay attention to them. (And hadn't I been guilty of saying something very much like that to that first senior class?) I hurried to my sixth period.

But those warning signals were still blinking faintly later that day when I thought over our noontime debate. I had recently read James Moffett's views on "transpersonal" writing. I picked up the book I had been reading and looked up his article. I agreed with Moffett's statement even more the second time I read it. He said:

> Applying scientific criteria that would be unacceptable to most real scientists making the breakthroughs out there on the frontier, many people have come to think that subtracting the self makes for objectivity and validity. But depersonalization is not impartiality. It is, quite literally, madness. (1983, 172)

It was, I thought to myself, another kind of madness to give a writing assignment without having a clear understanding of its purpose and value. You could argue, of course, that all these justifications of the research paper might be defensible to varying degrees. But I could find in none of them a compelling motivation. It made the whole exercise sound as lifeless and trite as the papers I had gotten, and deservedly so, from that first class of seniors. They were so generic they could easily have been generated by a computer. But without being able to give them a clear picture and a satisfying incentive for doing a research paper, how could I expect my students to do anything better?

Those students I had had that first year had written other papers that were really good. We'd had success with using response groups and the other techniques of the writing process developed by the National Writing Project: prewriting, peer response, revising, publication—I believed strongly in these things. The magazines of their best work that they put together as a final project were wonderful; they had been as pleased and proud of them as I. Some of the students had done individual magazines, others had worked in pairs or in groups, but all of them had taken advantage of each other as audience, as editors, and as resources for ideas as they were working, and they had needed only a minimum of direction from me.

The magazines had been really interesting—well written, lively, and visually appealing. Nothing at all like the research papers they had done.

To be trite, to be uninspired, to be so "objective" that nothing is alive in your writing—that surely isn't what we want them to "know for college" or for anything else in life, is it? Why couldn't the research paper be as worthwhile, satisfying and involving as the other writing my students had done? "Real" research usually was motivated by someone's intense curiosity about something; it was often based on a compelling *need* to find answers. Lawyers stay up nights searching their books to prepare for a trial; reporters put themselves at risk to get the best story; they're researchers, and they do it because there is a real payoff for them in finding things out. Was there a way to create that kind of motivation and involvement for my students? Why couldn't the writing processes I'd had success with be applied to the research paper? Was it desirable, or even possible, to put off the inevitable grousing over format and footnote style long enough for them to immerse themselves in the process of doing some self-directed research first? It seemed an obvious part of what I wanted to accomplish, once I had said it.

I was about to jump into the middle of a writing project without having any certainty as to the outcome, or even quite how I was going to proceed, except in the most general terms. I knew more what I didn't want than what I did. I had good reason to suspect I was approaching the research project in a manner of which some of my colleagues would thoroughly disapprove. I did have what I believed were sound theoretical reasons for what I was going to try, based on the reading I had been doing.

I was impressed, for example, by David Bartholomae's suggestions in his article "Writing Assignments: Where Writing Begins." He says that a good writing assignment "teaches by interfering. It interferes with a student and his writing." That is, the assignment should discourage writing that is "used to close a subject down rather than to open it up, to put an end to discourse rather than to open up a project"(1983, 308).

Ken Macrorie, in *The I-Search Paper*, explains his concept of the research paper as something that should actually relate to a person's real life (1988, 54-64). Developing that relationship in the minds of my students was what I wanted. Let them do a research paper that was worth doing because it was worth doing, not because they might need to know how to do footnotes in college.

But how did these theories translate in terms of what needed to happen in my classroom? No matter how much I read or thought about it, I was on my own behind that classroom door.

I had recently heard Dixie Goswami speak at a writer's workshop about teachers doing their own classroom research, and I felt encouraged to be more experimental, to take some risks, although I have to admit my first reaction to what she had said had been "I don't have time!" Still, what she said made sense. It made even better sense as days passed and the time to make some decisions about teaching research papers grew closer. I realized I was slowly being pushed into *making the time* to experiment. I was eager to try out some of the ideas I had been collecting, but timid about diverging from the traditions of the department. Stripping down to your theories and plunging right into what might prove to be very hot water can be daunting. Still, the "what ifs" were piling up in the back corridors of my mind, and I was increasingly certain that I wasn't going to revert to the methods of the previous year.

Plunging Ahead

One day soon after, I put up on the bulletin board a big banner that said: "What is Research?" Below this general heading, I put another banner which read: "What Should A Research Paper Look Like?" Under this, I displayed articles taken from different sources: a *Rolling Stone Magazine* essay about a reporter who goes to the exotic city of Peshawar in search of a story about the Mujahadin and the Afghan War; an article from the *Smithsonian* about how a tree becomes a baseball bat; an interview story about the rock musician, Sting; an honors student's research paper about English literature; a story about the Amazon rain forests from *Atlantic Monthly*, articles from *Seventeen*, *People*, and so forth. I even put up a couple of my old college papers. I avoided extremely technical articles; that was not what I was after. I made sure to include some articles that were attractively laid out and had eye-catching illustrations.

As the project took shape, I would put up new headings and staple underneath them copies of handouts, clippings, student comments or whatever else applied, so that as the bulletin board evolved it became a visual outline and chronology of where we were and what we had done up to that point. Many times students would stand at this board, reading some of the handouts or notes that were there, and it proved useful as a resource on the project's structure. We occasionally had guest speakers— for example, a friend from the university came in to demonstrate interviewing techniques, and we put up the notes they took from his lecture, and from their interviews of him.

I didn't say anything about the bulletin board for a few days, but I watched carefully to see what reaction I would get from my sixth-period seniors, who were about to become the subjects of my own research project, although they didn't know it.

Of course, some never knew it was there until I brought it up. Others glanced at it, temporarily curious. A few read through some of the articles. I listened in on their conversations with each other, enough to know they were wondering what I was up to. So, in truth, was I.

Choosing a Topic

One day soon after this, in my sixth-period senior class, I brought up the subject of selecting a college. How much time, I asked, had they spent in the last year or so making up their minds. Various figures were thrown out in response—ten hours, twenty, fifty, five, a zillion. I asked how many students had visited their prospective campuses. Half the hands in the class went up. How many had written for information? More hands. How many had read *Barron's* or some other guide? How many had a drawer full of pamphlets bulging with statistics? How many had talked to a sibling or friend or friend of a friend who had attended that college? How many were influenced by what their parents had to say? How many had determined to go to a college other than the ones their parents had attended? And why, I said, go to so much trouble just to pick a college; what was the big deal—it was just another school, wasn't it? A volley of answers rocketed back at me. Choosing the right college was *important*; it could affect how much money you made, who you married, where you lived—your whole *life*!

By now they were a-buzz, enthusiastically sharing their experiences about all the traumas and frustrations of choosing a college. Eventually, I asked them whether what they had been doing would qualify as research. This brought on some "a-has," some blank stares, some cynical "What is she trying to pull" expressions, and another debate. Several of the students were quite adamant at first that research, *real* research, was quite different from what they had done. So I asked them to explain to me what real research was, and what it was for.

The more they talked about it, the more students began to see that getting information about any subject that was important to them could *maybe* be called some kind of research. But they had to think about whether anything *they* were interested in was important enough to be called true research. They were "just high school students," after all.

The next day, I asked them to think of one thing they would really like to know more about—something that might truly affect the course of their lives or alter their thinking about an issue that was important to them. While they were considering this, I read with them an excerpt from Ken Macrorie's book *The I-Search Paper* in which he talks about choosing a topic, or "letting a topic choose you," and we discussed a couple of the papers from that book at some length. The first one, which I read to them, was about a young woman in her mid-twenties who wanted to return to college to become an architect, but was afraid that her age and her status as a single parent would prevent her. In the course of her investigations, she talked to a number of architects, and ultimately decided that it wasn't realistic to pursue her goal. The second one was an article about a man who raised wolves. Both the papers had the compelling ring of true experience, and my students were fascinated. Macrorie says you let a topic choose you by standing outside yourself and checking to see "what the fingers of your mind are scratching. That's how you'll locate the itch"(1988, 66).

I could tell that some of them were thinking about all this; there was that kind of hushed attention you get when an idea is sinking in. I reminded them that I had asked them to think of one thing they would really like to know more about, and to come the next day ready to talk and/or write about it. They were used to working in response groups, so the idea of having to discuss this with their groups wasn't anything new.

Taking a Stand

Naturally, on the day following our discussion about choosing a college, not all of them were ready or had a topic that I, or they, thought was feasible. It took several days, and more discussions of how important it was that they be honest with themselves. One student simply couldn't do it. Three weeks into the project, I finally assigned him a topic. I still wish I hadn't, but that's another story.

But enough of the class had caught on, enough of them believed me when I said I didn't want them to waste their time or mine by writing about something that wasn't important to them, that I felt we were ready to go on to the next step.

I asked them to put their subject as a heading on a piece of paper, and then to list everything they thought they already knew about it. Then I asked them to list all the questions they had—what they would like to find out by the time they were through, and what conclusions they expected they might arrive at. (I wanted them to be aware of any preconceived ideas they had.) Lastly, I asked them to explain why this subject was important to them.

We developed these notes into what we called position papers. Here are excerpts from some of them:

> I am researching the topic of learning disabilities. Right now what I know is that my 22-year-old brother has one, but I have never been told what exactly the problem is. I'm frustrated by his attitude. and by some of the things he does. . . . I don't know if it's just a game or really his L. D. . . .

> Do college entrance exams demonstrate the aptitude of its participants? I found the *ACT* to be extremely superficial. These tests do not measure the student's knowledge, they seem only to test a student's capability of acting under pressure. . . . After I am done researching and interviewing people . . . I think I will find that I was correct in my beginning assumption that they're not a good measure of your ability to do well in college.

Although I know quite a few college freshmen, I don't know very much about their studying habits or what the classes are like or anything for that matter. . . . I would like to find out the hardships and the fun side of life as a college freshman. I plan to interview some of the college freshmen I know. I also plan to observe students up at the university. I can get other information from booklets and handouts that I have collected from college fairs and at the university . . .

The reason I chose to do teenage suicide is because I have a friend who attempted it and I want to know what drives teenagers to take their own lives. . . .

Throughout time, women have taken a backseat in business. But today women are seen in the most industrious and demanding jobs, not just as secretaries, but as the executives themselves. My question is, what must be given up in order to attain such a high position? As yearbook editor, I have found that there are some very real sacrifices that go into becoming "The Boss." Do you have to be known as "The Gorilla" in order to be successful as an executive? I guess I just want to know if there is another way. If there isn't, then is it worth it? My goal is to find someone out there who has found that "right" way, because right now, I seriously wonder if there is one.

I'm researching the ski patrol and what qualities are needed for one to be on the patrol. Being on the patrol would be a good hard job if one loved medicine and skiing. . . .

We divided a second bulletin board into sections, one for each of the six groups. I asked them to do a final copy of their position papers and put them up in their group's section of the board.

And I put one up, too, explaining that I wanted to do research on how high school students did a research paper. They were quite amused by this, but they were impressed that I was going to do a paper along with them. Here is part of what I wrote (I won't include it all; it was too wordy and a little pompous—I was nervous, too):

Current research says that the best people to analyze what happens in a classroom are the ones who actually spend a lot of time there—the students and the teacher. I'd like to look at what a research paper really is about. Maybe we can design a way of doing such a paper that will be more effective and worthwhile, and maybe even more enjoyable. I'd also like to understand what students need from me in order to be successful researchers.

I went home wondering what on earth possessed me. But I had to admit that I looked forward to sixth period more than any of my other classes. I was as curious as the students about what I was going to try next, and how things were going to turn out.

With the commitment to let them choose a topic came some unanticipated problems, and a realization of the responsibility that I had to handle these problems with care. The girl who wanted to do a paper on teenage suicide because she had a "close friend" who tried to kill herself confessed to me privately that the "friend" was her older sister. We agreed it should remain "close friend" for the paper. The girl whose brother was learning disabled had often discussed this with her friends, and I was confident, and so was she, that she could handle the class knowing about it.

A third student came to me to say that what she really wanted was to find out whether homosexuality was a learned behaviour, because her father had recently confessed his homosexuality to her and the rest of the family, and had subsequently moved out of the family home. She was, she said, having a hard time with his wanting to remain close to her. We finally agreed, after much painful debate, that if this was the topic she really wanted to pursue, that she should protect her family's privacy. She had difficulty all through the project. I have to admit that a little "objectivity" might have made things easier for her. Her feelings were still too raw. She found little research that was definitive and a lot of controversial speculations, and what she was looking for were black-and-white answers, and that upset her. Given her preoccupation with this situation, however, she might have been just as distracted with a less compelling topic.

I had qualms about how the administration would look upon my encouraging a student to do so controversial a topic. Nevertheless, I had made a commitment to my students that they should be allowed to pursue a topic of legitimate concern to them, and this was something she really wanted to know. I believed I had an obligation to allow her to do so if I possibly could. Her topic was neither obscene nor illicit and it was very important to her. Looking back on it now, I think it all comes down to a question of how much risk a teacher is willing to incur in order to keep her word, and a careful assessment on the teacher's part of what the student really can handle. There's no way for me to be certain I made the right choice for this student.

About the Response Groups

Erica Lindemann, in her book *A Rhetoric for Writing Teachers*, says:

> We can also turn our classes into writing workshops to let students help each other develop and rewrite papers. Writing workshops have several benefits. They insure that students take time to compose papers in several stages. They encourage students to teach each other by exchanging

solutions to writing problems. They provide opportunities to discuss papers with audiences other than the teacher. When students give each other immediate feedback and work out strategies for expressing the message effectively, they gain a broader sense of audience and an understanding that good writing doesn't just conform to teacher-imposed standards. (1987, 184)

Response groups can fulfill these characteristics of a workshop that Lindemann describes. In order to be successful, however, a teacher needs to prepare students for working in such groups. Giving specific directions takes the fear out of response groups for students, especially at the beginning of the year when they don't know what to expect. A teacher should make it clear that students aren't going to be asked to evaluate the goodness or badness of a paper, but that what they are doing is simply reacting to the paper, honestly, giving their personal impressions, or doing some simple editing, without condemning or assigning value.

The teacher's reactions to students' first efforts at responding is crucial. If they feel they can't trust a teacher they won't be honest, and then you'll get nothing worthwhile from them. I find as many legitimately positive outcomes as I can and praise them well. I keep my enthusiasm going even when theirs is flagging and I do a lot of modelling of the kinds of responses I expect.

And I don't get discouraged when things don't work as I know they should. I've done enough response groups now to know that they don't always work the way they're supposed to. I accept that there are some groups that never work out well, no matter what you do. Some students just can't handle the more open procedures; they long for the nice neat rows of desks and the quiet order of a tightly structured class. They're comfortable behind their masks of indifference or passivity and they don't want to take them off.

I'll be the first to admit that learning to use response groups was a process of trial and error over the course of several years. My first attempts were dismal and discouraging. If I hadn't been convinced of their potential worth, I would never have stuck with it. They can be intimidating and unpredictable and demanding. But when they do work, and work well, there's just nothing better for getting some good writing done. I had the good fortune of attending a series of writing workshops taught by members of the National Writing Project during my first few years as a teacher. I sailed home from these workshops absolutely on fire, eager to try peer response and prewriting and all the rest. I thought my junior high school students would be just as excited as I was. They weren't. I bombed miserably. My second and third attempts weren't much better. The classroom in my head was far, far better than the one in which I stood facing thirty-seven squirrelly seventh graders who couldn't even spell response group, much less do one. I discovered in a hurry that knowing what you want to do isn't the same as being able to do it. But dissatisfaction with the other methods available forced me to keep trying, and eventually I worked out what I could be comfortable—and successful—with in my classroom.

Sometimes I begin training students for response groups by asking them to give me a topic, and I will write a paragraph or two, and then, using an overhead projector, we will go through it and revise and edit it together. I will ask them to help me analyze how I can improve it, and to tell me what isn't clear or needs expanding, and so forth. I ask them to point out mistakes (always make a few obvious ones the first time through). This helps them to see that revision is something that I consider a natural and comfortable process and an integral part of writing. I'll make notes in the margins to reflect what they tell me, or highlight sections according to their comments, or underline, or cross out and write in above the line the corrections—all the ways of revising and editing that one normally does when going through a paper. Then I'll ask them to do a draft, perhaps on the same topic, and I'll ask for a volunteer or two, and we'll do some evaluating of their papers using the same procedures. There's usually a student or two brave enough to volunteer once they have seen you take the risk yourself. Modelling what you want them to do before you put them into groups takes a lot of the uncertainty out of the process for students.

It's valuable to develop a file of student papers that have gone through the revision process in a group, and to keep evaluations of response group efforts from previous years so that students can see what others have done. When we're finished with the first response groups, I select some that have worked out well and particularly those who have done some substantive revisions, and put them on the bulletin board, with all the drafts included in the display.

When a response group session doesn't go well, it is important to admit it, and to discuss what might be done to improve things the next time. I often ask students to evaluate their group's work at the end of a project, and to make suggestions. It isn't realistic to assume that all response groups are successful all the time. What students need from the teacher is candor, and the acknowledgment that just because one session or even one project didn't succeed doesn't mean others won't. They need to understand that you will be willing to help them fix what's broken, that failure isn't going to perpetuate itself within the group, and that we can recover from a bad session and get on with things. I try to be honest. I feel I can say, "O. K., this went really well, but this part didn't work out the way I expected. Here's what I thought should happen. We need to analyze why it didn't and come up with some ways to fix it." I circulate among the groups and sit in with them from time to time in order to let them know that I'm interested and available. Both they and I need to be comfortable with an interactive relationship that allows for mistakes and corrections in procedure.

Response Groups and the Research Paper

I had begun response groups from the beginning of the school year, so by the time we were ready to do the research paper, the fundamentals were already in place. I planned a minimum of one response group a week while we were engaged in the research project. These groups would keep track of individual members' progress and keep a running tally on a chart posted on the bulletin board, so that we would all have a perspective of how well we were keeping to our deadlines. (I was utilizing peer pressure, I admit, but it did work well.) In general we kept to this schedule until the final week when they were putting together their research magazines. There were times when groups asked for additional time, which I allowed as much as I could, and, with some exceptions, they used the time profitably.

In selecting people to work together I decided to give them the option of choosing group participants. I had mixed feelings about this, and I have mixed feelings about the results. The danger, of course, is that friends choose friends rather than people who might actually be of more benefit to the group. All but one of the groups worked out fine, although there were the inevitable frustrations when group members were unprepared or didn't take a task seriously or were uncooperative. This one group, all boys, all very independent—it wouldn't be inaccurate to characterize them as loners—just never gelled. I let it go too long before I finally regrouped them, adding them in, one to each of the other groups. Consequently they were all, except one, behind the groups to which they were assigned, and every one of them was the last in their group to come up with a final paper. If I had it to do again, I think I would have made myself a member of their original group and worked with them on a more individual basis.

Ideally I was hoping that, as the project progressed, response groups would evolve into a "community of scholars" in which working together on assignments as was appropriate would seem a natural thing to do, whether we formally announced a response group or not. They were pretty good about evaluating each other's work when requested to do so but they—and I—were a long way from the kind of spontaneous interdependency that I had in mind.

I had been deeply influenced by an article by Parker J. Palmer: "Community, Conflict, and Ways of Knowing." It was one of those readings that awakened a passionate response in my own mind. Palmer discusses what is meant by objectivity. He argues that we take this to mean that we must keep knowledge "at arm's length." This idea of objectivity "distances the knower from the world . . . it divorces that knowledge—a part of the world—from our personal life. It creates a world 'out there' of which we are only spectators and in which we do not live. . . . We make objects of each other and the world, to be manipulated for our own private ends." He calls this a kind of "trained schizophrenia." Students are taught to report on a world which is "not the one in which they live" (1987, 22).

I wanted my students to live in the world they were researching, and to see what they were learning as an integrated part of that world. I wanted them to care about what they were doing; I also wanted them to care about what other members of the group were doing, and I believed that the key to both of those accomplishments lay in their finding a genuine enthusiasm and curiosity about what they were doing, individually and collectively. I wanted them to forget their shyness and self-preoccupation and lose themselves in what they were discovering. I believe now, as I did then, that such involvement is an important part of any true research. I was struggling for ways to facilitate the response groups as a support for this kind of research.

One of the things I did to encourage interdependency was to announce that we would, at the end of the project, publish group magazines that would include a research paper by every member of the group. I emphasized that no magazine would be acceptable that didn't contain a completed research paper from *each* member of the group. I did this to encourage group cohesiveness, and for the most part, it was successful. I know it caused some frustration, but I don't think being frustrated is always a negative thing; sometimes it is the precursor to growth and change.

A side benefit of encouraging peer interdependency and mutual responsibility for each other is that many discipline problems just fade away. Goof-offs soon learn that other group members are not long amused by their antics. Acting out doesn't bring the payoff it might in the usual classroom arrangement. Even better, they and their group are involved in meeting a set of deadlines in competition with the other groups, and if one member fails to complete the task, the whole group suffers. This kind of peer pressure can be a positive incentive. The risk, of course, is that a student may feel a failure in the group's eyes and drop out, literally or emotionally. A teacher needs to keep a careful eye on group dynamics and make changes when necessary, or counsel with the group or the individual, or both.

I did notice an increased intensity, as the work proceeded, in their responses. I felt that for the most part students were taking their work seriously. Their evaluations expressed an involvement with each other and an ability to measure themselves against the progress of other group members that seemed useful. They were able to say things to each other without offense that I might have been hesitant to say in written notes on their papers. Here are some comments from one of the early response group evaluations we did:

I found that I know a lot more about my subject than I thought. Discussing it, I had the opportunity to defend what I believed about my subject.

I realized I need to follow [a] stricter outline. The only way this will succeed is if I apply myself more regularly.

I learned that I'm doing better than I thought I was. I've been comparing my progress to _____ this whole time, who is ahead of everybody. I'm not so discouraged about my progress and I am ready to get going again.

I have come so far on my project alone that I've already researched the aspects that they might come up with. Some people are just screw-offs and can't deal with an adult subject.

One person is going to lend me a book he has that will help me a great deal.

I was very close to changing my subject until I talked to my group. They think I should continue with it. Now I think I really will.

I realized that I was speaking from one viewpoint and not realizing the different aspects of my subject.

I learned a better way to structure my interviews to make them more productive. I also learned that I'm not the only one who's a little confused and frustrated about this paper.

They [the groups] allow for an effective exchange of ideas and information. We should have more critical discussions.

I think the groups are an excellent idea. I liked to hear about everyone else's project, and how they were coming along. Now I don't feel so isolated. I also got some new viewpoints and opinions on my subject.

It takes up time I could be using for research and using the computer. We had a *little* fun. I did find a little bit out, by how they were conducting their research.

I feel very stressed! It's *HAW* [an organization for female students; this girl was an officer] week and nothing is ready for the dance. I'm going to have to depend on myself this week because my best friend won't be here. There's a ton of things to do and the last thing I need is more homework!

I think it would be more helpful after I've done more on my project.

Sometimes I would ask them to pair up and interview each other about how they were doing on their research projects, and then give me some oral or written feedback. Here are some examples:

> Brad is still gathering his data and isn't ready to start interviewing. I told him I thought he should set up a time for his first interview, and then he would have something to force him to get going . . .

> Hilary is working on an interview guide. She wishes we had a phone in the class so she could do interviews by phone.

> Mimi has *major* library information—pages upon pages. Ready for interviews. Very well prepared. She has 8 sources and has done one interview. Set to present a report to the group on Friday. Currently typing up completed interview.

> Michelle is having a hard time with interviews but *OK* on library sources. Creating a survey, currently.

I don't suppose we came very close to creating Palmer's ideal community of scholars, but we did do well in achieving a new kind of "conflict"— what Palmer describes as learning to confront each other "critically and honestly over alleged facts, imputed meanings, or personal biases and prejudices." Some of the groups were very open and frank with each other, and it was not uncommon for one member to bring in an article that he thought someone else in the group could use, or to comment on a possible source they might find helpful. Conflict, Palmer says, in a real community of scholars should be "open, public and often very noisy"(25). We certainly managed the noisy part. I sometimes wondered what administrators or other teachers might think if they passed my room during one of our loud group sessions.

Project Logs

Kirby and Liner, in their book *Inside Out* suggest using a project log, and I decided to try one (1983, 18-30). When I gave these to the students we discussed learning styles and I gave them some examples of different patterns of learning behaviors. I asked them to think about what their learning style was. Did they, for example, do a little bit each day on an assignment, or did they set aside time to study on a weekly basis, or did they catch an hour here or there without planning ahead? Were they the type to wait until the night before a deadline and then get busy? How could they make their learning styles work for them? I asked them to keep a record in one section of their log accounting for the time they spent on their project. I wanted them to write down what they actually did, not what they thought they should do. It was kind of like asking dieters to keep records of what they ate. I hoped it would help them to see the patterns in their study habits. I also hoped it would motivate them to get their research done. This part of the project was not very successful; there were only a couple of students who actually kept up with their logs, and we got so involved in the research papers themselves that the logs were an early casualty. It would have been a better idea to examine learning styles at another time.

The other sections of the log worked out well, though. We divided the logs into sections for library research, interviews, on-site observations, brainstorming, and the learning log. In the library section they were to put all their printed research material and notes, numbered to correspond to a list of sources. In the first two pages they were to make their record of sources, a bibliography in other words, and give each a number. I included sample entries of how to do this for each type of source. Then in the following pages they were to do their notetaking, summarizing what they read, and identifying their notes with the number of the source. What they did, in effect, was use a notebook instead of note cards. Since much of what they gathered was Xeroxed copies which they annotated, having a pocket in a notebook to keep them in worked out fine. They also had room to summarize articles. We had already done a lot of precis writing, and I encouraged them to distill what they were reading and put it into their own words as they would in a precis. It was as convenient as the note cards, and gave them more room.

We did classroom exercises in each of these areas as I introduced them, as well. For example, we did exercises designed to heighten their awareness of what body language and dress might reveal about a person they were interviewing. I sent them to various parts of the building—the television studio, for example, and they wrote up their observations of how the site related to the work done there, and how it might affect the people who worked there. These were added to the bulletin board.

The last section I called "Flashes of Brilliance" and suggested that that was where they could do their mental "doodling"—put all the thoughts and notes that didn't seem to belong anywhere else at the moment.

Although the learning log didn't last until the end of the project, there were some entries by some of the students that were well worth reading, such as the following:

> I agree that research papers should be required, because everyone at one point in their life is going to have a question and want to find an answer. Learning the process to find it is helpful for everyone. I think a teacher shouldn't restrict the student to a certain topic or make it busy work, just to fill up a week.

According to one of the workers at Wasatch Canyon Hospital, there is no cure for depression. I find that hard to believe. Maybe there is no drug, but I believe there is a cure in the mind.

Interview question: define depression? What are some ways to control it? How common is it? How serious is it? How can one avoid depression? How does it relate to stress? Who is it more common in—male, female, old, youth? How does it affect the thinking or thought process? Is it inherited? How can you deal with a depressed person?

I went to the school library from 1:30–2:10 and had a hard time finding books. I'm wondering if I'm really going to find what I want. Maybe it's because I'm not really sure what I want to know.

I interviewed my brother John sort of for my own information and that's when I decided not to change my topic. . . . I sat down with him for an hour and 1/2. It was the longest I've ever seen him really listen. I learned a lot from talking to him. I found out it's kind of hard for him because he feels like he's in his own world. He runs away when people raise their voices because he feels threatened. He also is afraid to learn and wants to do everything his way. It's frustrating that he doesn't want to learn a new way. But something I thought was interesting—he does think he'll get better. See, no one's ever really talked to him about it. I've never understood what was actually wrong with him. How can he manage money or support a family? He quits all his jobs, too. I was glad I talked to him. I felt I really learned a lot and maybe he did, too. He kept asking why I cared and I said 'I just want to understand you'. It kind of brought us closer.

I went to the university library and looked in the blue abstract books. It took me a while to figure them out. But after I did I found there was so much information and so many topics. There are several types of learning disabilities and tons of aspects and problems.

What I need from the teacher is more time. I've had a hard time finding things—I've also had a hard time just finding time. Maybe she could be more specific on exactly what she wants.

I was keeping a log, too. Here is what I wrote for my first entry:

Today we began our research papers. I'm really nervous because I'm plunging off into the unknown in structuring this assignment, but I'm excited to try something new. . . . They were really involved in the paper [about the woman who wanted to become an architect]. I hope it gave them a fresh perspective on what research is. I've given them another paper, "The Great American Baseball Tree" and asked them to identify what parts of the paper must have come from library research, what from interviewing and what from personal observation. I want them to see that a research paper isn't something only high school seniors do but that much of what's in print is really 'research papers' done up with lots of appeal.

Structuring the Project

Don Murray, in "First Silence, Then Paper," suggests that teachers are responsible for providing the following:

(a) Silence in which to think and to work.

(b) Territory. Meaning freedom for the student to choose a topic and that the teacher do nothing that "reveals you think the student has nothing worth saying, and makes the student depend on you for subject matter."

(c) Time. The teacher should provide deadlines for each portion of the project and not just the final draft.The teacher may want to make quantity demands also. Freedom to fail along the way must be encouraged, too.

(d) Need. Students need the "egocentric experience of hearing the voice they did not know they had."

(e) Process. The student needs to understand the writing processes. Teachers can set up groups, conference, share stories of other writers' experiences, give techniques, etc., but she should leave the options open to the student as to how he will proceed.

(f) Text. Text will be the student's own writing. "There is a blank page, and then, with luck and work, a messy page." Students and teachers should learn to read unfinished writing.

(g) Response. The student writer needs response "when it can do some good, when the writing can still be changed. Students would have opportunities to share their writing with others, both peers and the teacher, in an atmosphere of faith and trust" (1983, 228- 234).

I used these suggestions as the basic pattern around which to develop the project. Overall, it proved to be a good basic outline.

Types of Research

I decided, in keeping with Macrorie and others, to require three types of research for the project:

1. (a) Print media, utilizing authoritative, up-to-date sources.

2. (b) Interviews of people in the community who were knowledgeable on some specific area relevant to the project.

3. (c) On-site observation. For example, a student who did a paper

on television anchor people went to the studio and made notes of what a studio was like during a broadcast.

I encouraged them to do their library research before they went out to do interviews, so that they would be knowledgeable when they talked to people.

Format

The format for the paper was an adaptation of the basic structure for a university research paper. It was to be organized in the following manner:

1. Background and statement of problem. This was to be a polished and expanded version of the position paper.

2. Literature review. This was the place for their findings from library research.

3. Interviews and observations. Here they would include what they had derived from their own interviewing and observing. We discussed several options as to how the interviews could be included in the final paper and whether and how much direct quoting from the interview they might want to use. They could also explain how they did the interviews and observations, why they chose the people they did, and under what circumstances the interviews and observations took place.

4. Findings and conclusions. In this final section they were to draw some conclusions of their own, both in summarizing what they had learned and interpreting the implications of this knowledge.

We also discussed the language and tone of the paper, and whether it should be written in the traditional third person. I discussed choosing a point of view based on audience and content, and explained that all research papers need not be written in the third person. I thought it would please them to have the freedom to choose the appropriate point of view depending on the subject matter of their papers. But for some of them, this was frightening. I wanted them to put themselves into their papers? How could this be? Of all the unorthodox ideas I had been proposing, this was the most threatening. Some of them ended up using the old familiar third-person style. We had done so many things during the project that were different from what "everybody else" was doing for their senior research papers that perhaps this was a comforting reversion to orthodoxy.We agreed to use endnotes but they had the option of doing footnotes if they chose. There was a great deal of anxiety over proper use of notes and bibliographies, despite my attempts to downplay this aspect of the project until they were ready to do the final draft. Sometimes I felt that, despite my best efforts, they were more concerned with the appearance of their papers than what they had to say. I wanted them to realize that the appearance and correctness of their papers should function as an enhancement of the content, and not something of greater importance than the knowledge they had gained and written about.

I tried to keep the focus on research and not on the style of their writing until they were through with their research and ready to do a first draft—but it was hard! Questions about how to do notations and bibliographies were ongoing.

Drafting

As we moved into the drafting stage the need for response groups increased. Those who had kept up with the deadlines and were ready to write a first draft really began to flower here. They found friendly ears, both within and without their groups. We used both oral and written evaluations.

The girl who was writing about women executives provoked an interesting response to her first draft:

> You did your paper nicely, and I can see that you put a lot of work into it. At some places in your paper it was hard to follow your train of thought, but I have gained some insight on what troubles there are for women in the business world. And I will try to treat them fairly, and on an equal basis while still trying to be a gentleman. If you want to discuss any of what I have said, or any of the things in your paper, I would be glad to.

Another commented that her "quotes and ideas don't flow into each other. Your paper seems to be jumpy. Another questioned what she meant by "women have humanized the business world."

A student who was writing about teen depression got this as feedback:

> I like the way you incorporate yourself into the paper, like you're there watching the whole time. This is a hard topic to deal with effectively and I liked how you admitted that it affects you, too. Your interviews are *very* shocking! How did you feel when interviewing these people? Could you add your reactions (how you felt about these people, what you thought of them, etc.?) I was really impressed (but shocked) at your statistics about depression. My only other suggestion would be to expand the section on the different types of depression and what depressed people experience. Other than that, your paper really made me think. I found myself relating your paper to the times I've felt depressed.

A girl who researched why birth mothers give up their babies because she herself was adopted, got this suggestion from one of her group:

In your conclusion you state that you understand a birth mother's real motives in deciding to give up her baby—what were the reasons? You don't explain.

Another said: "You said that birth mothers don't forget those feelings . . . what feelings do they have?"

What I see in these comments are students reacting to what they have read in two ways, both of which are useful to the author. First, they have things to say about *how* the paper is being written, and secondly, they reveal their own personal reactions to *what* is written. By the time students can respond meaningfully in these two ways without my imposing outcomes for them, response has moved from what the teacher wants to what the students need, and that is when real interaction in the groups begins to be meaningful.

Sometimes, just to reassure myself that groups were working out, I asked students to respond to the criticisms they received during a group session. Here are some of their comments:

> I thought my paper was O. K., considering it was a first and rough draft. It lacks insight and depth. After some work, I think it will turn out to be a pretty good paper. The ideas were not grouped together but other than that, I thought it was a good paper. I need to group the ideas in a logical order and get rid of unnecessary words.

(He was right; he said many of the things I would have said about his paper; how much better that he could see these problems for himself!)

> I think the suggestion to put aside the writing for a few days and then come back to it is helpful. You gain a new perspective and it is easier to come up with new ideas.
>
> Some sentences were run-on and were there to take up space. There were even some points that I didn't even really believe. The thought comes across differently than it was intended. I had several ideas squished into one.
>
> In reading over my paper I was kind of disappointed in what I had written. I still am. But I also feel I looked deeply into the topic. I have to think about what to do next.
>
> Taking several perspectives on my paper helps me to assume new roles which can make my writing more whole. I need to work on verb tenses; I keep changing from past to present.
>
> I think I need more guidance from the teacher. I don't want to make a fool of myself. You should help us see our errors.
>
> I need to bypass the fillers and come down to the 'meat' of my paper.

This kind of evaluation is far more valuable to a student than the comments a teacher might write. Students often know far more than they want to admit, either to the teacher or to each other. If you can get them involved enough to forget to play dumb, and to have confidence in their own analysis, they are frequently very good editors. It's just that we so rarely encourage them to express that quality.

Conferencing

The works of Moffett, Graves, Murray, Macrorie, and others had convinced me that I needed to do an individual conference with each student, but the time constraints concerned me. I had thirty-six students doing this project. We had a forty-minute time period each day, which realistically amounted to thirty-five. How was I going to do an individual conference about a fairly lengthy paper with each of those students? I simply decided to go ahead and do it, and let the time constraints work themselves out. I scheduled three students per period. Two would have been better. We had to do some filling in and finishing up over lunch and after school. Doing these conferences added more days to the project, which was already much longer than I had anticipated, but I still feel it was worth it.

They handed in their draft in whatever stage it was the day before the conference, and I read it and made notes, not on the manuscript but on a separate paper. I encouraged the student to lead the conference, to tell me what he thought still needed doing, and I referred to my notes to point out where I felt the student had overlooked things that had to be covered. I made sure to point out where the papers were really working well, too, after asking the students to tell me where they thought it was going well. Some of the conferences were really profitable, I thought; others were strained because the student was ill at ease being asked to take the initiative. I needed to practice this type of discussion more, and if I had it to do again, I would have tried to do more informal reading of drafts as I circulated from group to group earlier in the project.

All but three students made their conference time, which was worked in between the second and final drafts. (These same three students had met few of the deadlines along the way, and were the ones who held up their groups at the end, bringing in papers that hadn't really gone through the revision process. They were all in the group of "loners" who'd had trouble with the process from the beginning.)

Publishing

I had already seen benefits of publishing student work, and I felt there were some real plusses in asking students to design and publish their work in magazine format. First, it gave them an incentive to read and analyze current periodicals and develop an awareness of the things that magazines do to present their material in ways designed to attract the reader. Most important of all, it lent credence to the idea that what they were writing had weight and deserved an attractive and contemporary presentation. And of course knowing that others are going to read what you have written is a powerful incentive to do your best and take your work seriously.

Since the final drafts of their papers had already gone through the drafting process, including feedback and revision and a conference with me, I expected that the finished product that made it into their magazines would be polished and relatively error-free. Once we had conferenced, I didn't see their papers again until they appeared in the finished magazine. It was the end of the quarter, we were out of time, and this was more a matter of practicality than a conscious choice on my part.

Each group made enough copies for each member of the group and one for me. On the final day, we all sat around reading each other's magazines. There were a lot of satisfied, if initially nervous, authors, and once they saw how pleased I was, a lot of smiles. I certainly was pleased with the outcome of our labors and I believe they were, too. There were errors, of course. I would have liked to edit all their final papers and make them error-free, at least from a structural standpoint. But that would have detracted from what the students had accomplished, and I'm glad I didn't. They were, as they should have been, a reflection of the effort of their authors. Like the magazines students had done the year before, these were lively, creative, and readable, only this time they included research papers representing topics of real interest to their authors. I was satisfied that what we had accomplished was well worth the sleepless nights it caused all of us. I don't know if what we did made writing papers in college any easier, but I am convinced that most of those students know the meaning of the word *research* in a very personal way. "To look again"—to really study something that you need to know about for your own enlightenment—that, they understood.

Looking Back

I learned in the classrooms of my childhood that you sit in straight rows and don't talk and you listen-listen-listen, and then *maybe* the teacher will let you in on some of what he knows. But if you try to do things your own way, if you're a "rebel," you'll be punished. Such a system encourages passivity and excessive dependence on the teacher. I don't think I ever heard a teacher say "write about what interests you." In truth, I did very little writing when I was in high school. Or at least I don't *remember* writing, except for one attempt at creative writing when I was a junior. My teacher wrote on my story something to the effect that he hoped I'd write more and that he thought I could be a writer. That one small bit of encouragement gave me the courage to take creative writing classes in college.

But 'creative' writing was perceived as something only a few could do and it had no connection to the "real" world of work. It was almost a secret vice, the "chocolate cookie" of writing, a stepchild to the serious members of the family, who went about under the surname of "composition." Many schools still have this same outlook. In my high school, for example, students cannot get English credit for taking a class in "creative" writing.

When I began to attend that series of writing workshops taught by Healy, Cooper, and others from the National Writing Project, I was an immediate and zealous convert. They opened up the concept of writing for me. Instead of pigeonholing writing into categories such as "technical" and "business" and "creative," I began to see the various modes of writing as points along a spectrum and that "creativity" ought to be a part of any writing assignment, not just a label for works of fiction. I also began to see how much more social an activity writing could be. As a teacher, it was a relief to move from the authoritarian model of teaching to a more student-oriented one. Peer evaluations, doing response groups, moving writing away from doing handouts on sentence structure delighted me. I remembered how much I had learned from writing seminars in college and it seemed so logical that some of those same techniques could be included in the teaching of writing in high school.

Sometimes I think response groups are a way of trying to put back into education what we have leeched out of it by the time kids have reached high school: the ability to interact freely when engaged in learning. We tend to assume that independent effort and interdependent effort are always mutually exclusive. We encourage the belief that the only effective critic of student work is the teacher rather than enabling students to develop their own critical skills. Even the standard arrangement of the classroom encourages a student to keep to himself and look only at the teacher—to believe that learning is private business. It's true every scholar needs time to be alone, of course. But who should decide when a student needs "alone" time and when she needs to discuss things with her peers—the student herself, or the teacher? I wanted to create a writing environment where that decision could be in the hands of the students as much as was feasible. I wanted to move them from passive responders to active initiators of response.

I have come to look very suspiciously at the concept of "objectivity" and what its place is in the writing of high school students. I can see the extension of some of our notions of "objectivity" in writing, and in education in general, in the offices of just about any corporation in the country, where workers sit in isolated spaces divided by those padded, neutral-colored screens. Interactions of the staff are limited and discouraged, I suppose, on the premise that if workers remain isolated, they will be more willing to give their undivided attention to the company and not "waste" it on each other. We all know this isolation can be dehumanizing, yet we all find reasons to perpetuate it. We replicate this isolation in the arrangement of desks in the classroom.

Much has been made of the Japanese corporation's sense of loyalty, of "family," toward its workers and of our need to reconsider our management styles in order to compete with the Japanese, but we still haven't taken a serious look at educational practices that continue to develop a work force that is not only unwilling to move toward interdependency but is defiantly proud of its unwillingness. The education of the individual in American schools remains objectivity-oriented, and not creativity-oriented, as well. Footnote style is more important than the curiosity of the student. Fortunately, there's enough room for initiative in our society that many succeed in spite of negative educational traditions. But at what cost?

Of course there are times when the third-person, formal structure of language is appropriate and necessary, but it should be seen as only one choice out of a range of communication options, even when it comes to researched papers. The student should own the writing, and not the other way around. Writing methodologies that protect and encourage this ownership are more effective, more interesting, and more humane.

In subsequent classes, I have organized a sequence of preliminary concepts in advance of the quarter we actually do the research project—observation techniques and interviewing techniques, for example, can be a unit in themselves. In this way the actual time to do a research project is streamlined and will fit within the time constraints of a crowded curriculum. I try to incorporate every time-saving modern research technique I can. I've kept a scaled-down version of the log rather than note cards, and added the computer search programs of local libraries as part of the methodology. I've added more times in the writing lab, spaced at intervals instead of one big block at the end; knowing these writing days are coming up helps groups to meet their deadlines.

I also work to incorporate the good things I learned from this experience into other writing assignments. Among the things I try to remember are:

- Raise the anxiety level. I keep in mind what Murray said when talking about the first requirement for writing (silence): "Sometimes as I come to the writing desk I feel trapped in an arctic landscape without landmarks, an aluminium sky with no East or West, South or North. More often, I feel the emptiness as a black pit without a bottom and with no light above . . . Despair." That, he maintains, is the starting point for good writing. It's good to wonder if we have anything to say and to "fear that we do not" (228). Both I and my students felt this kind of anxiety at times. Realizing that this was healthy gave me confidence to wait it out when things get tense.

- Allow students to choose their own topic. This is essential to many writing assignments. As one student said, "a topic should be something a student is interested in because then the student learns more than he thinks he can."

- Work for a sense of community. Promote peer response, cooperative editing, group production of publications, and other procedures that encourage students to work together and to develop their editing and revising skills, and discourage over-dependency on the teacher for these skills.

- See yourself as a writing facilitator rather than the gatekeeper at the storehouse of knowledge. It's a less adversarial, less dictatorial relationship.

- Set goals and deadlines, in cooperation with the students, and stick to them. I'm responsible for the structure of a writing assignment. Students do need boundaries and deadlines. A good teacher helps them to impose as many qualifications on an assignment as possible voluntarily, but when it comes to enforcing agreed-upon deadlines and requirements, the teacher should hold the line and stick to the schedule as closely as possible, with exceptions being just that.

- Encourage student evaluations of class projects. This is useful and enlightening, both for students and for me. Such self-work also helps them to judge the importance of what they are doing in the classroom. I may not always like the assessment a class gives a writing assignment, but it keeps me thinking about why a writing assignment ought to be done. If they don't understand why a writing assignment is important, I haven't presented it properly and may not have thought it through sufficiently before I began it.

- Conduct classroom research. It is well worth the time and effort required, and can be a real boost to a teacher's enthusiasm and to the learning atmosphere. A teacher who is willing to try new things models an important aspect of true education—calculated risk in order to discover new knowledge.

The realities of the classroom may limit the extent to which an ideal can be realized, but it shouldn't preclude experimentation designed to achieve educational outcomes that are closer to those ideals.

As I write this account of the project, I'm struck by how much of a learning experience it was for me, as well as for the students—but I can't help noting that I'm feeling a certain amount of—what—guilt?—surprise, perhaps?—that this is true. After all, why shouldn't teachers be learners? What better modelling can we do for students than to reveal to them that we teachers can get excited about learning something new, too. James Britton says, "a classroom should be an interactional place, essentially social in nature—teachers and students learning with each other and from each other" (1983, 221). And there's another benefit: the emotional investment the teacher has in seeing a class succeed goes way up when she is involved in the excitement of discovery along with the students, and that usually translates into a better rapport with students and a more dynamic learning atmosphere, as well.

The project raised as many questions as it answered. There's plenty of room for me to do further research about this and other ways of utilizing response groups in the classroom. I now see that teacher research is valuable enough to merit the extra effort it requires, and I like the concept that I can do such research for myself. It interfered in healthy ways with my perceptions of the classroom and of the research paper as a high school writing assignment. And it confirmed my theory that the writing methods that are so effective for other writing projects are equally dynamic in helping students to develop a research paper.

Works Cited

Bartholomae, D. (1983). "Writing Assignments: Where Writing Begins." In Stock, P. L. (Ed.), *FFORUM*. Portsmouth, NH: Boynton/Cook.

Britton, J. (1983). "Language and Learning Across the Curriculum." In Stock, P. L. (Ed.), *FFORUM*. Portsmouth, NH: Boynton/Cook.

Kirby, D., and Liner, T. (1983). *Inside Out*. Portsmouth, NH: Boynton/Cook.

Lindemann, E. (1987). *A Rhetoric for Writing Teachers*, 2d ed. New York: Oxford University Press.

Macrorie, K. (1988). *I-Search Paper: Revised Edition of Searching Writing*. Portsmouth, NH: Boynton/Cook.

Moffett, J. (1983). "On Essaying." In Stock, P. L. (Ed.), *FFORUM*. Portsmouth, NH: Boynton/Cook.

Murray, D. M. (1983). "First Silence, Then Paper." In Stock, P. L. (Ed.), *FFORUM*. Portsmouth, NH: Boynton/Cook.

Palmer, P. J. (1987). "Community, Conflict and Ways of Knowing." *Change* (September/October): 20-25.

Part IV

Closing the Circle
*Response Groups in College
Writing Classes*

11

Breakthrough

William Strong
Trudy Griffin

It's a quiet morning, this day of final exams, as teachers-to-be bend to the task of evaluating their blue writing folders. For most, it has been a busy week, first conferencing with me, then putting finishing touches on Macrorie-style "I-Search" papers and getting ready for a retrospective exam. Today, working from learning logs, outlines, and portfolios, they will try to put the term's learning in perspective.

To my right sits Trudy Griffin, Diet Coke at hand. Her hair is blonde and curly, cut short, and she sports a tan from weekend skiing. She pauses frequently, chewing the end of her ball-point pen. For Trudy, writing is still a sentence-by-sentence struggle, yet her commitment and perseverance are evident as she rereads extensively, pushing herself forward. She has come a long way in the five weeks since she made her breakthrough.

I'm still not sure how it occurred. Maybe inner pressure had been building for years, and Trudy finally got tired of "faking" her writing. Or maybe it was collaborative circumstances—in-class workshops coupled with out-of-class conferences—that served as catalysts for her decision to get serious about learning to write. Whatever the cause, Trudy's story has prompted me to think about the collaborative relationship that writing can promote. Maybe, as Shakespeare once put it, "the readiness is all," for all of us.

In what follows, I describe the circumstances surrounding Trudy's emergence as an engaged, struggling writer. Let me emphasize, however, that this chapter is truly a collaborative effort between Trudy and me. Our aim here is to consider students who have not yet faced themselves as writers—those, particularly, who fake their writing, to some extent. My job is to establish context for this piece; Trudy's task is to fill in details, in her own voice.

By providing teachers with a story to share with their students, Trudy and I hope to prompt discussion about what happens (and doesn't happen)—in collaborative writing classrooms. The two of us contend that many students learn to produce empty writing in high school. We want to show how such learning can have dark consequences later on.

Writing About Teaching and Learning

The course in which Trudy enrolled was thematically organized, with four major process assignments, plus a final exam, distributed over a ten-week term: (1) a narrative dealing with a significant learning experience; (2) an essay comparing and contrasting two teachers from the past; (3) a case study in literacy learning; and (4) an "I-Search" paper on a self-selected topic related to teaching/learning issues.

For background in writing process, the text for the course was Donald Murray's *Write to Learn*, second edition (Holt, 1987), with Strunk and White's *The Elements of Style* (Macmillan, 1979) available for students who claimed they had never mastered the "basics" of mechanics and usage. True to form, most students relied on me far more than on print sources for advice about process and conventions.

I asked students to bring their writing as far as possible, with help from peers, so that I could work with well-developed texts, not rough drafts, in out-of-class conferences. Because I believe that grades undermine writing instruction, I refused to grade individual essays. However, I did provide extensive comments and editing tips as I met with students. Evaluation was "open-ended." Students could revise repeatedly, though final deadlines were eventually established.

Since the class comprised teachers-to-be, all writing tasks related to themes of teaching and learning. In the first writing assignment, for example, we considered important learning experiences and the environments in which they occurred. The handout accompanying the workshop for this paper emphasized that learning always occurs in some kind of context, never in a vacuum—that we learn in baby cribs, alleyways, repair shops, gymnasiums, cafeterias, and other places.

A series of in-class activities moved students from here-and-now writing to memories of dinner table environments, where we all learn lessons about manners, social roles, and the meaning of family. Thinking about the dinner table helped students discuss lessons embedded in their experience. At the end of the workshop sequence, the directions for memory search and personal application became explicit:

> Think about other environments where vivid learning has occurred. To find a focus, brainstorm on paper. Think back to elementary school, junior high, and senior high classrooms. Which ones stand out in your

memory? Also, consider learning environments such as summer camp, athletic fields, jobs, hospitals, garages, or places in the community where you learned interesting or important lessons, either positive or not-so-positive. Quite often these learning environments will have one or more "teachers" (in the broad sense of the term) who play a role. After looking over your options, decide on a learning experience that interests you.

From my viewpoint, the task was wondrously clear. Students had workshop activities, an accompanying assignment handout, even a model paper.

"Any questions?" I asked. Trudy did not raise her hand.

During the next class, we moved into peer response groups, and I mentally noted that Trudy had not developed a rough draft. Sitting near the door with her partners, she looked embarrassed and avoided my eyes. Two weeks later, when many students had signed up for conferences, Trudy's name was not among them. By then we had started on the second assignment.

What was going on here? Was she writing on her own or procrastinating? In class, I urged anyone who had not conferred with me to do so. Ducking her head, Trudy made for the door.

For me, these were fleeting questions and perceptions. I had work to do, and Trudy understood the rules of the course. Besides, I rationalized, what about student responsibility for learning?

Finally, a Paper from Trudy

Toward midterm Trudy's name appeared on my conference sign-up sheet. The paper she had submitted was something less than two pages, with no title and no paragraph indentions. Her topic was skiing:

> I approached Park West at 9:00 a.m. Sunday morning, the sun shone brightly not a cloud in the sky. I knew today would be a better day. The run "slaughterhouse" which I had no success on the previous day was not going to annihilate me again.
>
> It all began when I slipped my right foot into my cushioned model 82 Salomon boots. I then placed my black, tinted vaurnets on and was ready to create an act of excitement unexplainable to mortal man.

Okay, I sighed: a beginning. The writing was melodramatic and rough, but at least a start. Trudy seemed to be straining for effect, trying to "load up" on details.

> Grabbing my Rossignal skiis and Scott poles I headed for the lift. I felt the confidence and excitement circulate within my body with each step I took. As I patiently waited in line I glanced up at what I was about to attempt again. The fear of being defeated by that mighty mountain ate

at the lining of my stomach like acid through metal. I said to myself, "today I will not be defeated, I will conquer that run no matter what it takes." As I rose slowly up toward my destination I felt a calmness as the morning sun warmed my face.

Confidence, excitement, patience, fear, resolution, calmness—six emotions in five sentences. What about focus? "Beware of overwriting," I wrote in the margin, then braced myself for more purple prose.

I then looked down upon that treacherous hill in which I saw skiiers crash right and left. It was as if I felt an excruciating pain myself. When the ride ended I put on my black gortex gloves and adjusted my boots as tight as possible. I looked down at the run I was about to take once again. It was covered with a foot of fresh powder from the previous nights storm. This would add a new twist to things but I was determined not to let this stop me. I saw only few moguls as I stood at the top contemplating which way to go.

Trying too hard, I told myself. I corrected the mechanics of the first sentence, checked a few details of punctuation, and complimented her on "setting the scene" for the reader—a little encouragement from a fake reader.

Choosing the right line and taking a deep breath I was off and alone, I had no fear, only a challenge. I could feel the adrenaline as it was pumped to every part of my body. I gripped the handles of each pole and off I went. In and out of the powder using every possible leg muscle.

Wait a minute: Two separate sentences that dealt with starting the ski run. More description for its own sake? I noted the fragment.

I could feel the pain from skiing so vigorously the day before. Suddenly I sensed I was out of control. Trying to regain my composure I lost control of my skies and was left in a cloud of powder. My skies and poles were scattered, I could barely pull myself together. This incredible run had challenged and defeated me several times in the past but I was not about to fail again. Standing up and brushing the soft powder off my frozen face I took control of my equipment for the second time. Skiing mogul after mogul I finally reached the peak of difficulty.

The peak of difficulty? I made a question mark in the margin to accompany checkmarks for punctuation review. As for the plural of "ski," I had more important matters to think about just now.

I was shocked by the strength that my body possessed. Being familiar with what awaited me I pushed myself more and more. I went up, around, down, and beneath the average amount of gravity. My heart was

> pounding and I could never have reached a more pleased and satifying
> attitude. A bright, enlarged smile broke across my face as I glanced back
> at the overwhelming mountain at which I had just mastered.

More question marks in the margin. There was something about this writing that felt unreal or detached to me. The sentences seemed warped, oddly misshapen. I reread them and shook my head.

> Accomplishing this great task with determination made me realize to
> never quit or give up. It reminded of when I was young, I learned that
> when you get bucked off a horse the best thing to do is climb right back on.

I scanned the paper again. Writing as a Sunday school lesson, perhaps? Maybe what Trudy had in mind was a sermon. I'd have to raise that as a question—gently, of course—during our conference. Trudy and I had work to do.

Moving Toward a Breakthrough

A day or two later, Trudy knocked tentatively at my office door, then slipped inside. Her smile was nervous and polite as I moved into my chatty teacher routine, hoping to break the ice. Everything about her asked the same question: How bad is it?

I asked about her choice of topic, and she spoke vaguely of a recent ski weekend. The paper had potential, I remarked, but I wondered about its focus—what it was really about. Was she skiing alone or with others? When I learned about her three companions, I asked whether she felt embarrassed taking a spill in front of them. Was competition with friends a part of this experience? Her answers would help me see why this learning was significant.

Trudy seemed edgy and unable to deal with this question, so I finally backed off, switching to the problem of "overwriting." We discussed William Zinsser's idea—that "the secret of good writing is to strip every sentence to its cleanest components." I offered suggestions on trimming back description. Turning to the conclusion, I urged her to write simply and clearly about whatever her experience meant. "Don't try to impress your readers," I emphasized. "Be honest and direct. Remember, this isn't a Sunday school lesson. No need for a moral."

A week or so later there was another knock at the office door—Trudy again, just under the deadline. She left a new version of the first assignment before beating a hasty retreat down the hall.

This essay had an interesting title, plus conventional paragraphs. As a piece quite different from her skiing narrative, it would answer many of my questions about her earlier effort.

"The Easy Way Out"

Here I sit at 12:00 midnight. I am trying to revise my English paper that is to be turned in tomorrow. With sunflower seeds in one hand and a Diet Pepsi in the other, I am just now starting my paper. Well, I should say starting my paper over.

English has always been my worst subject in school. Ever since I can remember, I have hated to read and write. I am a senior in college, and I still feel I cannot write. This is where all of my problems begin because I do not have any confidence in my *own* writing.

Voice, I thought. This sounded real, not like the exaggerated voice of the skiing incident. The sentences were direct and clear. And the word *own* was underlined. I wondered why.

Relieved at the thought of having to take only one more English course, I strolled into William Strong's course. I had missed the first class period, so I was already a day behind. Our first assignment was a descriptive/narrative learning experience, the assignment I am writing now. Mr. Strong went on to explain the assignment in more detail. The more he explained, the more horrified I got. I said to myself, "I cannot do this. I have nothing to write about."

The class consisted of about twenty students. We all sat in rows facing each other. Everyone commented and asked questions right and left, while I just sat back, still trying to decide how I was going to write this paper.

The following class period focused on evaluations. We were put in groups of three. In those groups, we offered suggestions on each other's papers. Of course, I was not prepared because I had not written my paper. I had put it off because I do not enjoy writing. So then I was about a week behind on that paper. The following week we started a new paper on two different teaching styles. I put paper number one in the back of my head, and went on to paper number two.

Now I was hooked. In three succinct paragraphs Trudy had neatly folded in background information about her midnight situation—a predicament that resulted from a lack of confidence in her own writing ability. She was doing so many things well here that it was hard to believe she had written the skiing piece.

A couple of weeks later, I realized I still had that horrible paper to finish. The first thing I did was to try to find an easy way out; next I went to my filing cabinet where I kept all my past class work. I dug up all my old English papers. Thumbing through them, I found a descriptive/narrative paper on skiing that my two roommates has helped me write two years ago that had gotten an "A." Actually, my two roommates wrote it, I just typed it and turned it in. I was sure I could just change it a little and turn it into a learning experience.

Sitting at my sister's house the night before my conference was quite an experience. We laughed and stressed over the paper for three hours. It was so dramatic and descriptive that I had to change and eliminate half of it. I was to the point of not caring, and it started getting late so I just hurried and finished it so I could turn it in.

So "the easy way out" referred to strategies that Trudy had used to slip through writing courses. Her pattern had been one of "getting by"—of faking her work, with some success. The phrase "not caring" seemed significant as I read it again.

This is where the humiliation began. I turned my paper into Mr. Strong and met with him the following day. Feeling very nervous and scared, I went up to his office for our conference. He invited me in, and we began talking about my paper. We were facing each other, staring at what you might call an English paper. I felt very uncomfortable and knew my paper was a joke. I was sure Mr. Strong knew it, too. He was just too kind to say it. I sat there and listened while he gave me suggestions. I could tell he could not make sense out of my paper. I felt very embarrassed and just kept making reasons and excuses for why I had written what I did.

Leaving his office twenty minutes later, I was no further ahead than when I had started. My paper needed a lot more work. Where was I going to go now? Who could help me? What was I to do? Maybe I'd try to find another paper. All of these thoughts ran through my head.

I couldn't help but smile as I thought back to Trudy's foot-dragging during our conference. Little did I know that she was on the threshold of insights far more important than a few cosmetic changes.

None of these thoughts were the solution. By this time in class we were working on assignment number three. My second paper was coming along much better than paper number one. Starting on the new assignment, I put my skiing paper away for the second time. The next week in class, Mr. Strong set some due dates for our papers. He sounded a little stern and the class knew he was serious. He told us to quit putting them off and to just get them done and turn them in. Now I was in for it. I had one week to get a final copy of my paper.

A little stern? I recalled quoting from the course syllabus—how "procrastination is a writer's worst enemy." For Trudy, then, fear had been a motivator. She had known for whom the bell tolls.

This takes me back to tonight. It is Wednesday evening, and I returned home at 10:00 p.m. I pulled out my English paper and climbed on my bed. Sitting here, trying to revise my paper, I started giving up after ten minutes. My roommate, who was sitting across from me on her bed, started laughing because I was getting so frustrated. Finally she started to help me.

As I started reading my paper to her, I could not help but be very embarrassed. I just then realized what a total joke my paper was. For one thing, I was trying to write a simple paper on skiing and was using lines like "unexplainable to mortal man" and "it ate at the lining of my stomach like acid through metal." These were just a few lines, but there were many more just as bad or worse. My roommate said it sounded like I was going to Mars or something.

This paper was the combination of four people's ideas thrown together like a jigsaw puzzle, which might have worked for another situation but I found it very inappropriate for this assignment. Continuing to read the lines, we ended up laughing hystericallly.

She was amused by my paper, but I was laughing because of embarrassment. I said to her, "I cannot believe I actually handed this in. He must have thought it was a joke." I continued writing for five more minutes, laughing and trying to change this mess I was trying to call a paper.

I pictured two college girls sharing real laughter over fake writing. The two were an "interpretive community," to use contemporary jargon, and their collaboration marked a turning point for Trudy, just in the nick of time.

Around this time, it was close to midnight. I could not believe how much work I still had to do. But what upset me more was how much time I had wasted because of my procrastination and most importantly my fear of writing. Then I looked up at my roommate and said, "This is the best learning experience ever." This is what I get for trying to take the easy way out, for underestimating my abilities, and lastly for putting things off until the last minute. Now I had something to write about that was true and not being made up.

It is now 1:30 a.m., and I have just finished a very, very rough draft of paper number one, which was assigned five weeks ago. I have definitely learned a great lesson from all of this. Now I know that in the future when given an assignment, I will sit down with my own ideas and write it myself!

I wondered about being seduced by a voice of intimacy here. Was this perhaps a fake confession rather than a real one? Or was Trudy genuinely working *toward* the truth here? Rereading her paper over and over that afternoon, I realized that real writing had made me a real reader once again.

Revisiting Trudy's Collaboration

So how is it that Trudy's skiing essay is clumsy and self-conscious while her first-draft midnight effort is clear and interesting? The answer lies, I think, in the *quality* of her commitment. To explore this idea, let's consider what her laughter might reveal.

At her sister's house, she writes, "we laughed and stressed over the [skiing] paper for three hours." Is it unreasonable to suggest that the laughter here is basically conspiratorial? In this case Trudy and her sister are cunningly engaged in trying to outwit an instructor with whom Trudy has no real or continuing relationship, only a temporary one. Probably everyone has had similar experiences where an "enemy" creates a powerful bond.

On the second occasion, by contrast, Trudy's laughter may have a different ring to it. She and her roommate are laughing *about* the skiing paper, not about the game of faking her writing. Her laughter represents a critical judgment and the beginnings of a turning point. For the first time, perhaps, Trudy considers her essay from a reader's viewpoint. Ironically, her embarrassed laughter signals that she has finally begun to take herself—and her writing—seriously.

Let me emphasize, however, that Trudy's laughter is only a first step toward changed behavior. In other words, while it is one thing to laugh (or cry) over an unsuccessful effort, it is quite another to face the blank page again. Such an effort takes courage. As Trudy begins her midnight essay, she uses writing to face herself. By telling her story and naming her experience, she sees that her own identity, not just her grade, is at stake. She writes for herself more than for me.

In her final examination, Trudy discusses what "The Easy Way Out" meant to her in terms of confronting herself:

This paper was the beginning of my improvement. It will have a major effect on me the rest of my life. In this paper I admitted to myself and my classmates and most embarrassingly my professor what I had done. In writing this paper I realized just how immature I had been. I was sick and tired of not being able to write. . . .

The turn-around in my writing all started the day I handed this paper in. I took it to Dr. Strong's office, smiled, and left. Two hours later I went back and picked it up. I was so nervous and embarrassed, and I was praying he was not there. I got my paper from him and immediately left. I remember on the front of it, it said, "Applause, very intelligent; let's work on this." I was so pleased because it was my own work. Right then I realized I could do it if I would just try.

The following week I handed in paper number two. When I picked it up I could not believe the feedback that was on it. Dr. Strong wrote,

"Great paper; you're doing a really good job." I thought he was just saying that so I would not feel bad. But whatever Dr. Strongs intentions were, it worked. I was finally beginning to think that maybe I can write, maybe I will get a grade in his class.

In the exam, Trudy then considers the classroom factors that contributed to her improvement in writing. According to her analysis, the three most important activities were evaluation from her peers, revising on her own, and conferences. This was a *new* kind of collaboration for her, one that does not depend on conspiring with friends and family against a teacher/ enemy; and it is *she* who makes the switch.

She remarks that although she was embarrassed at first, "towards the end I really enjoyed sharing my work with others." She says that once she had a rough draft, she "found it very beneficial to read over it many times" and that "the more I read and revised, the better my paper was." Finally, she notes that as time went on, "I began to enjoy conferences. I wanted help and feedback so I could improve my writing. For once in my life, I wanted to learn more about writing."

The root of the problem, Trudy comes to find out, is that "all these years I have had a negative attitude about writing, and so therefore I have not tried." She understands how attitude has undermined her self-confidence, making her "hesitant." She comments that "one thing I have found in writing is that you cannot be hesitant. You have to sit down and write. Don't let anything hold you back."

Finally, her exam also reveals how she developed "a plan" for the assignments that followed her breakthrough:

> First, I just sat down and started writing everything I was thinking. Second, I made an outline, and third I wrote the paper. Then I had my group give me suggestions and then Dr. Strong. I found this to work much better than how I used to do it. At the beginning of this class I just sat down for three hours and wrote it, no outline, no plan. I just wanted to get it over with.

Trudy's plan is a process that works for her. In dealing with matters of organization and structure *after* a freewriting draft, she has discovered anew what I had been unable to teach her directly.

She has also discovered, however, that "personalizing" the task of writing—finding a way into it—"makes it much easier." Perhaps this is why she concludes that "I am excited, pleased, and satisfied" and that "I no longer have a fear of writing."

Learning to "Fake It"

As I hinted above, fake writing from students inevitably leads to fake reading from teachers. Real writing, on the other hand, leads to "breakthroughs" of understanding and teacher/student collaboration, the kind of learning that makes a life-long difference. Fakery undermines collaboration, whereas honesty supports it.

Honest teachers will acknowledge just how seductive fakery can be. Under duress, we have all "faked it" on occasion, either on paper or in our day-to-day teaching. Moreover, an honest perspective reminds us why our response groups sometimes give fake feedback when they don't know what else to do. The truth is that fakery is easy, and honesty is hard—both for us and our students. Honesty depends on certain habits of mind.

So how is it—and why is it—that many students learn to fake it in writing classes? Trudy answers this question straightforwardly: "For years I have always tried to write like someone else. I always felt that the other persons style of writing was correct and mine was wrong." What she learned, she says, is that "when it comes to writing the worst thing you can do is fake it."

While the possible reasons for fakery are many, Trudy and I want to suggest three root causes as starters. First, because many students feel little ownership of their own topics and texts, writing is often seen as "something you do to get a grade" and little more. Second, because an adversarial environment exists in some classrooms, many students become committed to a quiet (or sometimes not-so-quiet) conspiracy against learning, "teaming up" against their teacher's best efforts. Finally, because of the problem of numbers—large classes, period after period—it is easy for teachers to develop callouses of the soul, a detachment from the human interchange so basic to effective teaching.

No one should be surprised that fakery flourishes under these conditions. What is surprising, perhaps, is that the best teachers continue to struggle for real, authentic interchange, despite the odds and despite the fakery. They do so because of their belief that writing enables us—all of us—to become more fully human, more fully empowered.

But students are not victims—and neither are teachers. Both of us have power to shape the relationship between us. At first it will likely be tentative, but over time it will develop, one way or another. If it is a positive relationship, it will be built on a foundation of trust and mutual respect, of course. And like any relationship, it will be damaged or destroyed through carelessness, neglect, or fakery. We need to remember this basic fact, so central to collaborative learning.

As I think about Trudy's story, I see again how important this relationship is. After all, it was Trudy who made the basic decision to trust a teacher. Until she had done that, nothing could happen in terms of real collaboration and learning. I wonder what the message was that triggered her willingness to risk the give-and-take of collaboration. Could I say it, perhaps, to other students?

Maybe this: Take a chance. Because your voice counts. Because making mistakes won't be penalized. Because being honest, not faking it, is where we all begin. Because we will work *together* on this. Because it's hard for everybody, not just for you. Because you can do it, even though you're afraid. Because you might be the next Trudy Griffin.

Will such an appeal work? Is it possible for teacher and student to trust each other as partners? What does "trust" *mean* in a writing class-room? And if collaboration is built on a foundation of trust, how do we point to fakery—in ourselves or in each other or in written text?

Trudy and I don't know the answers to these difficult questions. We do know, however, that teachers who have read to this point are looking for *breakthroughs*—and that those who share these ideas with their classes have made a strong statement about their faith in students.

After all, fakery is our enemy, not each other.

References

Macrorie, Ken. 1988. *The I-Search Paper: Revised Edition of Searching Writing.* Portsmouth, NH: Boynton-Cook.

Murray, D. 1987. *Write to Learn.* New York: Holt.

Strunk, W., and E. B. White. 1979. *Elements of Style.* New York: Macmillan.

Zinsser, W. 1985. *On Writing Well: An Informal Guide to Writing Non-Fiction.* New York: Harper & Row.

12

Spiraling Toward Maturity
Peer Response as a Window on Social and Intellectual Development

Karen Spear

In his 1981 essay, "Cognitive and Ethical Growth: The Making of Meaning," William Perry proposes, "perhaps the best model for growth is neither the straight line nor the circle, but a helix, perhaps with an expanding radius to show that when we face the 'same' old issues we do so from a different and broader perspective" (1971, 97). Writing, as one of the most complex socio-cognitive tasks of education, certainly reflects this expanding spiral. New audience relations and more complex topics ask writers continually to reinvent themselves as they traverse new intellectual terrain. This chapter continues the story of secondary students' social and intellectual development as we see it unfolding in the peer response groups of freshmen and advanced college students. The similarities and differences here with the seventh through twelfth graders portrayed in earlier chapters bears out Perry's proposition that growth is indeed a spiraling journey. In fact, although the theorists cited here are principally concerned with the social and intellectual development of college students, their observations are strikingly appropriate to secondary students.

For some years I have been tape recording students' conversations in response groups, initially in freshman composition courses and later in advanced composition courses. While the various theories of cognitive, social, and ethical development provide valuable global descriptions of each stage and of the stresses and strains of transition between them, process-oriented writing teachers need more context-specific depictions of how these stages manifest themselves in writing classes. Students' conversations as they respond to each other's writing and anticipate how to revise their own work offer a useful window into the dynamics of writing development in its fullest sense of a complex social and intellectual process. The repetitions, regressions, integrations, and reintegrations that punctuate these conversations help us better understand the nature of these strands of development in their relation to writing.

Developing Expertise

Like so many classroom research projects that begin in frustration, mine grew out of aggravation that my beginning students' final papers were often their least successful pieces. As I indicated in the third chapter, my courses take students through a carefully designed sequence of writing assignments, one of which is related to their investigations of nuclear weapons. In addition to James Moffett's theories about hierarchies of discourse and my own investigations into a sequential writing curriculum, this design has also been influenced by James Voss's research on problem-solving strategies among novices and experts and their relation to domain-specific knowledge. Voss used a think-aloud protocol methodology, asking university faculty (experts), graduate students, and undergraduates (novices) to think aloud about how they might solve the problem of low productivity in Soviet agriculture. Although the undergraduates had just completed a course on Soviet domestic policy, their knowledge still consisted largely of "bits and pieces." Voss observes, "although the individuals acquired information related to the agriculture problem during the academic course, they were not successful in utilizing this information when given the problem at the end of the course" (1983, 206).

This lack of integration is all too familiar in writing classes. In contrast, Voss finds evidence in the expert protocols of generalized problem-solving strategies and, more important, of considerable use of declarative, domain-specific knowledge. The experts show three structural characteristics in their protocols:

1. Construction of continually expanding conceptual networks that highlight relationships among facts, concepts, principles, etc.

2. Construction of causal relationships to establish interdependencies and to allow for argumentation.

3. Development of hierarchical structures which probably assist in information retrieval.

These characteristics of expert problem solving are also hallmarks of strong expository writing. Not surprisingly, although Voss is not a developmentalist, these descriptions echo the characteristics of later stages of intellectual development, descriptions of which are remarkably consistent from one theorist to another. My goal then, in constructing writing courses around a single theme has been to help students move toward a degree of expertise in a subject by reading about it, writing about it, and discussing it—all from a variety of complementary perspectives: historical, political, economic, social, scientific, personal, and cultural.

The assignments emphasize analysis, interpretation, synthesis of diverse sources, understanding multiple ways of knowing, writing to varied audiences, and finally, pulling their reading and thinking together in a position paper. It's clear from the following freshman discussion that the students have learned a great deal about nuclear weapons, but are groping with how to integrate the material in a final essay.

Rob: It looks like what you're working on is just an analysis of the economics involved in defense spending and the more commercial spending and a kind of critique of current policy and what you can do to change it. That's kind of what I see. You can do a lot with Star Wars . . . to demonstrate how it is so wasted . . .

George: I need to argue my point. I mean, yeah, this all sounds good to say. It's like, you know, some people would say I don't think we're spending too much money.

Rob: I could be one to argue that point, after all, I've been depending on it all my life.

George: You see, I—

Rob: That's the weakest part. OK, What you've got set up is examples of areas that we should emphasize more that are being reflected, such as fusion; hydrogen is another one; solar power is another. OK, and then the areas that are getting emphasis that are an absolute waste. And you were bringing up Star Wars as a classic example. You would need to show it very clearly and completely and leave absolutely no doubt. And if you bring into it the ideas that Bundy and Kennan and all those guys, if you bring into that the ideas that it's intended to protect against ICBM's, that it cannot possibly get all of them, and that it doesn't even address the problem of submarines and bombers or the old time thing of suitcase style bombs. If just one missile gets through, it's failed.

Although Rob has acquired a reasonably impressive and useful store of knowledge about nuclear weapons, he is not able to listen to George's plans and questions. Instead, he twists George's draft into something that matches a position Rob already holds (and is actually working on in his own paper), and he lectures George on how to write that paper. Like Voss's novices, these students have accumulated bits and pieces of material—all accomplishments that they (and I) considered exciting, empowering, and engaging. But they are not yet able to create the structural handles that expert problem solvers use to help them generate and

understand complex arguments and alternatives. Johanna, the silent
third member of the group and an otherwise competent student, got so
lost in the details and possibilities of the topic that she found herself
unable to write the final paper at all.

Expertise, then, seems as much a developmental phenomenon as it is
one of exposure to and accumulation of information. Voss contends that
"the most obvious factor contributing to expertise is the varied exposure
to issues and problems of the particular field. Such experiences . . . provide multiple patterns of organization that are constructed and stored"
(1983, 207). Yet it is also clear that Voss's experts, like the faculty members that Michael Basseches interviewed for his studies of adult intellectual development, are also more cognitively mature than undergraduates.
Developmental theory can explain how experts manage that varied exposure and how they experience multiple patterns of organization. Thus, to
track the developmental spiral that Perry so eloquently described, I
began offering the nuclear course under an advanced composition title,
altering only two of the later assignments to match what I thought would
be a greater sophistication in reading and conceptional integration
among the older students.

Tracking the Helix

I begin both courses with a relatively simple data-based assignment that
helps writers review how controlling ideas work in paragraphs and probe
the relationship between fact and inference, supporting detail, and gen-
eralization. In both these beginning sessions, the writers are working with
the social and interpersonal challenges associated with peer response. At
this point, they grope for a vocabulary and safe style of interaction, and
they try to define the boundaries of my instructions. For both sets of writers, the teacher is clearly a presence in the response group activity and in
the writing assignment. Both groups raise questions about what "she"
wants. The freshmen, however, are nearly paralyzed by these worries.
They cannot find a way into the drafts or beyond the surface of each other's language. Although the freshmen diligently follow my instructions to
read their paragraphs aloud twice and to ask the group specific questions
about revising, their comments focus on the subject, not the draft. They
define the task primarily as an exercise in changing things.

Mike, for example, comments after reading his draft:

> What do we got to do next? Um—OK. I guess I'm supposed to say what
> I think wasn't too good about it. I think I need to, when I re-do it, go
> over and adjust the order a little bit and try to maybe put where they can
> answer yes, no, or uncertain; maybe add that to the topics or something,
> try to tell that they were asked questions. I'm going to need to work on
> the order a little bit.

Mike then turns to another member of the group and invites her to read her paper. She obliges. The whole session, with three members, takes about ten minutes.

Students at both levels admit that the process of sharing their drafts is intimidating. While Mike handles his discomfort by getting the first session behind him as quickly as possible, Patrick, another freshman, expresses some of his frustrations more personally in a revision session on the next paper, a narrative. Here, Patrick responds to Lori: "I think, um, you know, you need to practice what you preach to me. It's easy, you know, when you read someone else's and say, 'You need to do this.' When you're writing it doesn't come well."

Nevertheless, Patrick gives Lori an excellent response to her paper including the advice, "I think you should expand, try to show Omaha, Nebraska—the grass, the prairies, the wheat fields, Bruce Springstein on the radio. Let me see Nebraska. I want to see Nebraska. I want to see you walking through the hay fields, vast plains and farms. People content with their existence and doing nothing but hoeing their fields." In spite of the fun Patrick is having with his own hyperbole, he is giving Lori useful feedback. Yet he ends the session in frustration and a little annoyance:

> I mean you told me exactly on mine. You know, you could read mine and you just say "you need to do this, this, this, and this. I don't like this." It's a bit more difficult for me. I know you're good. Your insights on my paper are perfect.

In contrast, the advanced students quickly subordinate their self-consciousness to the collaborative problem of creating clear meaning, but the beginning students are still much concerned with competition and an urge for self-protection. The advanced students are equally aware of the need to do the assignment correctly, but for them doing it right is not just a matter of divining my secret intentions. It's finding a way to make the piece work on its own. They can talk about the thought processes that led to a particular decision, as, for instance, when Nadine says, "Well what do you think? Right off the bat I've got this wrong. I was thinking . . . " and she goes on to describe how she interpreted some of the data she used in the draft.

Unlike the freshmen, these writers become a genuine audience for the drafts. They are able to suspend the notion that this is an assignment and instead read each piece on its own terms. Instead of being paralyzed by the dualistic need to know the right way to do the assignment, they bracket that question by attending to their reactions as they hear the piece being read. Nadine herself, one of the most hesitant writers in the class, recognizes as she reads her own draft that "it's a little bit too much with all of it."

The other significant characteristic of this discussion is that the students move it toward closure. The freshman discussion has a random,

halting quality to it, what Gene Stanford described in his book on classroom groups as "skyrocketing." Each student shoots up a flare and they all
watch it drop, waiting for the next one. The advanced students talk about
the need to balance generalizations and interpretations with factual detail.
Their comments spiral back on that theme, becoming fuller each time the
issue surfaces. At the end of Nadine's second reading, Debbie comments,
"You know what? I think this whole beginning part sounds fine as a good
introduction about what's going on, what's happening, but then you start
getting into the percentages and all this—it's a little bit too much, I think."
Some moments later, Debbie sums up the emerging consensus:

> I think there's still a little much of percentages. I think it's kind of the
> same thing. You need to just generalize more without using all the num-
> bers. Just generalize, like 'twice as many.' There are ways of doing it
> without this percent or that percent. It's true you know. When you're
> writing you don't really realize it, but as you go along, you start reading
> numbers, you just lose whatever the words mean.

By the time students in both classes have begun revising their third major
assignment, they have worked in response groups at least five times in
planning sessions, drafting sessions, and revising sessions. They are more
comfortable with each other and familiar with the process. By now you
hear more give and take between writer and reader. Writers retain ownership of the draft, but readers are able to justify their suggestions on the
basis of their needs as readers. Writers talk more about what they are trying to do and readers do more than give empty admonitions. The groups
as a whole focus more on possibilities and options, and they begin to
attend to structural issues in the drafts, not just individual details. Here,
for instance, Kristin (a freshman) observes,

Kristin: I never thought you were writing to me.

Paula: Well, what is it you don't like about it?

Kristin: It just sounds like you have no facts backing it up at all. It's
just like, OK, I know you think this way. It's just too much.

Paula: What did that make you think? How did that make you feel?

And a few exchanges later, Kristin begins reading Paula's piece again,
and tries to explain the difference between what Paula apparently
thought she was saying and what Kristin understood. She concludes that
Paula was assuming her readers would know more than they could.

Still the differences between the groups are sharp. Ron, one of the
advanced students, begins this session with a list of ideas that center

around a theme he describes as "how the government has taken advantage of the public ignorance on the subject of nuclear war." As he talks about his ideas, his peers quiz him on the sources he has in mind and how he is going to prove his assertions. Lynn eventually asks whether he really knows what the main focus is, and Debbie attempts to draw out a number of possibilities. Unlike the freshmen, these writers are poised to shift to a more abstract understanding of Ron's situation. They are comfortable, in other words, with metacognition—thinking about their thinking. Joyce advises: "Maybe you need to sit down and ask yourself questions, like for instance . . . ," and she supplies several good ones. Debbie offers the perspective of a seasoned student: "Think about the sort of time constraints you are dealing with."

Ron's readers continue to press him to define his topic more clearly. Where the pattern of discussion in freshman groups tends to show a series of one-to-one exchanges, without much sustained development of ideas, this group is more typical of advanced students who are able to make finer discriminations and to analyze shortcomings in meaning. In other words, the freshmen tend to work with what's there in a draft; the advanced writers consider what's missing. Continuing with the same discussion, Ron tries to clarify what he wants to do and Joyce points out, "You've got two different ideas here." Ron tries again and Lynn follows, "Well now, that's the third thing you've said." Debbie clarifies for him the differences among his several proposals and Ron finally concedes, "I gotta narrow it down, I know."

But his colleagues are still not content to turn Ron loose. Debbie and Joyce talk to him in very separate ways about where their own ideas come from when they write, and each gives Ron some specific advice. Unlike Rob's directives to George on *what* he should write, Debbie and Joyce concentrate on *how*. First, from Debbie, "just sit down and start writing. I used to just sit there and try to come up with an idea but then I lost all the creativity that went with it because I was trying to narrow so hard I lost all the other things. This time it's a bunch of drivel on the pages, but, you know, I saw a couple of ideas coming through more strongly." Joyce follows up, suggesting that he record the separate ideas on 3 x 5 cards and combine and recombine the cards until the juxtapositions produce something new.

This advice represents an important cognitive turning point that Piaget termed decalage—the ability to lift a pattern of meaning from a very specific context and to express it in more general, abstract terms. William Perry argues that decalage signals a shift into relativistic thinking in which mature intellectual commitments are possible: "The shift from 'what' (content) to 'way' (generalized process), being a move to a higher level of abstraction, frees the 'way' to become context, displacing the 'what' and relegating it to the status of a particular" (1971, 88).

From Received Knowledge to Constructed Knowledge

In all this discussion among the advanced students, there's an emerging understanding that meaning is something the writer creates, and that new meanings can be brought into being by tapping what you already know and putting it in new combinations with other materials. Michael Basseches describes dialectical thinking as a final stage of adult reasoning. It's "a process of creating order by discovering what is left out of existing ways of ordering the universe and creating new orderings that embrace and include what was previously excluded" (1984, 11). The dialectical thinker seeks out multiple frames of reference and takes on the intellectual and social challenges of synthesizing these perspectives so that both the perspectives and the people holding them can co-exist. The creation of meaning through mutuality is particularly evident among the advanced students, and it stands as a crucial gateway in achieving the higher stages of intellectual development that Perry termed "commitment in relativism." By this he meant that students are able to move beyond the intellectual paralysis of relativism, which students usually express as "everybody is entitled to their own opinion." Instead, they are able to develop and apply standards of evaluation that they recognize as relative but that they accept because of the need to make commitments to one position or action over another. Another developmentalist, Lee Knefelcamp, refers to this stage of reasoning as "courage in spite of." For freshmen, responding critically to each other's writing is not the act of aggression they initially think it is—an interpretation that grows directly out of their inability to temper relativism with commitment. For advanced students the process of peer response becomes much more quickly an act of community, of helping a classmate do the best job she can.

Ron was unquestionably the weakest student in the advanced class—twenty-two years old, a community college transfer, working full time and maintaining a fairly lackadaisical attitude toward school until, each term, his grades started to slide and he rediscovered earnest commitment. Nevertheless, it's as natural a move for him as for his classmates to see this assignment as an extension of the previous readings and discussions, and most importantly, as an outgrowth of the ideas he has been developing in previous writings.

The group's review of Lynn's draft dramatizes this awareness more fully. Lynn's concern is less with what she's going to say than with finding a form most appropriate to her intentions. Here again is the shift from what to way, content to context:

> I want to know how to set it up. I already know my ideas. I want to know
> what kind of format to put it in. Because that's the main thing I've seen
> in everything I've read and everything like the interview we did—
> everything. The main thing that keeps hitting me is the propaganda to

> build a distrust between the two countries, and I don't see how we can
> ever solve anything when we basically distrust.

As the group searches for models of organization, Debbie pulls out of her backpack a magazine essay she had been reading that she thought Lynn might find useful, and the group evolves a plan for incorporating into the paper a quotation from a previous reading that Lynn wanted to use. The common ownership of the assignment evident in the discussions of Lynn's and Ron's drafts suggests another significant departure from the egocentricity of the freshmen groups. It's clear to everyone that Lynn must make the final decisions about her paper, but it's also clear that each reader can assume and argue hypothetically for one proposal or another. Perry describes a fundamental shift from multiplistic to relativistic ways of knowing as a shift in self-definition from being a holder of meaning to being a maker of meaning. As these students coach each other in strategies to achieve that shift, they are taking on that new self-definition.

Perhaps the most difficult transition for both sets of students has to do with their discomfort over the relationship between fact and interpretation. Both sets of students appreciate the multiple frames of reference in which the readings and the sharing of each other's writing immerse them. Students at both levels see themselves as having become more critical, discerning readers of both professional and peer writing. They comment in almost identical language that they've learned not to assume something is true just because it shows up in print and that they've learned to be more critical of their own work by reading so much of their peers'. But they still prefer readings that they characterize as "factual." An assignment late in each course asks them to assume the role of a staff editor, writing a memo to an imaginary journal editor to recommend one of two articles for publication. One possible pairing, and the most frequently chosen, links Howard Scoville's historical reconstruction of the United States-Soviet standoff since 1945 with George Kennan's analysis of the cultural differences between Soviet and American society. Beginning and advanced students alike judge Scoville's the better piece because they see it as objective and reliable. Scoville's piece is historical; therefore, they conclude, it states "the facts." Because Kennan's piece is so much more obviously an analysis, they describe it as emotional and opinionated, therefore unconvincing.

Ironically, while they prefer to read pieces that are highly structured, "objective," and conclusive, both sets of students prefer to write assignments that allow the most room for "creativity." What the two groups mean by creativity, however, is strikingly different. The freshmen cite only the early narrative assignment in which they tell about a personal turning point. They do not view the position paper as a creative activity. The advanced students, on the other hand, agree that the narrative is a "creative" assignment, but their definition of creativity has become more inclusive. A later assignment that I termed an "interpretive essay," asked them to draw on various readings to discuss the impact of the nuclear dilemma on our everyday cultural life. Though they found this a difficult assignment, they describe it, too, as "creative," and they value the challenge of pulling their interpretations together in a uniquely expressive way. In other words, what they dislike in Kennan's approach to making meaning they are coming to prefer in their own work.

These differences highlight a fundamental principle of developmental theory. Developmental theory holds that individuals prefer reasoning at one stage beyond their current level of functioning. Significantly, their preference is anticipatory: they cannot yet do what they nevertheless find challenging and provocative in more sophisticated constructions. With their broader definition of "creative writing," the advanced students seem poised to reconcile what they now see only as a dichotomy between fact and opinion. Actually, Debbie's comments about Kennan suggest that it's not really his "lack of objectivity" that makes his essay less effective, but that he does not offer viable solutions: "Kennan tells the reader why we should be concerned but not what to do about it in real life terms. . . . He doesn't give you anything to work with."

I take the advanced students' expanded definition of creativity as a transitional position. They are beginning to accept the disquieting prospect that creativity and objectivity are not polar opposites, but that what appears so "objective" is as much an act of construction as what they want to condemn as emotional or opinionated. Perry and other developmentalists emphasize the sense of loss that accompanies students on their cognitive journey. Robert Kegan's description of the ambivalence that comes with development is especially appropriate for the uncertainty the advanced students face as their faith in the absoluteness of facts begins to crack:

> The career of the truth is not a cognitive matter alone, but the history of loss and recovery, death and rebirth, painful separation and triumphant liberation. The process conception of personality which a neo-Piagetian framework yields is not a list of consecutive philosophies but a reckoning . . . of the costs to the soul . . . of making and surrendering meaning; not alone the story of successively more true organizations of reality, but from the point of view of *being* one who develops, the story of successive losses of the very meaningfulness of the world and myself in it. (1979, 33)

Kegan's work emphasizes that teaching is not an address to a stage, but an interaction with a person engaged in a continuing process of making new meanings and losing old. Like Perry, Kegan stresses the necessity of interpersonal supports. Cognitive development is not an isolated experience but one that simultaneously relies on and creates community. The portraits presented here show how the peer-centered writing course contributes to the creation of a mature intellectual community.

Closing the Circle

The story of this research, like Perry's developmental spiral, ends in a sense where it began. By any absolute measure, the advanced students' final papers were certainly better than the beginning students', though they were still not what I had hoped. I now see the problem as more mine than theirs as I pushed them beyond what they were intellectually ready to produce. But while I didn't get the review essays I had asked for, I nevertheless received a stunning set of book reviews, characterized by a tone of authority and a more self-confident and fully internalized sense of the nuclear conversation. The students had evolved from observers to participants.

Beyond the papers themselves, though, were clear indications that writing with peer response had become a more fully realized process of creating meaning. Nearly every advanced student worked on their final papers outside of class in student-initiated response groups. As they came by my office to turn in their portfolios, the students routinely and proudly proclaimed that their final pieces were "really good," "the best work I've done this semester." And they were right.

Both the beginning and the advanced writing courses serve similar functions but at different stages of students' intellectual development. In the Piagetian sense, they occasion the consolidation of intellectual positions that have otherwise been largely latent or subliminal. To evoke a feminist metaphor, collaborative writing courses are, in the very best sense, midwives to intellectual development by helping students bring into being what is there but not yet functioning independently. Writing collaboratively has all the characteristics that theorists of cognitive development maintain are essential for the intellectual commitments of adulthood: The experience is personal. The response groups promote intellectual risk taking within a community of support. They allow students to focus on issues that invite the application of academic knowledge to significant human problems. Thinking and writing are grounded in discussion and debate.

Reading and responding to peers' writing asks for interpersonal and personal resolution of multiple frames of reference. In this sense, collaborative writing courses at all levels provide an essential opportunity to practice becoming members of an intellectual, adult community. In such a community, commitments to ideas and to the people who hold them become equally important. My college freshmen sound much like Kathyrn and Heather's AP seniors in their hesitation and tentativeness, while my college juniors sound more like Becky Reimer's seventh graders in their readiness both to support one another and to argue over the ideas in the writing. The paradox is that what look like the same issues from one year to the next—community building, learning to give response, and reading thoughtfully—are never really the same because even the same student is never really the same.

Works Cited

Basseches, M. (1984). *Dialectical Thinking and Adult Development*. Norwood, NJ: Ablex.

Kegan, R. G. (1979). "The Evolving Self: A Process Conception for Ego Psychology." *The Counseling Psychologist* (9) 5–40.

Moffett, J. (1968). *Teaching the Universe of Discourse*. Boston: Houghton Mifflin.

Perry, W. (1971). "Cognitive and Ethical Growth: The Making of Meaning," In Arthur Chickering and Associates, (Ed.) *The Modern American College*. San Francisco: Jossey-Bass. 76–116.

Spear, K. (1983). "Thinking and Writing: A Sequential Curriculum for Composition." *Journal of Advanced Composition* 4: 47–63.

Stanford, G. (1977). *Developing Effective Classroom Groups*. New York: Hart Publishing Co.

Voss, J., Greene, T. R., Post, T. A., and Penner, B. C. (1983). "Problem-Solving Skill in the Social Sciences." In Bower, G. H. (Ed.) *The Psychology of Learning and Motivation* Vol. 17. New York: Academic Press, Inc.

Notes on the Contributors

Cheryl Ause has taught in public schools for seventeen years and has been using her version of the writing workshop with students since 1979. Of the peer review process, she says: "In Utah, peer review in the classroom is more than a preferred methodology for teaching writing. Because of our overly large classes, it's often a matter of survival." In 1986, she received an N. E. H. summer grant to study Southern women writers with Barbara Ewell at Loyola of New Orleans. The experience rekindled her desire to return to graduate school. In 1991, she received an M. A. in British and American literature from the University of Utah. Currently, she teaches English and is the yearbook adviser at Cottonwood High School in Salt Lake City. She also teaches freshman composition part time at Salt Lake Community College.

Heather Brunjes is currently pursuing a Ph.D. in composition, rhetoric, and literacy at the University of Utah. She has thirteen years of experience teaching writing in the public schools, grades K–10. She is a site director for the Utah Writing Project and has been a writing teacher-consultant for more than a decade. Heather specializes in collaborative learning and questions of gender in writing development, and in the politics of teacher and student agency in the writing classroom. She is well-known throughout Utah for her workshop presentations featuring elementary students demonstrating the dynamics of peer group response.

Marjorie Coombs is principal of the Rowland Hall-St. Marks Middle School in Salt Lake City, and teaches writing in the computer writing lab, which she designed. She was the Writing Coordinator, K–12, for the Salt Lake City School District for three years and has been a writing teacher-consultant for the Utah Writing Project since 1983. Marj is a past president and board member of the Utah Council of Teachers of English, and was Project Director of *A Guide to Literary Utah*. She was named Utah English Language Arts Teacher of the Year for 1992. She has enjoyed twenty-four years of teaching and learning, primarily in seventh- and eighth-grade language arts classrooms.

Trudy Griffin graduated from Utah State University in 1991. She teaches Spanish at North Layton Junior High in northern Utah, where she is enjoying her success. Because Trudy was assigned to teach English in 1992, she enrolled for a special one-week summer workshop offered by the Utah Writing Project. Her interests include all kinds of sports, especially skiing.

Nolyn Starbuck Hardy is currently teaching English at Highland High School in Salt Lake City. She is a dedicated free-lance writer in her private life, and has published both fiction and non-fiction. She has a B. A. from Brigham Young University, where she was a teaching assistant, a member of the Academics Committee, editor of the literary magazine and an honors scholar. Her M. Ed. and teaching certification in English and Journalism were obtained at the University of Utah. She has taught literature and writing for twelve years, in college and high school classes, and has been a presenter for regional language arts workshops.

264

264

Beth Johnson ~~DATE DUE~~ ning and
earned her master's degree at Westminster College in Salt Lake City in 1987.
She has taught English in public schools for twenty years, currently at Jordon
High School in Sandy, Utah. She is committed to her students and loves teaching.

Kristi Kraemer is currently teaching seventh, tenth, and twelfth grade in the
Davis, California, public schools, and freshman composition at Sacramento City
College. Over the last eighteen years, she has taught English in grades 7–12 and
both lower and upper division college composition courses. She has been a
teacher-consultant with the Area III Writing Project in Davis for fifteen years and
spent six years working with education students at the University of California at
Davis Secondary Credential Program in English/Language Arts. She received her
M. A. in Language and Literacy with an emphasis in the Teaching of Writing from
the University of California at Berkeley, and began her doctoral work at UC
Davis in the fall of 1992.

Rebecca Laney is currently teaching and serving as English Department Chair at
Alta High School in Sandy, Utah. A native of Colorado and an adopted native of
Utah, she loves the outdoors and enjoys writing about the land and people of the
West.

Becky L. Reimer teaches seventh-grade English and is currently completing a
Ph. D. in curriculum and instruction at the University of Utah. She specializes in
reading and writing development, using a whole language approach. Becky has
published her work on teaching and teachers in various professional journals, and
is a frequent workshop leader throughout Utah.

Karen Spear is Professor of English and Dean of Arts and Sciences at Fort Lewis
College in Durango, Colorado. As a composition specialist, she writes about collaborative learning and cognitive development, but she works with equal intensity
on undergraduate, liberal education. She is a past president of the Association for
General and Liberal Studies and editor of the Jossey-Bass sourcebook, *Rejuvenating Introductory Courses*. She consults nationally on liberal education and on
collaborative learning and writing program development, and she occasionally
steals time to boat and hike at Lake Powell, Utah.

William Strong is Professor of Secondary Education at Utah State University in
Logan, Utah, where he teaches courses in writing, teaching methods, and content
area reading/writing. His most recent book is *Writing Incisively* (McGraw-Hill,
1991). He is Consulting Author for Composition of *Writer's Choice, A Composition Series for Grades 9–12* (Glencoe/Mcgraw Hill, 1993). He is the founder and
continuing director of the Utah Writing Project, and in his spare time rides a very
large and powerful motorcycle.